Disinformation and You

Identify Propaganda
and Manipulation

ABOUT THE AUTHOR

Marie D. Jones is a fully trained disaster response/preparedness member of Community Emergency Response Teams (CERT) through FEMA and the Department of Homeland Security, and she is a licensed ham radio operator (KI6YES). She is the author of over 15 nonfiction books on cutting-edge science, the paranormal, conspiracies, ancient knowledge, and unknown mysteries, including Visible Ink Press' *Celebrity Ghosts and Notorious Hauntings; Demons, the Devil, and Fallen Angels; The Disaster Survival Guide: How to Prepare For and Survive Floods, Fires, Earthquakes and More; Earth Magic: Your Complete Guide to Natural Spells, Potions, Plants, Herbs, Witchcraft, and More;* and *The New Witch: Your Guide to Modern Witchcraft, Wicca, Spells, Potions, Magic, and More.* She is also the author of *PSIence: How New Discoveries in Quantum Physics and New Science May Explain the Existence of Paranormal Phenomena; 2013: End of Days or a New Beginning; Supervolcano: The Catastrophic Event That Changed the Course of Human History;* and *The Grid: Exploring the Hidden Infrastructure of Reality.* She is a regular contributor to *New Dawn Magazine, FATE, Paranoia Magazine,* and other periodicals. Jones has been interviewed on over a thousand radio shows worldwide, including *Coast-to-Coast AM.* She makes her home in San Marcos, California, and is the mom to one very brilliant son, Max.

Marie D. Jones

DISINFORMATION AND YOU

IDENTIFY PROPAGANDA AND MANIPULATION

iv

Visible Ink Press®
43311 Joy Rd., #414
Canton, MI 48187-2075

Visible Ink Press is a registered trademark of Visible Ink Press LLC.

Most Visible Ink Press books are available at special quantity discounts when purchased in bulk by corporations, organizations, or groups. Customized printings, special imprints, messages, and excerpts can be produced to meet your needs. For more information, contact Special Markets Director, Visible Ink Press, www.visibleink.com, or 734-667-3211.

Managing Editor: Kevin S. Hile
Page and cover design: Cinelli Design.
Typesetting: Marco Divita
Proofreaders: Larry Baker and Christa Gainor
Indexer: Shoshana Hurwitz

ISBN: 978-1-57859-740-6

Cataloging-in-Publication data is on file at the Library of Congress.

Printed in the United States of America.

10 9 8 7 6 5 4 3 2 1

MORE VISIBLE INK PRESS BOOKS BY MARIE D. JONES

Celebrity Ghosts and Notorious Hauntings; Demons, the Devil, and Fallen Angels
ISBN: 978-1-57859-689-8

Demons, the Devil, and Fallen Angels
ISBN: 978-1-57859-613-3

The Disaster Survival Guide: How to Prepare For and Survive Floods, Fires, Earthquakes and More
ISBN: 978-1-57859-673-7

Earth Magic: Your Complete Guide to Natural Spells, Potions, Plants, Herbs, Witchcraft, and More
ISBN: 978-1-57859-697-3

The New Witch: Your Guide to Modern Witchcraft, Wicca, Spells, Potions, Magic, and More
ISBN: 978-1-57859-716-1

ALSO FROM VISIBLE INK PRESS

Conspiracies and Secret Societies: The Complete Dossier, 2nd edition
by Brad Steiger and Sherry Hansen Steiger
ISBN: 978-1-57859-368-2

The Handy American Government Answer Book: How Washington, Politics and Elections Work
by Gina Misiroglu
ISBN: 978-1-57859-639-3

The Handy American History Answer Book
by David L Hudson, Jr.
ISBN: 978-1-57859-471-9

The Handy Communication Answer Book
By Lauren Sergy
ISBN: 978-1-57859-587-7

The Handy Geography Answer Book, 3rd edition
by Paul A. Tucci
ISBN: 978-1-57859-576-1

The Handy History Answer Book: From the Stone Age to the Digital Age
by Stephen A Werner, Ph.D.
ISBN: 978-1-57859-680-5

The Handy Law Answer Book
by David L Hudson, Jr.
ISBN: 978-1-57859-217-3

The Handy Military History Answer Book
by Samuel Willard Crompton
ISBN: 978-1-57859-509-9

The Handy Presidents Answer Book, 2nd edition
by David L Hudson, Jr.
ISBN: 978-1-57859-317-0

The Handy State-by-State Answer Book
by Samuel Willard Crompton
ISBN: 978-1-57859-565-5

The Handy Supreme Court Answer Book
by David L Hudson, Jr.
ISBN: 978-1-57859-196-1

Plagues, Pandemics and Viruses: From the Plague of Athens to Covid 19
by Heather E Quinlan
ISBN: 978-1-57859-704-8

PLEASE VISIT US AT WWW.VISIBLEINKPRESS.COM.

CONTENTS

PHOTO SOURCES

Artcraft Films: p. 48.

David Bailey: p. 93.

Bain News Service: p. 123.

Michel Bakni: p. 323.

BBC Radio: p. 269.

British Museum: p. 19.

Noam Chomsky: p. 155.

Cranach Digital Library: p. 25.

Executive Office of the President of the United States: p. 204.

James Gathany, Centers for Disease Control and Prevention: p. 126.

General Artists Corporation-GAC-management: p. 72.

Julian Gomba: p. 144.

Harper's Weekly: p. 39.

Library of Congress: pp. 32, 50, 63, 146.

Life Magazine: p. 250.

Lilly Library, Indiana University Bloomington: p. 31.

McLennan County Sheriff's Office: p. 259.

Joseph Mercola: p. 176.

National Archives and Records Administration: p. 215.

National Institute of Standards and Technology: p. 214.

Naval Historical Center: p. 53.

Naval History and Heritage Command: p. 223.

Pentocelo (Wikicommons): p. 14.

Laura Poitras/Praxis Films: p. 160.

Prologue Magazine: p. 66.

Rameshng (Wikicommons): p. 70.

David Shankbone: p. 112.

Shutterstock: pp. 2, 5, 7, 21, 36, 42, 46, 79, 82, 86, 89, 98, 101, 105, 106, 108, 110, 118, 127, 130, 132, 135, 138, 152, 159, 162, 165, 170, 172, 174, 177, 179, 181, 183, 184, 190, 191, 196, 197, 199, 202, 212, 218, 228, 233, 240, 242, 245, 247, 253, 255, 258, 263, 268, 270, 274, 277, 280, 286, 290, 295, 301, 304, 309, 315, 319, 321, 324.

Gage Skidmore: pp. 115, 142.

AUTHOR'S NOTE

At the time of this book's completion, America (and much of the rest of the world) is still under lockdowns, and the mass media are pushing fear about rising Covid-19 cases and virus mutations. Yet, during the contentious November 2020 presidential election—itself a perfect example of propaganda and disinformation playbooks—people were told by the CDC that even if they were infected with the virus, it was okay for them to go vote in person. Meanwhile, the mass media was calling the election winners before one vote was cast, a propaganda technique called optics that is meant to push a narrative that may or may not be true to encourage voter suppression. Both sides of the political spectrum are guilty of allowing these "shenanigans" to continue unabated, with the media and social media fully complicit, but no one is more guilty than the American public for allowing this kind of mind manipulation to cloud the truth. No doubt, by the time this book is released there will be a host of new false flags, misdirection campaigns, fear mongering, media manipulation, and disinformation to last everyone a lifetime. The only difference? You will be able to recognize it because you read this book.

Therein lies your power.

One of the biggest challenges in writing a book about propaganda and media manipulation is that it never ends. Each new day brings more news and events filled with spin and hidden agendas, so that a book that covers the entire current history would comprise about ten volumes and have no "The End" point. Since authors have deadlines to get books into production, that means ending a book when the subject matter is still ongoing.

The most important thing, though, is to help readers learn to identify the uses and techniques of propaganda in the past and present so that readers can then see it unfold in the future. By the time this book is released, there will be some major new world and national developments worthy of additional chapters…. But it has to be cut off somewhere.

My greatest hope is that once you read this book, you can go back a few months, or even just a few days, and be able to pinpoint what was fact, and what was not fact, and then this book will truly have done its job because no matter what is going on in the world, or who is in power at any given time, there will always be those who seek to manipulate, coerce, and control you.

Don't let them.

ACKNOWLEDGMENTS

I would like to thank Roger Jänecke and his entire staff at Visible Ink Press for their ongoing support for my work. Having a publishing home like Visible Ink Press is priceless for an author. They are the best of the best, and it's a dream to be working with them. Kevin Hile, you are an editor worth your weight in gold ten times over. Thank you for always keeping me sharp and on point.

My agent, Lisa Hagan of Lisa Hagan Literary Agency, as always, is not just a dear, dear friend but also a guide and guardian angel in every possible way. Thank you for always being there for me and working on my behalf to get my ideas out into the world over these years.

To my mom, Milly, for always believing in me and supporting me no matter what I was doing. To my dad, John, who passed away years ago but is still a big part of my quest for truth. To my sister, Angella, who is my best pal and cheerleader, and my brother, John, and his wife, Winnie, who are always there for me. To my extended family, dear friends and colleagues, and colleagues who have become friends: Thank you for all of your love and support over the years.

To the radio hosts who have been so gracious to me when I appear on their wonderful shows and podcasts, and to my fellow writers and researchers who always generously share ideas and direction: Thank you so very much! I am so spoiled, having been treated so well in response to my books.

To anyone who has ever read or purchased one of my books or taken one out at the library, you are the best! Thank you so much, and I hope I continue to keep you curious and wanting to learn more! Without readers, writers don't flourish. We need you guys! To truth-seekers out there, I truly thank you for your ongoing dedication to spreading information, standing in truth, speaking truth to power, and being a part of a great awakening.

But most of all, to my son, Max, who is my sun, and moon, and stars. You are the light of my life and the heart of my heart, and I pray some of what I do can help bring about a brighter future for you and your friends. You have taught me so much in return, and I marvel at your intellect, curiosity, instinct for truth, and insight daily. I'm so proud of you, kiddo!

Keep reading and keep buying books!

INTRODUCTION: AGENDAS ARE EVERYWHERE

Propaganda is making puppets of us. We are moved by hidden strings which the propagandist manipulates.
—Everett Dean Martin

Every living thing has an agenda. It can be as simple as survival and finding food, shelter, and water—oh, and a mate to make babies with. It can be to access goods or material items from others. It can be to find true love or that dream job or just see your grandchildren grow up happy and healthy. Individuals have agendas, and so do collective bodies such as governments, corporations, industries, and segments of society. Not everyone's agendas match up or align, and then you have to find ways to either coerce, control, or eliminate those who stand in the way of fulfilling your agenda.

Some of those ways involve the use of coercive techniques such as propaganda, which is designed to influence or even scare others into joining your individual or collective agenda. There are so many different tools and techniques involved—from persuasion to outright threats, using rhetoric and dialectics, and creating viral campaigns to lying outright enough times that those whose minds you wish to change go ahead and buy into your agenda lock, stock, and barrel. There is disinformation, misinformation, malinformation, conditioning, bias, spin, and a host of other methods by which you can make someone, even an entire nation of someones, do your bidding. Even the world.

This book will examine the long history of propaganda and disinformation and how it has influenced our historical evolution. It will also look at current events and offer examples of concepts and ideas presented in a way everyone can understand. Knowledge is power. Sort of. Knowledge is not really power unless it is utilized, so this book will also serve to educate, enlighten, and offer tools for detoxifying yourself of propaganda so that you don't continue to spread it virally and become a part of the problematic contagion instead of the solution. Bad information tends to spread faster than good. Negativity and fear are all over the mass media because that's what sells. "If it bleeds, it leads." For every dozen or so bad stories that depress or sadden us, we are lucky to see one that lifts our spirits. Why is this? What is it about goodness that scares the living crap out of so many people? Or is it just the people behind the propaganda that benefit from our staying permanently entrenched in a state of fear, doubt, confusion, and uncertainty?

The use of propaganda is always accompanied by a host of other types of persuasion, tools, and techniques that are rooted in mind control and behavioral manipulation. The masters of propaganda are often masters of sales, public relations, marketing and how to "close the deal" when it comes to driving a particular point of view deep into the minds of those they wish to manipulate. To sell someone, or an entire population, a certain ideology isn't all that much different from selling them a car or a washing machine. You give them enough reasons to choose one brand over another, and they will choose your brand almost every time, unless they know they are being manipulated, and that awareness allows them to make better and more informed choices.

Propaganda and disinformation provide us great understanding of human behavior and psychology, and it's fascinating to learn why we think and act the way we do, especially when we are exposed to external influences. It is also eye-opening to find out we are just as guilty as the next person of buying into these lies and distortions as long as they fit the political, religious, or social narratives we have come to accept and hold onto for dear life. We will fight to the death to stand behind our support of propaganda as long as we agree with it, even if it hurts others or harms the world at large.

Once awakened and aware, though, it becomes harder to miss the manipulation. Once we spot the manipulation, it becomes harder for those external forces to control our responses and reactions. Once seen, it cannot be unseen. Therein lies the power to truly change the narratives that keep us all in the dark, falsely informed, ignorant, and lashing out at the wrong people instead of demanding the perpetrators of the propaganda come clean.

Somebody once said that knowing the truth would set your free, but first it would piss you off. Maybe that's why we love to "buy the lie" instead of dig for the truth. It keeps us in a comfort zone, warm and safe, not having to think for or act for ourselves. But the truth doesn't vanish just because we don't look for it or acknowledge it. It is always there, and like another famous someone once said, it's better to know a hard truth than a soft lie. You will have to face and deal with the reality of a situation sooner or later, so why not give yourself the advantage of making it sooner with an empowered mind and centered point of view to operate from?

Ultimately, you can read a million books on propaganda, but until you learn to discern the tools and techniques used on you, and how to avoid them or dissipate their power, they will control you. Understand why you are being manipulated in the first place, by whom, and what you can do to stop it. Then the truth will set you free.

Propaganda

What Is Propaganda?

Aldous Huxley wrote in his 1958 classic *Brave New World Revisited*, a retrospective on his famous 1932 novel of the same name, that there are two kinds of propaganda. The first type is "rational propaganda in favor of action that is consonant with the enlightened self-interest of those who make it and those to whom it is addressed." Rational propaganda makes use of things like logic, reason, and facts. And there is nonrational propaganda, which is not aligned with any enlightened self-interest but instead is dictated by passion and avoids fact and logic to influence by repetition of catchwords and phrases. Nowadays, awash in slogans and memes, we are drowning more in the latter than the former.

You've no doubt seen the posters of Rosie the Riveter in her red bandana, flexing her muscles and saying, "We Can Do It!" This powerful piece of World War II propaganda is a perfect example of a technique for promoting, publicizing, and pushing a particular point of view or call to action. The image was used as a rallying cry to include women in the support for the war efforts. In a similar way, the famous "Remember … only YOU can prevent forest fires" campaign that began in the 1940s by the U.S. Forest Service used artist Rudolph Wendelin's advertising icon, Smokey the Bear, to include common citizens in an environmental cause.

(In 2001 the slogan was changed to "Only YOU can prevent wildfires.") For more than five decades, this campaign served to place the responsibility for stopping forest fires on ordinary citizens by pointing the finger of guilt their way and claiming forest fires were the result of errant and untended campfires and other types of outdoor fires (but not the prescribed fires monitored by the U.S. Forest Service). With enough news stories of just such fires starting by just such means, it was easy to make citizens feel like they, and only they, had the power and ability to stop forest fires.

"Uncle Sam Wants You!"

"Give a hoot, don't pollute."

"See something, say something."

And in the year 2020 when the virus that caused COVID-19 swept the world, millions repeated the mantra "Stay inside, save a life." Oh, and do so "for the greater good."

These are all examples of propaganda at work, attempting to influence and achieve a desired reaction or response from the public to a particular situation, event, or circumstance, sometimes for better and other times for worse. It is everywhere.

These advertising campaigns skillfully employed the use of proven propaganda techniques that have been sharpened and molded over the course of history. Not all propaganda is bad, as we can all certainly agree that getting people to clean up their campsites so they don't burn down the forest after they leave is a good thing. But not all propaganda is good. Today, whether good or bad, some type of propaganda, coercive persuasion, media manipulation, rhetoric, social engineering, neurolinguistic programming, groupthink, cult speak, predictive programming, or other tool to shape our thoughts and actions exists in our everyday lives whether we spot it or not. It even exists in our own personal interactions with other human beings, and if we look at history, we'll find that it always has. It is often directed at us, and it is often directed by us.

Propaganda often uses bold and idealized imagery to inspire strong feelings of patriotism, camaraderie, and heroism.

Yet people still deny they fall prey to it and would rather point to the "other guy" or the "other side" as being a tool or victim of propaganda. That is also one of the techniques utilized to create a particular mindset or behavioral outcome. As we will soon see, the methods of mental manipulation run wide and deep, and they are not always easy to pinpoint, acknowledge, or ultimately avoid, which is why they work so well.

HOW DO WE DEFINE PROPAGANDA?

Propaganda is defined as the use of information to promote or publicize a particular point of view or perception. It is often used to spread one-sided, biased information to create support for a particular desired action, such as war or revolt. It can be used to sell a product or get the public to embrace a specific call to action, such as cleaning up their environment or stopping forest fires. It is used to influence an audience to accept an agenda, but rather than use unbiased facts to accomplish this, using propaganda often means resorting to lies, half-truths, misinformation, omitted facts, and disinformation to get the point across. Propaganda is, quite simply, manipulation of the masses. It can also be directed at an individual by another individual using the same tools and techniques. The bigger the circumstances, events, or issues around which the propaganda campaign is built, the bigger the propaganda campaign.

The word itself comes to us from the Latin *propagare,* which means "to spread or propagate." The word could be translated to mean "that which can be propagated." The earliest use of the word comes from 1622 when it was used in the name of a group called the *Sacra Congregatio de Propaganda Fide* or Holy Congregation for Propagating the Faith, which was meant to spread the faith of the growing Catholic Church in non-Catholic countries. In the 1790s, the word was applied to secular activities like politics and took on a rather negative tone.

The word could be translated to mean "that which can be propagated."

One of the best descriptions comes from a master of public relations and propaganda himself, Austrian American Edward Bernays (1891–1995), who wrote in his influential 1928 book, *Propaganda*: "The conscious and intelligent manipulation of the organized habits and opinions of the masses is an important element in democratic society. Those who manipulate this unseen mechanism of society constitute an invisible government which is the true ruling power of our country. We are governed, our minds are molded, our tastes formed, our ideas suggested, largely by men we have never heard of." Had the internet, mass media, and social media been around then, Bernays, who is considered one of the most influential men of the twentieth century, would no doubt have added their influence as puppet masters over the minds and bodies of humanity.

Propaganda is utilized particularly in politics and advertising, two arenas where altering and controlling public perception is critical to success. Advertisers employ it to proclaim their product's superiority to any other on the market. Politicians and governments use it for, well, everything, from coercing the public into unnecessary war to persuading voters to support one candidate over another. Political ads, signs, commercials, slogans, and memes are all part of the propaganda campaign to get you to do what they hope you will do—or what they need the entire population to do.

PERSONAL PROPAGANDA

Before looking at the history of propaganda tactics, we should note how our own individual behavior is rampant with it in some form or another. When it comes to human relationships, whether platonic or romantic, among friends or family, or related to school or work, we all resort sometimes to manipulations, distortions, and outright lies to get what we want—usually to get another person or persons to act, think, or behave the way we want them to. We may not design posters or come up with ad campaign slogans, but we use our words and actions as tools to influence another person to gain a particular outcome.

Personal propaganda can include things like flattery, giving gifts, offering services, supporting or even financing someone's dream, or just generally being there for them in ways others aren't. Think of all the times in your life someone has tried to get something from you, and the times you wanted something from someone else. What techniques, tricks, and tools did you resort to in order to sway or manipulate that person into saying "yes"? Perhaps you charmed them with flattery, offered to do things for them, bought them gifts, confided in them to build trust, among a host of other tactics designed to get them to see your way. Now imagine those same tactics on a larger scale, and you better understand how governments, world leaders, corporations, religious leaders, cult leaders, advertising agencies, PR (public relations) people, and the mass media all try to get you to see things their way.

The power of fear is a mighty weapon in convincing someone to do just about anything. Fear of dying, fear of being physically hurt, fear of loss or abandonment, and fear of fear itself drive the types of mass panic that often make propaganda a huge success, especially when used by nations to turn their people against other nations. In a personal situation, it might be used as a way to coerce someone into willingly giving up something you want, simply because you made them afraid of potential judgment or a perceived loss.

Personal propaganda involves tactics for getting something from someone by appearing to be more appealing yourself. Strategies such as flattery, giving gifts, or granting favors can all aid in ingratiating yourself to others.

On the flipside, you might use the promise of love to do the same thing. Romance and dating are riddled with propaganda between two people trying to impress each other, or from single people trying to elevate themselves and stand out over the crowd. The battle for a mate is often where the gloves come off and people use manipulative tactics to misinform, sway, coerce, and influence their intended target and snag a mate. He or she who best knows the tactics can have a great advantage, although one must ask how long the relationship will last once the mask of manipulation comes off!

Relationships between people are rampant with the art of "spin," which is to take a situation and "spin it on its head" to present a different view of it. One fun example appears on the television show *King of Queens* when Kevin James's character, Doug, is talking to his wife, Carrie, played by Leah Remini. Carrie says to Doug, "The doctor said your cholesterol is through the roof," trying to persuade him to take better care of his health. Doug's response is classic spin as he answers, "Maybe he meant that in a good way, as in 'woot woot,'" and he makes the "raise the roof" hand gestures. It's a funny scene and the perfect example of how we often spin negatives into positives to excuse our own behaviors—in this case, bad eating habits. Positives can be spun into negatives, too.

Do parents use propaganda on their children? Of course, they do. Recall the guilt trip of "children in China are starving, so be thankful for your dinner and eat it." Or perhaps you were exposed to the "don't make that face or it will stick that way" scare tactic. What about the "Santa is watching, so you'd better behave" manipulation? Adults tell children all kinds of things to control them and get them to behave a certain way. Parents don't necessarily use these tactics to be sinister control freaks but rather because they, too, were exposed to fearful propaganda as children to keep them in line, and, hey, if it works, keep working it.

But using propaganda can become toxic and even dangerous to a person's well-being. Manipulation and the use of fear, love, guilt, or shame can backfire by becoming abuse, and we have seen everyone from parents to world leaders going this route many times. We might be less aware when we ourselves become guilty of crossing that line, however. If our relationships with our friends, family, loved ones, colleagues, and even strangers rest only upon our ability to lie, manipulate, and coerce, perhaps the problem is with us, not them, and we are taking this propaganda thing a little too far. Domestic abuse survivors, rape survivors, and those who have been emotionally abused often are told, "If you tell, you die," or some equivalent threat. Victims who try to speak out against powerful figures are told, "You will never work in this town again," or, "It's your word against mine." Is this true propaganda? Yes, if it is used to influence a certain outcome, which in this case is silence.

Human behavior since the dawn of our time on this earth has been filled with opportunities to control each other and bring others around to our way of thinking and seeing the world. Our primitive ancestors had just as much to gain as modern humans by trying to influence the actions and thoughts of other tribe members, and they had just as much to lose if they were on the receiving end of the manipulation. From our earliest days, we learned to use others and to allow ourselves to be used.

Today, our personal identities tend to be so locked into whatever political party we belong to, what religious viewpoint we ascribe to, or what country we happened to be born in that we support and promote propaganda that supports us while absolutely and steadfastly denying any against us, even if it may be fact-based or truthful. Propaganda works hand in hand with things like denial, confirmation bias, and cognitive dissonance to play to our egos and make us want to be right more than anything else. We may even prioritize our stance over keeping relationships intact, preferring to manipulate others' thoughts or actions instead of just allowing them to think and feel the way they want to. It's easy to control people today. Just play to their political or religious identity, and you've got them in your grip.

OVERT AND COVERT

Overt propaganda is easy to spot. Think Smokey the Bear and Rosie the Riveter. Think Hitler's speeches and Nazi Germany. Think Uncle Sam. Overt uses of art, symbols, messages, slogans, and advertisements are obvious. Not so obvious are covert methods involving manipulating human behavior on a more insidious and sometimes subliminal level. In chapter nine, about tools and techniques, we take an in-depth look at this, but for now, look at your personal behaviors, actions, and thoughts and note where you are using overt tactics to get what you want, and where you are being more covert. It can also be easy to see in others. For example, if you are in public office and someone offers you a bribe of ten thousand dollars to support their bill, that is pretty overt. But if that same person instead befriended you and worked their way into your life, then started to attempt to sway you toward their goal, it would be more covert and would be harder to spot as it was happening. Why? Because we like to give people the benefit of the

Overt propaganda, such as is seen in this North Korean military parade, uses overt images, slogans, and symbols to convey a strong message.

doubt and see the good in them. We want to trust others and have them approve of us, even like us. An overt attempt to threaten or push you to do something doesn't play into those basic egocentric needs and often won't work, unless you are willing to act immorally, whereas a cover attempt might work quite well.

As we delve into the history of propaganda and the various forms it takes, using examples of real events and situations, it will become much easier to spot it at work in your own life. The methods don't change, only their degree. We may never stop using these methods on our children, friends, lovers, and colleagues, and in some cases where the result is a positive one, it may behoove us not to stop, even though honesty should be the best policy. It's the more insidious and destructive uses of propaganda we need to discern and fight, because they are not beneficial to anyone but those inflicting the deceptions upon the populace.

This is not to say we all must become clones of one another and join the same political party or all follow the same religion. We don't have to all believe in the same things and have the same points of view. We're human and we are different, and that needs to be acknowledged and celebrated. But propaganda rears its ugly head the minute we decide others need to be just like us—that others should believe as we do or they are bad, evil, or otherwise awful. There's a huge difference between acknowledging individuality and pressing others to accept your individual characteristics and beliefs. They are not you; you are not them. Live and let live, and can't we all just get along?

Taking personal responsibility for our thoughts, feelings, actions, and behaviors could be the most radical step we can take....

VICTIM OR PERP?

One of the most important things we must do, whether in our personal lives or as members of society, is decide in any given circumstance whether we are the victims or the perpetrators of propaganda, and act accordingly. Because of our need to be right, to feel righteous and just, and to deflect blame and guilt onto others, we often excel at identifying where and when we are the victims but fall way short of admitting we are the perps. Taking personal responsibility for our thoughts, feelings, actions, and behaviors could be the most radical step we can take to fight the rising tide of propaganda and manipulation we face daily, especially when we turn on the television and watch the news or get on social media and expose ourselves to the groupthink machines.

Asking ourselves questions such as the following can be useful in helping us make that distinction.

- Do I lie to others to get what I want?
- Do I manipulate others to get them to think my way?
- Do I defend my own religion or political party when it does awful things by pointing out the awful things of the opposing religion or political party?
- Do I coerce others into thinking as I do?
- Do I try to persuade others to be like me?
- Do I deny things that don't align with my identity or belief system?
- Do I blame others for my own shortcomings?
- Do I engage in "us versus them" behaviors?
- Do I close myself off to other points of view?
- Do I only promote and publicize things I agree with because I need others to agree with them too?
- Do I really believe in what I believe in, or am I indoctrinated into a belief system?

These are just some of the questions we can ask ourselves to stay in check with our own behaviors and thoughts. We can ask some bigger questions too.

- Does my ideology really serve my authentic self?
- Do I fully trust the media I watch?
- Do I tend to shun or deny media reports that go against what I believe in?
- Do I refuse to talk to anyone with a different worldview?
- Do I only spread news and media that aligns with my identity?
- Do I make fun of those who question authority, especially my authority figures?
- Do I excuse the behavior of politicians, celebrities, and other famous figures I like, while pointing out the same flaws in those I don't like?
- Do I buy into a certain worldview without questioning it?
- Do I ever question authority or what the media tells me?

We can go on and on, but the above are just some of the questions that might shine some light on how much we are influenced by the pull of propaganda personally and as part of the greater collective.

When it comes to propaganda, those who perpetrate it truly hope you never ask any questions.

A BROAD REACH

According to the American Historical Association, propaganda can be defined as any ideas or beliefs intentionally propagated, and this can include the positive, negative, and neutral ones. The website's page "Defining Propaganda I," an excerpt from the association's 1944 pamphlet *What Is Propaganda?*, states: "Of course propaganda is used in controversial matters, but it is also used to promote things that are generally acceptable and noncontroversial. So there are different kinds of propaganda. They run all the way from selfish, deceitful, and subversive effort to honest and aboveboard promotion of things that are good." This manipulation, for whatever purpose or effect, can be done in secret or out in the open for all to see, and it can be emotional and inciting, or rational and logical, depending on the message and the intent.

Historically, when it comes to war and politics, propaganda incites fear, appeasement, agreement, and action on behalf of the messenger or perpetrator. Despite its origins in the goals of the Catholic Church to "propagate" religious action for the betterment of humanity, ostensibly spreading the joy of faith in Christ throughout the lands, it has today become known as a tool of control and deception that works no matter who chooses to use it.

A Historical Look at Propaganda

"Quis custodiet ipsos custodes?"
("Who will guard the guards themselves?")
—Juvenal, Roman satirist and poet

Information tells the story of our human past. The problem is, how do we interpret that information correctly without knowing the agenda or motivation of those who left it behind? Experts in anthropology, archaeology, linguistics, history, and a host of other scientific arenas must piece together examples of human actions and behaviors along the historical time line and look for patterns, commonalities, and differences and what might have caused or influenced them. It is no easy task. Information during the dawn of humanity did not go viral as it does today, but it did leave clues in rocks, cave art, pottery, tools, drawings, etchings, carvings, glyphs, architectural features, art … you name it.

But it still fell upon the brains of the world to figure out what it all meant. Agreeing on an accurate assessment of our historical past is no easy task because so many of the clues we've found are open to interpretation.

Here, for example, is a simple example of how many different directions a simple drawing can take us.

A group of archaeologists discover a large cave wall drawing depicting a big, burly primitive man. At his feet are three antelope-like creatures, clearly dead. The man is holding up his arms to the sky.

The above description tells the facts—what is seen in the cave wall drawing. The possible interpretations can include:

- Grog (the man in picture) just killed three quarlocks (their name for the dead prey). Yay, Grog! He wins employee of the month!
- Grog is telling anyone who enters the cave that there are plenty of quarlocks around to feast upon. Take heart!
- Grog says the prey around here is his and he will kick your ass if you attempt to hunt near this cave. Be warned!
- Grog is clearly the best hunter in our tribe. Vote for Grog in the tribal elections next Tuesday!
- Grog is not a vegan.
- Grog found three dead quarlock carcasses. Anyone want a snack?

It may sound silly, but when presented with a certain amount of information, whether in words or images, we, the interpreters, are forced to fill in the blanks unless we find other drawings or accompanying information that clearly sets forth the artist's agenda … or Grog's.

The addition of information fine tunes the story being presented. Let's say Grog is holding a spear, and let's also say there is a dead human body next to the quarlocks. Let's also say Grog is wearing a weird mask made of quarlock fur. Now we might interpret the story as:

- Grog pretended to be a quarlock to infiltrate their herd and kill three of them, and he also kicked some guy's ass who was trying to steal the meat from him. Yay, Grog!
- Grog is a god who thankfully provided our tribe with three quarlocks to eat, but, sadly, Joog was killed by an errant horned boar in the process.
- Grog has power over dangerous animals and bad humans alike. Long live Grog. Elect Grog tribal king next Tuesday! Vote!

Applying personal meaning to the cave art is a form of personal propaganda if we don't really know all the facts about the images or their purpose. On a grander scale, applying meaning to an entire tribe or a rival tribe entering said cave is also a form of propaganda, meant perhaps to lift Grog to higher status among his peers and enemies, get primitive voters to vote for him for higher office, warn off enemies, or perhaps thank the real gods and goddesses by leaving them a really cool drawing of the miraculous intervention they achieved through their human vessel, Grog. One of these explanations may benefit one group of people over another. None of them may be true. It's also possible the drawing was just made out of boredom or for entertainment and was meant to convey nothing more than its face value. Or maybe Grog's kid, Creech, drew the image of himself while fantasizing about the hero he hoped to be when he grew up, overthrew his father, Grog, and led the tribe to greater glory.

The history of propaganda and other manipulative tactics begins here, with information and interpretation, with agenda and meaning and purpose.

The history of propaganda and other manipulative tactics begins here, with information and interpretation, with agenda and meaning and purpose. It begins with the dawn of understanding that we could use images, and later words, to convey a message to others, friend or foe, depending on what we wanted or needed from them.

PROPAGANDA THROUGHOUT HISTORY

Ask someone if they can give an example of propaganda, and chances are good they will make a vague reference to Uncle Sam or to the Nazi Party if they are over the age of 50, and to advertising campaigns to sell some junk food or material object if younger. A generalization, yes, but also highly indicative of how our ages and demographics are influenced and molded depending on what is important at a given time. Young people have no world war to reference from their own experience, but they can point to propaganda from the 9/11 era or the Iraq War, if they remember that far back or studied it in school. Most people today would point to political campaigns and product advertising as examples of propaganda. Propaganda parallels current events.

Our education about propaganda is minimal in history books and usually focuses on a few key programs utilized in the United States or overseas involving politics and world wars. History, however, is filled with examples of how these tactics were used, going all the way back to ancient civilizations and cultures, whether in art, architecture, literature, or politicking. Even cave and rock art. Remember Grog?

In fact, history itself is nothing but the propaganda that made it to current times. History is written by the conquerors of the world, which means that what we think we know of our own past has already been spun and skewed in favor of the cultures and civilizations that won the most wars, survived to tell the tales, and destroyed the knowledge and teachings of the losers. Case in point: the Mayan civilization lost many of its written sacred texts during the Spanish conquest of the Yucatan in the sixteenth century, which brought in Christianity and colonialism. Most of the lost texts were ordered destroyed by Bishop Diego de Landa in July of 1562. Others were burned by Catholic priests. What was left were four codices from which historians and anthropologists attempted to put together what little we now know of Mayan culture and beliefs before the sixteenth century.

To the victor go the spoils, and the story.

Located on a cliff at Mount Behistun in Iran, the Behistun inscription was an important archaeological find that helped experts decipher cuneiform script because the writing is in Old Persian, Elamite, and Babylonian. Its importance is comparable to the Rosetta Stone.

THE BEHISTUN INSCRIPTION

Three hundred thirty feet up a limestone cliff in the province of Kermanshah in western Iran is a sixth-century relief with text carved into the rock. This is known as the Behistun Inscription. The cliff sits above the Royal Road of the Achaemenids, known today as the Kermanshah-Tehran highway. Dating back to approximately 515 B.C.E., the relief and text tell the story of the Persian King of Kings, Darius I, who lived between 522 and 486 B.C.E. The inscription includes three different versions of the same text, written in three cuneiform languages, Old Persian, Elamite, and Babylonian. It was allegedly authored by Darius himself as a way to document his victories in 19 different battles in a one-year period while putting down numerous rebellions against him throughout the Persian Empire. This allegedly resulted in the deaths of many impostors and coconspirators who rose up against him as he took the throne of the Achaemenid Empire in 522 B.C.E.

The life-size bas relief shows Darius I, the Great, holding a bow, a symbol of being a king, and standing with one foot upon the chest of a man lying on his back. The man is thought by scholars to be one of the imposters, Gaumata, a king Darius forced into submission. To the left of Darius are two servants. To the right are nine figures with their hands tied and ropes around their necks, clearly those he had conquered. Darius is looking up to a *faravahar*, a Persian symbol of divinity (the Supreme God Ahura Mazda), floating above him and blessing him as a king. The text inscription is about 39 feet high and 82 feet wide on a limestone cliff and contains 414 lines in five columns.

The inscription was authored sometime between Darius's coronation as king of Persia in 522 B.C.E. and his death in 486 B.C.E. and is now used by scholars as the foundational tool for translating Near Eastern languages. The account of Darius's bravery and heroic battles has been challenged by scholars and historians as more self-promoting propaganda than total fact.

Darius came to power after Cyrus II the Great had founded the empire. According to the legend, this is how it happened. Upon Cyrus the Great's death, his son Cambyses II succeeded him and began a quest to conquer Egypt. While he was there, his brother Bardiya usurped the throne and proclaimed himself the king, forcing Cambyses to return to deal with the situation. Cambyses knew the usurper couldn't have been Bardiya, because Cambyses had murdered him before he left for Egypt! It was a Bardiya lookalike named Gaumata.

But Cambyses died of a supposed self-inflicted wound, and Darius I, who was a distant cousin and part of the entourage around Cambyses, took it upon himself to become the king. He was said to be aided by coconspirators, and the family accepted him because he was a (nonblood) relative to Cambyses, unlike Gaumata, the usurper. Thus, Darius I became the legitimate king of Persia.

The text of the inscription reads like pure propaganda, making the claim for Darius's legitimacy, bravery, and heroics, and using repetition and persuasive language to convince readers he was indeed a master in battle and the true king. It is a great piece of self-promotion and public relations. A renowned scholar of Per-

An impression from a Persian cylinder seal shows Darius I in a chariot with text declaring his greatness. Depictions of the Persian king often included propaganda writing to assert his legitimacy as ruler.

sian history named A. T. Olmstead (1880–1945) claimed that Darius I was in fact the usurper and Bardiya the rightful king based primarily on the lack of evidence of unrest or rebellion under Bardiya's rule and record of revolt when Darius took power. The obviously grandiose proclamations Darius I makes of his long and illustrious lineage and battle acumen in the text may not all be historically factual.

So some history points to some truth, but the Behistun Inscription is said to fall into the category of Mesopotamian Naru Literature—a category of literature that combines some historical events with fictional elements to enlighten the reader to a certain intent, give a reason for the events that took place, and impart a cultural value to the events.

In the article "Behistun Inscription: Darius's Message to the Persian Empire," published November 1, 2019, at *ThoughtCo*, reporter K. Kris Hirst refers to the relief and text as an "ancient billboard" and the "earliest known example of political propaganda." Though the text has the distinction of being an important advancement in the deciphering of ancient texts, thanks to its Rosetta Stone–like use of early forms of Old Persian cuneiform, the entire inscription also serves as an early education in what Hirst calls "political bragging." "Darius's main purpose was to establish the legitimacy of his claim to Cyrus the Great's throne, to which he had no blood connection," wrote Hirst. Historians point out that the whole work is so far above the road that nobody can read it, and few people were literate enough when it was carved to do so anyway. Historian Jennifer Finn, according to Hirst, "suggests that the written portion was meant not only for public consumption but that there was likely a ritual component, that the text was a message to the cosmos about the king."

ANCIENT GREEK PERSUADERS

The ancient Greek commander Themistocles was also a politician who rose to prominence in the early years of Athenian democracy. He was born in 524 B.C.E., died in 459 B.C.E., and served as the Athenian general to the Achaemenid governor of Magnesia. He was popular as a politician, especially among the lower classes, and often clashed with the wealthier nobility of the times. In 493 B.C.E. he was elected archon (chief magistrate) and uses his persuasive powers to convince the Athens navy to increase its power, something he did throughout his career as a general. His constant advocacy for a strong navy was considered instrumental in the Greek defeat of the Persians in 480–479 B.C.E.

He accomplished this by playing on the jealousy and distaste the Athenians felt toward the enemy Aeginetans and convinced them to support a larger military navy presence to control the seas around the country. At the time, more attention and emphasis was put on the land army, but Themistocles was quite the propagandist, and because of his passion, the Athenian navy was expanded enough to gain a huge victory not only against the enemy Aeginetans but also at the battle of Salamis, where the Athenians defeated the Persians in September of 480 B.C.E. He is remembered as being the primary influence behind the decision to focus on the navy and assure a later victory.

Themistocles was also adept at the use of disinformation, the spread of wrong or incorrect information to fool an enemy—in this case, Xerxes, the son of King Darius. He did this by instituting a campaign of classic deflection by sending messages to Xerxes by one of Xerxes's own sources that would claim Greek troops were on the verge

The Greek general and politician Themistocles (c. 524 B.C.E.–459 B.C.E.) used negative propaganda to convince his enemies not to deploy certain troops.

of revolt in some of the smaller city-states. This action caused Xerxes to not deploy said troops because he thought they'd be unreliable. Themistocles next disinformed Xerxes with messages claiming his troops in Salamis were going to leave, resulting in Xerxes sending half his fleet to stop them. A third disinformation campaign helped to weaken Xerxes's military threat enough for the Greeks to take victory and turn the war in their favor when they defeated the Persians at Plataea in 479 B.C.E. Scholars suggest the disinformation campaign succeeded so well because it was grounded in real possibility, believable enough that Xerxes had to entertain the possibility it was true and act upon it, to his detriment.

No doubt disinformation and deflection had been used before in warfare and general politics, but this was the first documented example where it succeeded greatly for the disinformer—in this case, Themistocles. It was a form of strategy that included great risk but, if executed properly, could turn an entire war around by making the enemy vulnerable and open for attack. The idea is to present information that sounds convincing enough to instill enough doubt in the disinformed so they will consider taking action counter to their projected battle plans. Using informants from the enemy camp, or planting information and evidence on enemy property, can convince a general or commander to make a quick decision because they trust the source it comes from.

Jump to 356 B.C.E. and the birth of Alexander III of Macedon, who would become known as Alexander the Great of the kingdom of Macedon. He was tutored up to the age of 16 by Aristotle and lucky enough to inherit, upon his father Philip II's assassination in 336 B.C.E., a strong kingdom and military. At the age of 20, young Alexander took up a massive and successful military campaign that eventually stretched from Greece to the northwestern part of India. Once he inherited the throne, he launched his father's plans to conquer the Persians and, in 334 B.C.E., invaded the Achaemenid Empire with a campaign that lasted ten years.

Alexander's battle prowess was unprecedented, and he was undefeated, to this day considered one of the greatest military commanders in history. His youth and relative lack of experience didn't seem to stop him, and he eventually overthrew King Darius III of Persia and conquered the entire empire. He died in Babylon in 323 B.C.E. before he could execute the invasion of Arabia, but his legacy lived on after him as his face appeared on coins, statues, and monuments, and his conquests in the written record.

When it comes to propaganda, Alexander the Great did not promote himself but rather was promoted by those who admired him after his death. Military leaders compared their courage and prowess to Alexander, who had set the bar high. The resulting admiration and even worship of the young Alexander's abilities lent itself to a deification of the man, clouding the historical record so that the stories we have today are not all truth but mixed with myth and fiction. An example involves a coin that appeared in the Kingdom of Thrace during the time of a successor of Alexander's. The coin featured Alexander with ram's horns on either side of his crown and had been issued in the city of Parium in what is now modern-day Turkey.

While he didn't bother to promote himself, Alexander the Great's legacy enjoyed posthumous propaganda from military leaders long after his death. His legend—sometimes exaggerated for effect—would serve as a touchstone for military greatness for centuries.

The coin's horns were symbols of the Egyptian god Amun, also known as Zeus in mythology, and suggested that Alexander the Great had achieved the status of a deity. He was a powerful symbol of military genius, power, and conquest, and eventually the telling of his story was suffused with myth. Many of the ancient narratives of his life written between 30 B.C.E. and the third century C.E. were courtesy of historians who lived long after his death and were interpretations of accounts by those who rode with Alexander into battle, according to some scholars.

There is also art depicting his great battles from which clues might be gleaned, but suffice it to say he was a major historical figure who was revered by some, despised by others, and his life story took on some of those shadings accordingly. One interesting story tells of his love for a good photo opportunity. Apparently, he used his sword to cut the famous intertwining Gordian knot that others before him had been unable to undo. The Gordian Knot was an intricate knot made of cornel bark that the son of a man named Gordius, who became king of the Phrygians, made to secure an ox-cart to a post. An oracle claimed that any man who could undo the knot would become the ruler of all of Asia.

Alexander arrived in the fourth century B.C.E. to find the ox-cart still tied to the post at the palace of the former kings of Phrygia at Gordium, now a province of the Persian Empire. Alexander perused the knot and struggled to undo it with no success. Then he figured out that he could just use his sword to cut the knot apart. He sliced it in half with one stroke and then found the knot's ends, untying them. That same evening a huge thunderstorm struck the town of Gordian, and Alexander claimed it was a sign that the gods approved of his unconventional method of undoing the knot. Another interpretation claims he pulled the knot out of its pole pin to expose the ends. Either way, he succeeded and became the stuff of legend at the same time.

The name Alexander the Great is used to this day in textbooks and books about war, success, conquest, closing the deal, and a host of other subjects....

The name Alexander the Great is used to this day in textbooks and books about war, success, conquest, closing the deal, and a host of other subjects, securing the young conqueror a place as an eternal symbol of certain traits and characteristics. The fact that he killed and pillaged his way across great swaths of land pales in comparison to his heroism and youth, deifying him as a man among men. Modern young men look to him as an ideal of being bold and going after what you want, thanks to the successful propaganda campaigns of those who lived during his reign or shortly afterward who spread the gospel of his victories, proving a person doesn't even have to be alive to be the impetus for propaganda.

ROMAN PROPAGANDISTS

Ancient Rome and the rise of the Catholic Church took the use of propaganda to a whole new level, starting with the emperor Julius Caesar and ending with the church's propagation of faith campaigns to spread the word and increase devotion and loyalty in non-Catholic countries. We will start with Julius Caesar.

Scholars and historians consider Caesar a master manipulator and propagandist, akin to Napoleon and Adolf Hitler. These men not only influenced the worlds around them; they changed and molded them into the visions of what they saw fit. As emperor, Julius Caesar was all about the spectacle and impressing the people with flash and flair, including marches and processions that represented various victories in battles and were expensive to put on. This kind of visual pomp and showiness was perfect for a man who stated he was descended directly from the goddess Venus and understood the power of symbols to convey meaning.

Julius Caesar's face was all over art, coins, and architecture, and his name appeared in the literature of the time. Via these and the elaborate public ceremonies and gatherings, he was able to proclaim to the public his own prowess and to portray the Germanic tribes as barbarians and blood-thirsty caricatures, and he did it effectively. (Coins were considered the favored tool of propaganda as they could easily be distributed as one traveled the lands. Even today coins portray the faces of famous politicians, public servants, and national landmarks.) He hammered out themes of Rome as the place of home, peace, comfort, and rule of law, and the enemy camp as chaotic and dangerous. One account of his Gallic Wars of the 50s B.C.E. has him stating that "the various tribes regard it as their greatest glory to lay waste as much as possible of the land around them and to keep it uninhabited. They hold it as proof of people's valour to drive their neighbours from their homes, so that no one dare settle near them." He goes on to describe the Germanic tribes as engaging in plundering raids and their soldiers as untrained and lazy. He would assure his Roman citizens that they were not like that and advise them: "Remember that you have to guide the nations." This is typical "chosen one" and "us versus them" language and worked well on the Romans at home cowering in fear from possible conquest by Germanic barbarian beasts.

Roman emperors used propaganda and their own chosen "spin doctors" to convey messages to their citizens and the soldiers of their armies. Often they would use fear as a tactic, but sometimes it was honor and valor that worked best. Emperor Hadrian (117–138 C.E.) promoted the concept of uniting the empire by a set of values and tastes to be aspired to. Hadrian and others like him focused on unifying their people by showing how the public loyalty to the state and its leaders would safeguard the values and tastes they believed in. They thought of themselves as civilized, not barbarians, and the people were persuaded to embrace the good of the commonwealth and its traditions and uphold its honor by agreeing with the emperor's decisions.

Via statues and coins bearing their likeness, along with art, mosaics, and literature, the leaders elevated themselves in the eyes of the common folk in a way that was gently coercive and inclusive, ensuring that the public was in allegiance with their leadership. Hadrian ruled during a time when

Roman dictator Julius Caesar was a master of self-promotion, putting his image everywhere in the empire, including money, art, architecture, and literature.

there were few aggressive wars, and he was able to provide the public with everything from bathhouses and theaters to a great wall as a type of controlled border. As he traveled around, he erected monuments, temples, and great buildings, ushering in a golden age during his reign.

But propaganda during these times told of a cycle that kept repeating. Times of peace and good things meant times of warring and death for anyone who defied the rule of law. Remember, this was also the time of gladiators fighting to the death, battles and conquests, enslaved soldiers and enslaved labor. Imperial propaganda of this era included traditional themes and values and, for a long time, paganism and pagan ideals and beliefs, such as the pantheon of deities to be worshipped in temples and other sacred places.

Until Christianity came into the picture.

THE CATHOLIC CHURCH

In 312 c.e., Constantine the Great launched an ideological war that would, by the end of that century, outlaw paganism and elevate and solidify Christianity's position as the state-sponsored religion. At the time, nobody accused Constantine as being a propagandist, but his actions were instrumental in either ending pagan belief systems or driving them deep underground. Roman emperors were deified for assisting the church leaders in the quest to squash down paganism and any future backlashes against the growing dominance of Christianity. They accomplished this by being portrayed as men of God—men sent from God to do God's work. How could the frightened public resist such proclamations? All of these men of politics and religion joined forces in an alliance that sought to quash any heresy with a bloodthirsty vision of destroying it wherever it raised its head.

Thus the appearances of these men in art, mosaics, coins, frescos, and even jewelry of the time.

The Crusades

For nearly 200 years, from 1096 to 1291 c.e., the bloody and violent wars of faith called the Crusades were fought, marking the Middle Ages as one of the darkest periods in history. Christian forces sought to control all of the Holy Land but first had to take it from the Islamic stronghold that held power in the region. The succession of Christian popes and monarchs during this period contributed to the fervor of the movement to consolidate power, control Muslims, and spread the influence of the Roman Catholic Church further east, challenging its rival, the Eastern Orthodox Church. It was all about power, control, and expansion for the Roman Catholic Church, and the Crusades were a tool of conquest.

To rally the troops and incite good Christian soldiers to participate in the Crusades, there were many exhortations and promises given, including absolution (the forgiveness of sin) and riches gleaned from conquered lands and people. Pope Urban II used good old-fashioned propaganda in his 1095 speech at the Council of Clermont where, amidst the majesty of the impressive event, well attended by bishops, cardinals, and wealthy nobles, he made his appeal for more military backup. The commoners were relegated to a place outside the event, but the pope made sure to go outside and stand upon a huge platform before the masses to speak about the atrocities of the Muslims and the threat of a horrible fate that awaited them all if they did not act against "the accursed race."

Pope Urban II utilized classic "us versus them" language, threats, fear, urgency, and a litany of the terrors of the enemy, including raping and pillaging, to incite the crowds to support his desires. He described in detail a horrific torture technique of Turkish soldiers that involved dragging victims by their extremities, binding them to stakes, and flogging them with whips, all of which succeeded in whipping the crowds into a frenzy. When he then asked on whom the "labor of avenging these wrongs" fell, it was pretty clear at that point the masses accepted the task willingly as their own. Urban combined the horrific vision of enemy conquest with the vision of what victory would be like as a land flowing with milk and honey, and he secured their support when he announced the Crusade to the chant of the crowd yelling "*Deus volt!*" — "God wills it!"

Pope Urban II used persuasive oratory to incite the Christians of Europe to launch a crusade to the Holy Land. He painted a picture of the Muslims as horrible barbarians who raped and pillaged Jerusalem.

"*Deus volt*" became one of the most successful propaganda slogans ever used to incite war as the masses accepted Urban's appeal hook, line, and sinker. In July of 1099, the Crusading forces finally entered the Holy City of Jerusalem and became a steadfast presence in the land for almost 200 years before losing control of the city. Despite the bloodshed, there were some beneficial and symbiotic exchanges of ideas, skills, and trade between the Christian forces of the West and their Islamic neighbors of the East.

Propagation of Faith

It was 1622 when Pope Gregory XV established the *Sacra Congregatio de Propaganda Fide*, or Holy Congregation for Propagating the Faith. Historians point to this action as the foundation for the modern concept of propaganda, as this was a widespread campaign to encourage and persuade Christians to follow the rules of the church and expand their faith, personally and collectively. Eventually, this organization would be called simply *Propaganda Fide* or *Propaganda*, and the term would be set in stone for all of history as a representation of a push to influence and shift public perceptions. For Pope Gregory, it was a new tool for bringing Catholicism to the Americas as well as strengthening the faith of those in European nations who might be persuaded to look elsewhere for their spirituality, especially with the growing threat of the Protestant movement.

In the Latin text, *Magnum Bullarium Romanum*, Gregory wrote, "Especially it is desired that, inspired by divine grace, they should cease to wander amidst heresies through the unhappy pastures of infidelity, drinking deadly and poisonous water, but be placed in the pasture of true faith, that they may be gathered together in saving doctrine, and be led to the springs of the waters of life." This was the basis for his founding of the sacred congregation to spread faith.

The provinence of the word "propaganda" as a concept for changing public opinions goes back to Pope Gregory XV and his establishment of the Holy Congregation for Propagating the Faith.

According to Garth S. Jowett and Victoria J. O'Donnell, authors of *Propaganda and Persuasion*, propaganda used for religious purposes will shift over time in accordance with social and political factors. The tone, then, is not set in stone. The authors write: "The somewhat humane practices of proselytizing of the early Christians were not followed in the coercive techniques of the Spanish Inquisition in the 16th century, and even today quite wide differences are found in the use of propaganda in different Christian denominations, such as fundamentalist Southern Baptist or Methodists." The authors point out that Islam, which is a part of life and not separated from secular interests, has undergone similar tone shifts, and today there is a "renewed propaganda effort by fundamentalist Muslims to use Islam as a means of achieving both the cultural and political goal of creating unity among Arabic nations," this as a means of counteracting Western influence.

Because propaganda worked so well, it was used widely as a debate tool, and it politicized the argument for the Roman Catholic Church separating from what became the Protestant Church when a German priest named Martin Luther (1483–1546) began to ask questions and stir debate about Catholic doctrines in 1517. Luther disagreed with the church's policy about the purchase and sale of indulgences, which were documents the church issued to forgive sins, impart the grace of God, and reduce the sinner's punishment. Luther believed selling these indulgences was a form of corruption, and he published this belief and others in a document known as the Ninety-Five Theses. These charges against the Catholic Church argued that the faith of each person, without an intermediary such as a priest or the purchase of an indulgence, was sufficient to find salvation, and his critical thinking about religious doctrine challenged the homogeneity of Christianity up to that point. This focus on individual faith as a way to salvation became the cornerstone of the Protestant Reformation.

Luther is said to have nailed the Ninety-five Theses on the door of a church in Wittenberg, Germany, on All Saint's Day in 1517, itself a symbolic gesture and propaganda ploy. This not only made the act public but let the church leaders know it was made public, and soon copies of this manifesto were printed and distributed all over Germany, a strategic method of assuring it was seen widely and not to be ignored or brushed under the rug. Accompanying this strategy was artwork created by artist Lucas Cranach (1472–1553), which portrayed Luther and his reformers as heroic and portrayed the pope and Catholic Church supporters in satirical caricatures

Martin Luther, an Augustinian monk who was a key leader of the Protestant Reformation, was against a variety of Catholic policies, such as the sale of indulgences. His posting of the Ninety-five Theses (complaints against the Church) on the church in Wittenberg was done publicly as a propaganda ploy.

such as the Whore of Babylon in the Book of Revelation. The art was sold in the Protestant sections of Germany and became hugely popular as precursors of the more modern posters seen during the twentieth-century world wars and the Cold War.

The Ninety-Five Theses served as the perfect persuasive "propaganda" for Luther's arguments and launched a period known as the Reformation. An order in 1521 called the Edict of Worms condemned Luther and anyone who agreed with his heretical ideas, which were spreading relatively rapidly thanks to the Gutenberg printing press, invented in Germany about a century before. The ability to print information and spread it far and wide was a game changer for those who challenged the status quo, but also for those who wished to preserve it. The printing of propaganda materials charged forward and never looked back. It was the first time that language, rhetoric, and information could go viral in such a way as to affect and influence people far beyond the confines of a village or surrounding vicinity.

Luther's theses opened the door for more challenges to the Catholic Church, such as the official split in 1534 with England when King Henry VIII established the Church of England, or Anglican Church. King Henry wanted a divorce, which was not permitted under Catholic law, so he officially declared that England would establish its own church and got his divorce.

Eventually a sect that became known as the Puritans moved to purify the Anglican Church, relocating to America and the colonies in the early seventeenth century when they faced persecution under King James I. In America they were able to establish their new religion in the form of a "New England." In the next century, with this new streak of individualism going viral, mass conversions to Christianity occurred in the context of huge revivals in a movement that came to be known as the Great Awakening. Occurring in several waves, the first two around 1730–1740 and 1790–1840, it was a time when social, racial, and gender barriers to religious traditions were challenged and diminished.

No great progress or revolution in thinking could be achieved without first using methods of persuasion and influence. In the religious world, where ideas and beliefs run from steadfast, fixed, unmoving traditions to fluid, malleable, flexible concepts and ideals, change came via the spoken proclamations and written teachings of the great leaders. The religious texts of major and minor traditions are themselves propaganda to rally believers and solidify their devotion and unity to a singular understanding of spiritual laws, often told via stories, parables, and proverbs. Each religion was challenged to keep the flock within the fold with strong and identifiable rules, warnings of what would happen if those rules were not followed (fear-based propaganda), and the promise of joy and salvation if they were (positive propaganda).

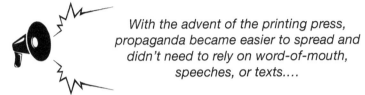

With the advent of the printing press, propaganda became easier to spread and didn't need to rely on word-of-mouth, speeches, or texts....

With the advent of the printing press, propaganda became easier to spread and didn't need to rely on word-of-mouth, speeches, or texts inscribed into singular murals, frescoes, rocks, or art that, if destroyed, took the original and the message with it. We saw this with Luther's nailing of his manifesto on the church door, backed up with copies spread throughout the country to make sure it was widely seen. This was the best way for information to go viral before the advent of telephones, televisions, radios, and the internet we enjoy in modern days. The printing press changed the game, and those who had access to one had access to a growing audience that went far beyond their own towns, cities, and nations to spread their ideas and incite change, maybe even revolution. Whether for religious expansion such as missionaries traveling to distant lands to spread "the Gospel," for political gain against one's opponent, or to highlight the good of one idealistic movement over another, the written word was a powerful and effective tool for planting the seeds of new thoughts into a larger field of fertile minds.

Jowett and O'Donnell point out in *Propaganda and Persuasion* that the Christians take the first-place award when it comes to the most effective religious propaganda campaign of all time—the G.O.A.T. (Greatest of All Time), if you will—by gearing its messages to the poor, the enslaved, and the downtrodden of the Roman Empire. "It had to compete with literally hundreds of other similar religions for this audience at the time of the dissolution of the Roman Empire," they write, "and considering that Christ and his followers did not have control over the existing communications media at the time, the ultimate level of adoption of Christianity must be considered one of the great propaganda campaigns of all time." The strategy and techniques the authors cite as being tantamount to success included the use of images and emotion through the spoken word, parables, religious writings, graphic metaphors, and dramatic gestures.

An example of metaphor was the labeling of men with powerful symbols. Jesus the Christ (messiah or anointed one) and Prince of Peace. Peter the Rock. Simon the Fisherman. All at the time were easily understood messages to the populace. Also effective, according to the authors, was having 12 devoted disciples who would take viral the messages and word of the Lord through their travels and good works, performing rituals such as baptism and communion, to bring more sheep into the flock. To this day, these symbols and rituals persist and convey a particular religious and spiritual message that has changed very little over the centuries, other than some modernization of the message for the masses. This was a classic example of a great word-of-mouth campaign, spreading the Gospel via teams chosen from the 12, who then most likely formed their own teams that went out and spread the word even further—kind of like Facebook or Twitter does today, with followers and likes and shares of posts and pictures.

Christians take the first-place award when it comes to the most effective religious propaganda campaign of all time ... by gearing its messages to the poor, the enslaved, and the downtrodden of the Roman Empire.

Behind it all was the simple message of hope, faith, and salvation—an easy sale to close in such challenging times.

War Propaganda

"If a victory is told in detail,
one can no longer distinguish it from a defeat."
—Jean-Paul Sartre

The propagation of new ideas continued through the times leading up to the American Revolution, when printing presses allowed both religious and political messages to be delivered throughout the American colonies via a network of newspaper and specialized printed materials, including posters and signage, that proclaimed either the ideals of the Patriots or those of the Loyalists. This was probably the origin of political junk mail, and historians identify a more negative aspect of propaganda dating from the French Revolution (1789–1799) through the mid-nineteenth century, when political propaganda had the power to create true social revolutions and also to stop them.

According to "The Story of Propaganda," from the American Historical Association's publication *What Is Propaganda?*, propaganda flourished throughout the Middle Ages and into modern times. "No people has been without it. The conflict between kings and Parliament in England was a historic struggle in which propaganda was involved. Propaganda was one of the weapons used in the movement for American independence, and it was also used in the French Revolution." The writings of Voltaire and Jean-Jacques Rousseau in the eighteenth century were said to have instigated opposition to Bourbon rule in France in much the same way that, across the ocean, Thomas Paine and other activists roused and inflamed opinions against England during the American Revolution. Always, it took a leader or several, well-spoken and articulate, to manipulate, influence, and coerce the masses to rise up and revolt, just as those they were revolting against used the same techniques to rally counterrevolutions against the outspoken and opinionated dissenters.

As we will soon see, the Patriot versus Loyalist battle of the American Revolution would be paralleled by the liberal versus conservative, Democratic versus Republican, and left versus right battles fought today in the mass media and via social networking. And, yes, you still get political junk mail, don't you?

Always, it took a leader or several, well-spoken and articulate, to manipulate, influence, and coerce the masses to rise up and revolt....

REVOLUTIONARY PROPAGANDA

"These are the times that try men's souls." So said Thomas Paine, the most famous propagandist of the American Revolution (1765–1783). This time-tested statement first appeared in a series of pamphlets collectively called *The American Crisis,* published from 1776 to 1783, in which Paine used rhetorical language to persuade others to embrace his justifications for supporting the Revolutionary War. Historians point to the colonial period as a time when the most powerful and influential figures shaping political history and creating a new government used various forms of propaganda to influence the intellectual debate and discourse and create a groundswell of support among the colonial peoples to rally behind the plan for a full-out revolution.

The rise of war propaganda began long before, during the times of Assyrian, Roman, Greek, and other ancient empires, but the printing press changed the landscape. By the time the American Revolutionary War came around, more efficient and potent tools for change existed for both sides of the enemy lines. Modernizing technology was making it a lot easier to persuade and influence larger numbers of the population than ever before, and the key figures of the Revolutionary War were no strangers to the power of the spoken word through speeches, via rhetoric and persuasion, to agitate the masses into action or at least anger them enough to support whatever outcome was desired by the propagandists. As an example of written rhetoric, scholars often point to the earlier works of John Locke, a seventeenth-century British philosopher and physician known today as the "father of liberalism," notably his 1690 work *Two Treatises of Government*, which he wrote to refute the power and divine right of kings and promoted the people as having sovereignty over their governments. Locke's work encouraged people to even overthrow government if their leaders could not be trusted or were not working in favor of the people. This concept would later influence sentiment during the Revolutionary War and all the way to the Vietnam War in the twentieth century, both ideological wars that spoke to the struggle between the power of the people and the power of those governing the people.

Pamphlets, posters, and speeches were tools of the Revolutionary War, used by the leaders of the colonists to develop an ideology that would be accepted by the mostly literate populace. Some of the more successful writings came from Richard Price, who wrote *On Civil Liberty* in 1776, and Thomas Paine, who wrote *Common Sense* the same year, which put forth the argument for liberation from England, and from statesman Benjamin Franklin via the *Pennsylvania Journal* and other outlets. Thomas Jefferson, George Washington, Samuel Adams, and other leaders of the Revolution made use of printing and selling books, booklets, and shorter texts as well as publishing articles in newspapers supporting the cause. George Washington ordered the reading of Thomas Paine's *American Crisis* to his soldiers to keep up morale and inspire emotional support.

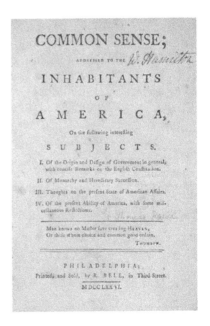

Written by Thomas Paine but published anonymously in 1776, the pamphlet *Common Sense* appealed to Americans' Protestant beliefs by sounding like a sermon while advocating for a distinct American political identity separate from England.

Newspapers became a major means of communicating ideas and information from the mid-1700s even as the British were attempting to tax all periodicals through legislation known as the Stamp Act. The *Providence Gazette* and *Boston Gazette* focused on organizing opposition to the Stamp Act and reporting on events such as the Boston Massacre, which occurred in 1770. The Boston Massacre was a prime example of a newspaper skewing news in favor of one side. In the skirmish, a crowd of rowdy citizens provoked British troops into firing upon the rioters, killing five of them. Even though the soldiers were taunted and provoked into firing, later newspaper stories made the rioting citizens out to be the victims and the British the bad guys, provoking subsequent attacks on the British via political cartoons, art, and other writings that continued to reference the so-called massacre. Paul Revere, a silversmith and engraver, was notorious for his various engravings and cartoons that played upon anti-British sentiment by embellishing facts, exaggerating events, and using images to incite further hatred of the evil—the British. These political drawings and cartoons were real propaganda and created with that purpose in mind, using plenty of death symbolism, color choices, and inflammatory race baiting to elicit a reaction from the American Patriots.

Ben Franklin followed suit with a famous drawing of a snake broken into eight pieces to represent each of the colonies, with the slogan "Join, or die." What a choice! The cartoon was part of a campaign for a "Plan of Union" and first appeared in the May 9, 1754, edition of the *Pennsylvania Gazette*. The cartoon was allegedly based on a superstitious belief that a snake with severed parts could be restored to wholeness only if the pieces were put together before sunset. It was both symbolic and urgent, and it served as a call to action to the colonists.

The color black was used often to represent mourning or the death of freedom, and often newspapers would put black borders around propaganda columns or cartoons for emphasis. In 1765, several newspapers were put out of business because of the Stamp Act, through which the British Parliament imposed a stamp duty on newspapers, legal documents, and commercial documents to raise revenue for the government. The newspapers that remained in business printed protests in dramatic black borders to represent the death of free speech and the repression of individual freedom by British rulers, and eventually opposition grew to the Stamp Act. It was repealed in 1766.

Benjamin Franklin's "Join or Die" political cartoon was published in the *Pennsylvania Gazette* in 1754. It proved to be an effective image for unity among the American colonies.

At the time the war broke out, there were three dozen newspapers operating in the colonies, and at the height of the war, there were over 70. (Many would stop publishing because of war losses, resulting in about 35 or so still operational after the war ended.) Suddenly, writers, editors, and publishers of newspapers were at the front lines of the cry for revolution, pumping out thousands of copies to provide the citizens with all the news fit to print, including art, cartoons, and slogans geared toward inciting support. Many leaders wrote under pseudonyms. Samuel Adams allegedly wrote under 25 assumed names to further spread his beliefs.

The power of repeating a slogan, idea, belief, or story, whether true or not, would often cross into the world of gray and black propaganda. White propaganda is positive and empowering, spreading truths and actual events. In the gray zone, all is a matter of interpretation. In the black zone are out-and-out lies, deception, misinformation, and disinformation. It was all considered acceptable for the good of the cause. Franklin was a proponent of using all such materials. He once wrote, "The facility with which the same truths may be repeatedly enforced by placing them daily in different lights in newspapers ... gives a great chance of establishing them. And we now find that it is not only right to strike while the iron is hot but that it may be very practicable to heat it by continually striking." Franklin understood the necessity of repetition as well as publishing propagandist materials in a news forum such as a newspaper, which lent credibility.

Slogans and political cartoons of the Revolutionary War still permeate U.S. culture. "Give me liberty or give me death" came from a speech by Patrick Henry to the Second Virginia Convention on March 23, 1775, in Richmond, Virginia. Advertisements and notices in newspapers allowed such slogans to be disseminated widely, just as today, social networking makes certain memes go viral. One of the most popular was "No taxation without representation," an abridged version of "Taxation without representation is tyranny," generally attributed to James Otis Jr., a lawyer and political activist in Boston in 1761 in protest of the British Parliament taxing the colonists at higher and higher rates but offering them no representation in government. Otis and his slogan were influential as a voice of Patriotism against British policy that led to the American Revolution. Today those who pay taxes demand they have a say in government, if only via their ability to vote.

Besides newspapers and speeches, there were other methods of promoting ideals and persuading the people of the colonies. There were songs, art, plays, assemblies, meetings,

The famous U.S. Declaration of Independence can be considered a seminal piece of propaganda. Author Thomas Jefferson's words are full of power and patriotism.

town halls, protests, letter-writing campaigns, performances, the planting of "liberty trees," and burnings of effigies, all to turn the public against the British.

Declaration of Independence

If there was one seminal piece of propaganda during the time of the Revolutionary War, it was without a doubt the Declaration of Independence. Thomas Jefferson drafted a masterful statement or manifesto said to include everything from the influence of John Locke to the ancient philosophies of Rome and Greece in a call to action for the colonists and Patriots to finally declare themselves free and sovereign. It began with a powerful proclamation—"We hold these truths to be self-evident, that all men are created equal"—and, via a litany of the sins and mistakes of the reign of King George III and British rule, laid out the entire justification for a revolution. Before it was accepted as an official manifesto, the Declaration was published in the *Pennsylvania Evening Post*. Two days later it was adopted by the Continental Congress, and the rest, as they say, is history.

The colonists had elected delegates to the Continental Congress, which eventually became the government of the Union during the time of the Revolution. The Congress delegates met in Philadelphia in 1775 and imposed rules of secrecy to protect the Congress and supporters. In June of 1776, Richard Henry Lee introduced a resolution stating the colonies "of right ought to be free and independent states." A committee of five people wrote up the reasons, and Thomas Jefferson, who chaired this Committee of Five, wrote the first draft. It took him three weeks of intense writing before presenting the document to the Congress, and much of it was edited and changed.

The final version was voted upon on July 2, 1776, and ratified on July 4, now known as Independence Day. The official printer to the Congress, John Dunlap, set the type and printed 200 copies, which became known as the Dunlap Broadsides. These were sent out to committees, assemblies, and Continental Troop Commanders. John Hancock's name was at the bottom, but the copies were not signed. Eventually a copy reached King George

III, and he wasn't happy with the misguided Americans, shunning their claims of independency.

Today, Americans celebrate the Fourth of July with fireworks, celebrations, and a strong sense of patriotism and the red, white, and blue of the American flag. All of these are symbols of the most important and widely embraced propaganda document of our nation's history, the one that inspired citizens to fight for their freedom from Britain and create the United States of America.

CIVIL WAR AND BEYOND

Prior to the years of the American Civil War (1860–1865), printing had become a more sophisticated and widespread technology, allowing for both the North and the South to carry out their ideological campaigns to larger audiences as the old-fashioned press gave way to steam-driven and then electric presses. Being able to better communicate their messages proved invaluable as the two sides rallied their forces on the issue of slavery, with the South in favor and the North against. Newspapers and other publications flourished, and so too did written and artistic propaganda.

Journalists and war reporters were a part of both the Northern and Southern armies, and it was common during the time for news reports to claim victories when they were defeats as a method of encouraging troops and public morale. One such false victory was the Battle of Bull Run, reported as a success for the North when it was a defeat.

The invention of the telegraph promised more and faster distribution of information, although in some cases, telegraph lines were destroyed to prevent factual news from reaching the newspapers and reporters, and the militaries of both sides engaged in censorship of anything that didn't portray their side as a stellar success. Magazines appeared around this time, offering more opportunities to spin the truth with articles and "front line" reports mixed with purely propagandic art, comics, and cartoons. Because photographs were not yet able to be printed in these publications, art was the order of the day, and it was common for partisan newspapers to feature only positive art to portray their side, and negative caricatures to portray the enemy.

Most scholars agree that the South utilized more partisan propaganda than the North. Although the Union, too, engaged in "fake news," it was a bit more likely to present factual reports from

The invention of the telegraph by Samuel Morse in the 1830s made possible the communication of news—and propaganda—at almost instantaneous speeds.

the front lines, using what information they could get. Reporters were not embedded on the front lines as they are in today's wars, but they were the closest sources of what was happening out on the battlefield.

Upon completion of the transatlantic cable in 1866, news, and of course propaganda, could now more quickly be disseminated overseas between Europe and the Americas. This corresponded with advancements in printing and engraving, including the inclusion of photographs, that contributed to the use of print as a weapon of mass propaganda. Adding to this were advertisements and those who paid for them, particularly into the latter part of the nineteenth century and into the twentieth. Advertisements were backed by corporations and business entities, and by politicians and political organizations, who pursued their own agendas. Whoever had the money to buy the ads had the advantage of reaching fertile audiences eager to take sides and spend their hard-earned money on the products that best played to their ethics, morals, beliefs, and emotions.

Abolitionists and Slavery

U.S. and British abolitionists turned to the forces of the press and propaganda to push their antislavery views and gain support for the cause of ending slavery. They focused on the horrid conditions in which enslaved people lived and how terribly they were treated by their enslavers, both white and black. Abolitionist stories often featured former slaves telling their tales of abuse and repression. Using both emotional and rational debate on the political, moral, and social repercussions of slavery, the North was able to gain a stronger foothold in popular opinion, even as the South used its own propaganda to push "tradition" and put a positive spin on the treatment of enslaved people. The rich plantation owners had a lot to lose if slavery ended. The key for the South was to try to portray some moral value in the good caretaking of enslaved workers, even as the wealthy elite were taking advantage of such cheap and plentiful labor.

Dueling ideologies, especially political but also religious and cultural, were at the forefront of the Civil War. The North portrayed the South's enslavement of humans as abusive, immoral, and inhumane and portrayed themselves as the progressive bringers of change and freedom to all. The South portrayed the North as dis-

Both sides used incendiary language, art, posters, cartoons, songs, and speeches to play upon the emotions of the people they hoped to influence....

regarding traditional values, wealth, and racial superiority and portrayed themselves as fighting not just to keep their traditions (including the right to own slaves) but also for fair trade tariffs and import/export laws and for the right to exercise self-determination. Both sides used incendiary language, art, posters, cartoons, songs, and speeches to play upon the emotions of the people they hoped to influence, including the enslaved people themselves.

By demonizing the enemy, both sides were able to recruit the necessary men needed for the war effort. Enlistment propaganda played on the patriotism of young men, urging them to take up arms and join the battle for justice and fairness. Posters and art called upon young men: "To Arms! To Arms! Your Country Calls! Volunteer for the War." They would include payment terms and the benefits of bravery. Songs of the time also played up the bravery aspects of enlisting, along with national pride. Often, pretty women sang those songs to encourage the young men to sign up. Some of the most memorable morale-boosters were "The Battle Hymn of the Republic," "Dixie's Land," "Battle Cry of Freedom," and "When Johnny Comes Marching Home."

White slave propaganda grew in popularity during this time, with a number of photographs, woodcuts, art, novels, lectures, and speeches by and about white-looking or mixed-race slaves. This was a method to secure money for the education of former slaves and to further the abolitionist movement by shocking white viewers with a reminder that slaves were not too different from them and shared the same humanity. The imagery often used children and adults who looked European. Harriet Beecher Stowe's famous 1852 novel *Uncle Tom's Cabin* features a quadroon slave character—someone whose ancestry is one-quarter Black—in Eliza, and mixed-race characters are found in other abolitionist novels of the time, such as Mary Hayden Pike's *Ida May: A Story of Things Actual and Possible*, which tells the story of an enslaved white person.

There were also plenty of nonfiction stories of enslaved Blacks who could pass for white or had a partial white ancestry, some of whom were freed slaves who penned their memoirs. Lighter-skinned enslaved people were sometimes treated better

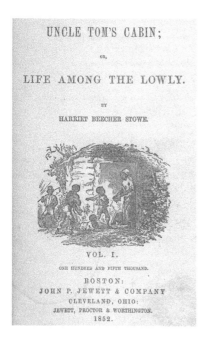

Uncle Tom's Cabin by Harriet Beecher Stowe served as antislavery propaganda for the North before the American Civil War.

or as more equal to free whites than darker-skinned enslaved people, causing more division. A *Harper's Weekly* woodcut from January 1864 bore the caption "Emancipated slaves, white and colored," and featured a number of former slaves, four of whom were more white-skinned in appearance.

According to Mary Niall Mitchell, a University of New Orleans professor of early American history, in her *American Quarterly* article "'Rosebloom and Pure White,' or So It Seemed," photographs of light-skinned former slaves were used by missionaries and charitable associations to appeal to the sympathies of white people to raise money for the education of freed slaves. Images of white-looking slaves could also be associated with the idea of white girls and women sold into Southern slave markets, striking fear into the hearts of wealthy white families who might worry about their own daughters falling to such a fate. Just as props were used in propaganda photos and images, these white slaves were used as props to further certain agendas.

Envelopes on the Rise

The North had access to more sophisticated methods of propaganda and began using slogans and imagery on envelopes as a way to spread its message and increase support and morale. Civilians and soldiers loved the envelopes and their messages of patriotism and bravery, and because the mail was the main type of communication method at the time, those messages could be seen by many people. Manufactured envelopes were relatively new in the 1860s and took off like wildfire as a method of planting a message to send to Americans who were far from their hometowns. Thousands of designs made their way onto envelopes, including those devoted to bringing the nation together after the Civil War ended.

With almost four million men in the North and South joining their respective armies, a lot of mail was being sent to loved ones and back. The printed envelopes were decorated with flags, birds, pretty women, short poems, the faces of generals, and other images, and at the height of use, more than 10,000 designs were printed for the Union alone. A hundred designs were sold for a dollar or so, and they were popular in the South as well, albeit not in the same numbers. Envelopes also featured the candidates of the 1860 presidential campaign.

Northern envelopes focused quite a bit on the preservation of the Union. There were not many that featured messages about slavery. Perhaps only 80 of the 10,000 featured African Americans on them. The South featured Confederate designs and slogans that flew off store shelves, including the Confederate flag with seven white stars on a blue rectangle and a red-and-white striped background. As new states seceded, the printers adjusted the designs by scratching in new stars or small crosses. Unfortunately for the South, they did not produce their own paper, importing most of it from the North or overseas from England, and had to get around a Union blockade of ships going to Southern ports.

Large numbers of these specialized envelopes were never mailed but were considered collectors' items, and they certainly are collectable today. Some of these postwar envelopes are quite rare, especially those with clearly racist images and sentiments sold in the Confederate states.

Ideological Art

The Civil War was a popular time for ideological artwork, cartoons, illustrations, and comics, which flourished as the population grew and printing became more sophisticated. According to the article "Visual Propaganda: Ideology in Art" at the website *IdeologicalArt.com*, "Between 1855 and 1860 the American lithographing and engraving industries flourished, several illustrated comic weeklies, including *Vanity Fair*, began offering their cartoon wares to the public, and most significantly three enterprising publishers established weekly illustrated newspapers: *Harper's Weekly*, *Frank Leslie's Illustrated Newspaper*, and the *New York Illustrated News*."

American readers now had ongoing access to cartoons and illustrations portraying current events, many printed alongside

A November 10, 1860, issue of *Harper's Weekly* features Abraham Lincoln on the cover. Lithography, which had been invented in German around the turn of the nineteenth century, allowed newspapers and other periodicals to include more illustrations that could prove as persuasive as text.

accompanying news stories. Obviously, many of those periodicals featured stories and images from the Civil War. These pieces of art showed the progression from the election of Abraham Lincoln in 1861 as the president of the United States, to the secession of 11 slave states after Lincoln made clear his agenda to abolish slavery, to the war itself from 1861 to 1865. There was even more fodder from the abolitionist movement—enough material to keep these newly established weeklies selling like hotcakes.

Another hugely popular written form of information was the almanac. The North had its *Anti-Slavery Almanac*, which included essays and news meant to instruct, persuade, and even frighten its readers against the slave system of the Confederates. These almanacs featured art and woodcuts of horrific abuse of enslaved people and racism meant to demonize the South and the ownership of humans. The South had their own almanacs that played upon the fear of people ending slavery and of white men having to compete with Black men for the affections of white women. One such image in a Southern almanac, "The Amalgamation Waltz" by Edward Williams Clay, shows Black men waltzing with white women while the white men watch from the balcony and was meant to insinuate that the abolition of slavery would result in former slaves seeking white women for their mates. Almanac cartoons were often meant to be humorous, but they still served to push one agenda over another.

Poetry became a weapon of words as writers, popular and unknown, wrote poems about the wartime experience that were meant to inspire men to enlist.

Poetry became a weapon of words as writers, popular and unknown, wrote poems about the wartime experience that were meant to inspire men to enlist. Some poems were set to music, and others were recited to soldiers to instill morale and pride. Writers submitted their propaganda poetry to the newspapers, who printed hundreds of verses over the course of the war. Male and female poets used their words to rally their fellow citizens to battle, as in Susan Archer Talley's "Rallying Song of the Virginians," which was published in July of 1861 in the *Richmond Daily Dispatch*. Some poems were written by professional writers, but others were penned by soldiers, wives, mothers, fathers, sons, and daughters getting their emotions on paper in the hope of convincing more young men to go off to war and to inspire those already fighting.

Both sides had their favorite poems and songs, urging their men to war and their women to support the men. Adding music made it easy for the people to remember the poems and sing along to them, with hearts full of patriotic pride. People began writing and composing their own patriotic songs to show their love of country and their devotion to duty and honor. Robert E. Lee, the commander of the Confederate Army, was moved to say, "I do not think we have an army without music." Commanding General (and later U.S. president) Ulysses S. Grant is said to have stated, "I know only two tunes; one of them is 'Yankee Doodle' and the other one isn't."

Music set the tone and mood of the times, whether somber and serious or cheerful and spirited, and evoked emotion and swelling pride when played in marches and social gatherings. The first song written specifically for the Civil War was "The First Gun Is Fired: May God Protect the Right" by the famous composer George Frederick Root. It became one of the most popular songs of the time and was played as often as possible to keep soldiers' spirits lifted and give hope to those at home waiting for their return. Soldiers reportedly brought fiddles and other instruments with them, along with lyric books, to keep the music going all the time. Another song by Root, "Battle Cry of Freedom," was a favorite among soldiers in the Union after they won the Battle of Stone River. It was played to boost their spirits after a demoralizing loss and was said to be playing outside every tent and by every campfire near the battlefield.

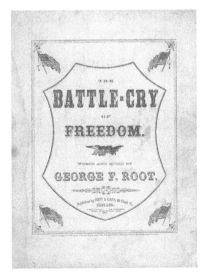

Recruitment posters featured imagery that by today's standards would appear racist and incendiary, but at the time was meant to provoke emotion, especially fear and anger, as a means for getting men fight for their chosen ideology. There were posters written in various languages to appeal to the growing number of immigrant populations, such as harps and shamrocks placed on posters in Irish-American neighborhoods. Nationality didn't matter; if you were on the side of the Union or the Confederacy, their army would be happy to have you. It was all about defining identity, according to the online article "Visual Propaganda: Ideology in Art": "This is primarily what purpose propaganda served during the American Civil War—the solidification of

Patriotic and inspiring songs such as "Battle Cry of Freedom" by George Frederick Root helped boost the morale of Civil War soldiers.

The Stories behind Popular Propaganda Posters

"I WANT YOU FOR U.S. ARMY" — Probably the most famous of all propaganda posters is Uncle Sam pointing at the viewer in a patriotic call to action. This military recruitment poster, by the illustrator James Montgomery Flagg, first appeared on the cover of *Leslie's Weekly* on July 6, 1916, as the United States was on the verge of entering World War I. The title above the poster asked, "What are you doing for preparedness?" Ever since its first appearance, this poster has been used in many variations and memes.

The iconic Uncle Sam Wants You poster was designed by James Montgomery Flagg one year before the United States entered World War I.

"Daddy, what did YOU do in the Great War?" — British illustrator Savile Lumley created this World War I propaganda masterpiece to compel men with families to enlist in the war. It played upon men's pride and their role as fathers, suggesting their children would one day judge them based on what they contributed in wartime.

"WE CAN DO IT!" — A woman wearing a red-and-white bandana and a blue shirt proudly flexing her muscles became one of the most iconic propaganda posters ever, created by J. Howard Miller around 1943 to boost the morale of women employees at Westinghouse Electric. This poster was later discovered by the feminist movement in the 1980s and used to show female worker empowerment.

The woman in the poster, based on a woman named Naomi Parker Fraley, who had worked in a naval machine shop during World War II, became synonymous with the name "Rosie the Riveter." It became even more popular than another famous propaganda poster, "Rosie the Riveter," which was created in 1943 by Norman Rockwell as a representation of the American woman working in the munitions and supplies factories during World War II. Rockwell's illustration was a call to arms for women to use their strength and capabilities to contribute to the war effort. Rockwell's "Rosie," who first appeared on the May 1943 *Saturday Evening Post*, was nothing like the arm-flexing image most people now associate with Rosie. This woman sat against the backdrop of an American flag with her riveting tool on her lap, eating a sandwich and stepping on a copy of Hitler's *Mein Kampf*. The name on her lunchbox reads "Rosie."

There was also a Chinese poster portraying a female riveter, created by artist Ning Hao. The 1954 work was meant to encourage women to work with men at factories to increase workforce numbers throughout China.

Jim Fitzpatrick created the iconic "Che Guevara" poster that was based on a photograph by Alberto Korda. This bright red-and-black image was visible during the Vietnam War protests worldwide and during the Paris student riots of 1960. It was used, and is still used, as a symbol of revolution and popular uprising.

A modern poster created in 2008 by Shepard Fairey features former President Barack Obama's face with different words beneath the image such as "Hope," "Change," or "Progress." The iconic poster was embroiled in controversy when the creator was accused of lifting the image from an Associated Press photographer, but it stands as one of the most popular and widely recognized modern propaganda posters.

North vs. South identity, pro-abolition vs. anti-abolition. The efficacy of each respective side's propaganda can still be felt easily today, close to 150 years since its occurrence." The article continues by stating that even today, that North vs. South divide lingers in the symbols and signs of pride and heritage, whether Yankee or Confederate.

In the twenty-first century, many of the symbols of the South and the Confederacy have been destroyed, dismantled, and removed by protestors and government officials out of respect for the people who were brutalized and killed by the system they celebrate. The removal of statuary and other memorials can be a powerful gesture, albeit a symbolic one, if the symbols are removed without changing the systems that gave rise to them.

THE WARS OF THE WORLD

The two twentieth-century world wars were perfect opportunities to escalate the use of propaganda to create divisiveness and promote enlistment. In World War I, German emperor Wilhelm II (Friedrich Wilhelm Viktor Albert) created the Central Office for Foreign Services to distribute materials to countries considered neutral during the war. Once war broke out, the British severed cables under the ocean connecting Germany to other nations, cutting off the country's main communication channels, although Germany retained a wireless transmitter to broadcast its propaganda throughout the country and to nearby nations. Germany also employed the use of cinema in the form of mobile movies sent to the troops to build morale and inspire a sense of pride and heritage.

The British launched their own campaigns through the War Propaganda Bureau, led by a journalist named Charles Masterson. Famed writers were invited to assist in creating messages, including Arthur Conan Doyle, Thomas Hardy, Rudyard Kipling, and H. G. Wells. A. A. Milne, creator of Winnie the Pooh, also wrote covert propaganda materials for the Brits.

Both sides offered plenty of exaggeration and embellishment, as well as misinformation and outright fabrication. The British portrayed the Germans as monsters committing atrocities, and the Germans did likewise, to the point of exhausting the public with a bombardment of propaganda by the time the war was over. The British campaign was said to have been so powerful that it helped persuade the United States into jumping into the war, and

German chancellor Adolf Hitler later studied British materials to formulate his own campaign for World War II, ideas for which he shared with propaganda minister Joseph Goebbels.

Famed writers were invited to assist in creating messages, including Arthur Conan Doyle, Thomas Hardy, Rudyard Kipling, and H. G. Wells.

Historians agree that the greatest war propaganda of the Nazi Party during World War II had its roots in the lessons learned from the campaigns of World War I and led to the art and science of propaganda as deserving of its own governing agencies. During the First World War, there was the German's Ministry of Propaganda and Public Enlightenment, the British Ministry of Information, and the American Committee on Public Information, all operating their own agendas and working hard to persuade nations to support them. The twentieth century had brought with it a new tool—radio—and radio broadcasts became the order of the day for their ability to reach ever-widening audiences across the lands 24 hours a day. Having listeners glued to their radios for firsthand stories and news reports meant the propaganda machine had a truly captive audience to take advantage of. Radio stations did broadcast real news and actual front-line updates, but they also broadcast opinion pieces, calls to action, divisive stories about "the enemy," deceptive advertising, emotional pleas, and a host of other "nonfactual" information, as well as music filled with propagandist lyrics and messages.

Motion pictures also served as a tool for promoting military and political agendas and portraying the enemy as evil by using visuals to create a sense of "us versus them" mentality and muster consent for ongoing war support. The Soviet Union sponsored films made by Russians to promote and glorify their Communist ideals, such as the 1925 *Battleship Potemkin*, and later both the Nazis and the Allies would make good use of cinema for their respective causes. During this time, which was considered the Golden Age of Propaganda, the German filmmaker Helene "Leni" Riefenstahl created one of the most widely known movies for such use, *Triumph of the Will*. Over in the United States, animated cartoons and films were promoting war support to the young people and stirring up patriotism with parodies and caricatures that made the Nazis look like either clowns or terrorists.

The Rise of Food Propaganda

"Eat less wheat!"

"Meatless Mondays"

"Local Is Best"

"Food Will Win the War"

These are just a few of the slogans used by the U.S. Food Administration during World War I to encourage the women at home doing the shopping and cooking for their families to do their duty to the country by keeping down food waste, buying the right products, and eating less to make sure the soldiers overseas had enough to eat. Just as other forms of poster propaganda proliferated during wartime, food propaganda had its place in history.

The themes were to conserve food and to volunteer to do what you could from the home front, including things like keeping your own chickens for eggs and drying peas to eat instead of meat products. According to David McCowan in his article "How WWI Food Propaganda Forever Changed the Way Americans Eat" for the *Takeout* on March 15, 2017, before the war broke out, food was a bountiful resource. Once the United States entered the war, food delivery infrastructure drastically changed, and feeding the troops became top priority.

President Woodrow Wilson created the U.S. Food Administration (USFA) to manage food resources for the U.S. Army and

the Allied troops, and he appointed mining executive Herbert Hoover to lead the efforts. Hoover soon became known as America's "food dictator," and the USFA began fixing the prices of certain critical foods, such as wheat, to stabilize prices for farmers. He also was behind commandeering rail lines and intervening to prevent food monopolies to make sure food transport was fast and reliable. He took no salary for the job (and he later became a U.S. president).

Part of the propaganda campaign included vilifying German foods and elevating American ones. Sauerkraut was renamed "liberty cabbage," and hamburgers became "liberty steaks." According to McCowan, "To ensure that support for the war remained high, Wilson authorized the creation of the Committee on Public Information

During World War II, Americans were asked to call this a "liberty steak" so as not to acknowledge its German roots.

(CPI) just days after the U.S. officially entered into combat." This propaganda organization was given the task of writing and producing press releases and pamphlets and provided quick lectures at parks, at social gatherings, in theaters, and anywhere they could put up a soapbox to spread the importance of food conservation and "the patriotism of growing one's own vegetables."

The CPI also fought its war with visuals, in the form of posters and buttons. It created over 1,500 different posters and buttons during the war effort, all meant to push the same message: "Food will win the war. Waste nothing." Eventually, the growing field of food science added its own messages to the food propaganda poster onslaught, featuring everything from substitutes for meat to unusual new products like "sea steak" and "sea beef," whale and porpoise meat respectively, which didn't quite take off.

Some historians believe that this food propaganda push had an indirect role in the creation of supermarkets because so many housewives wanted to try new products or find a greater variety of foods to choose from when they went shopping. They also wanted lower prices and more options than the local mom and pop corner shop could offer, thus changing the way people not only ate but shopped for their food.

Agitated Propaganda

In the 1920s, the Soviet Department for Agitation and Propaganda served the Communist Party of the Soviet Union. The department was responsible for political propaganda's dual purpose of agitating the masses and promoting Communist ideals using popular forms of media, including art, literature, plays, and street theater. "Agitprop theater" had the goal of enticing people to join the Communist Party through its use of politicized art forms. Agitprop could also spread information and news to the public. An agitprop train toured the countryside after the 1917 October Revolution to spread Communism via artists, actors, and performers putting on plays and theater at each stop. A printing press on the train allowed them to disseminate written pamphlets filled with propaganda as they rolled along, and radios let them communicate with the Communist Party and offer updates on the activities in each town. Ships also became traveling agitprop theaters.

Agitprop theater became all the rage in the latter 1920s, spreading into Europe and the United States as the term became synonymous with political theater. Today we have similar forms of

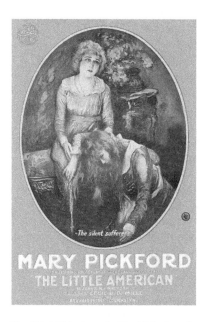

The World War I movie *The Little American* (1917), starring Mary Pickford, romanticized the struggles of the Great War.

street activism known as "woke theater" involving plays, coordinated protests and marches, readings, music, and stylized performance art to spread a social message or draw people toward a political movement.

Wartime Movies

War films became their own genre in the 1930s and 1940s and proved just as efficient as radio for delivering messages to rapt audiences eager for news, even if it was embellished. Stock news footage was also popular in theaters, where viewers were subjected to the realities of warfare, albeit edited versions, and even nonwar films often opened with a cartoon or short war propaganda piece to set the mood and stir up public sentiment.

During World War I, propaganda appeared to be meant solely to spread deception, disinformation, false information, and fake news stories to help destroy the enemy, and it took on an ominous and negative tone that it would carry into modern times. Forget morals, ethics, or truth—this was all about winning a war against a major enemy and its allies, and both sides employed it to the best of their ability, certain they were on the right side. It was up to them to convince their people of the same. All is fair in love and war, and with propaganda, making the enemy out to be monsters was considered fair, even if false or exaggerated. It was, to put it simply, information warfare.

The First World War also drove home to the Germans the power of the British propaganda machine in destroying troop morale and instigating the revolts of many German soldiers on land and at sea in 1918, a lesson they would use to correct course during World War II. Hitler went on to write his two-volume autobiography/manifesto *Mein Kampf* in 1925 and 1926, in which he expounded at length about the theories of propaganda that later served to elevate him to power and authority. The book represented his journey toward his political and religious ideologies and the plans he had for Germany. To those who fell under his charismatic spell, it served as a propagandist call to action that historians agree remains unmatched in its fervor and success.

World War II and the Nazi Propaganda Machine

"If you tell a lie big enough and keep repeating it, people will eventually come to believe it."

—Joseph Goebbels, Nazi Propaganda Minister

German chancellor Adolf Hitler understood that people would believe anything if they heard it enough times from authority figures and that a solid propaganda campaign would be able to counter and shut down any contradictory beliefs. Nazi Germany's Ministry of Public Enlightenment and Propaganda was headed up by another master of manipulation, Joseph Goebbels, and would often go head to head with the British Political Warfare Executive and the American Office of War Information.

According to "Enemy Propaganda," an article on the American Historical Association's website, "Hitler is the arch propagandist of our time." The article goes on to state: "Division, doubt, and fear are the weapons he uses within one nation and among Allied countries arrayed against him. His purpose is summed up in his own phrase—to sow 'mental confusion, contradiction of feeling, indecision, panic.'" His thinking informed the name he chose for the party he was to lead—the National Socialist German Workers' Party, popularly abbreviated as "Nazi." He knew each word of the party name would appeal to a particular group, and "that was what Hitler wanted—a name that would prove a catchall, an omnibus upon which many could ride," according to the article.

Hitler went on to use the old colors of the days of the kaiser, or German emperor, which he knew aroused nationalistic emotion in the people....

Hitler went on to use the old colors of the days of the kaiser, or German emperor, which he knew aroused nationalistic emotion in the people: black, white, and red with the swastika cross embedded upon it. It was a striking visual. The red appealed to the socialists, the white to the nationalists, and the swastika was to satisfy his anti-Semitic supporters. Then came the Nazi salute, with arm rigid and outraised to the sky. "Heil Hitler" became its own catchphrase. It was the salute of the people seen at the large rallies, parades, and gatherings in the town squares, along with the Nazi flag flying somewhere nearby. The marching soldiers known as storm troopers were a potent visual, a sight to behold that incited great emotion and frenzy among laborers and their families, party officials, and the thousands upon thousands of attendees at the rallies.

From the party name to the flag, the uniforms, the visuals, and the slogans, every aspect of Nazi life was meant to instill pride, invoke loyalty, and induce an almost hypnotic, cultlike following of the fearless leader, no matter how outrageous or immoral the acts he was soon to propose. The German people fell under the spell of a master speaker, performer, and politician who used language, rhetoric, phrasing, and emotional impact to sway his audience to his will.

The Ministry of Propaganda worked all hours to formulate the plans, the tricks, and the tools to utilize newspapers, radio, and other methods for control over the German people. Any newspaper that went against the Nazis was shut down or infiltrated and co-opted under Nazi control. There was no room for criticism or dissent. When propaganda didn't work, the Nazi leadership turned instead to vilifying certain racial and social groups to instill hatred and the old "us versus them" mentality. Those groups included the Jews, the Roma (Gypsies), Romanians, and other minority groups, including Communists and trade unions. These became the "enemy" that the Nazi leaders could point to as a distraction from the problems the country was facing and a way to keep dissent down before it could become a challenge to their authority.

This Nazi poster points a finger at Jewish people for causing the social and economic problems in Germany.

Of all the scapegoat groups, the Nazis unleashed the most hatred on the Jews. Their main argument was that the Jews were not of pure, so-called Aryan blood and therefore were defiled. Whatever the German people were suffering from, it was blamed on the Jews, and with the massive propaganda machine to support them, it was only a matter of time before Hitler and his colleagues had convinced the Christian Germans of this argument. Between 1933 and 1934, Hitler solidified his dictatorship over the people of Germany, and those who disagreed stayed silent for their own safety. In fact, one of the propaganda slogans used by the Nazis to justify their dictatorial abuses was "Fur ihre Sicherheit," which meant "It's for your safety."

Using fear and force, the Nazis became untouchable and unquestionable, often promising their detractors positions of power and influence if they would join them. With a network of spies and propagandists, they were able to dissect the potential dissent of different social groups in the country and find a way to buy, coerce, or force loyalty back to the party. Just as the Nazis used propaganda to fight their alleged enemies, they also used it to keep total control over their populace.

One of their favorite techniques was subversion. The Nazi leadership knew they could infiltrate allied nations by planting subversive agents in different localities' tourist bureaus, embassies, and other official agencies where they might work from the inside out. Known as "fifth columnists," these subversive elements would plant seeds of doubt and dissent, or lie in quiet wait for their instructions to do their damage without one soldier ever setting foot in that country.

Their main strategies were to divide with fear by raising doubt and suspicion among the Allies. Radio broadcasts to the British, for example, would tell them they couldn't trust the Americans and that it was their own leaders pushing for violence and war. But they would also use appeasement by claiming the Germans liked the Americans and were their friends. The broadcaster would claim the Germans had no desire to wage war or to stop democracy in the United States. It was sweet talking at its finest, trying to spread a message of friendly peace to a nation it was about to make war with. The idea was to keep the enemy off balance and filled with confusion. By sowing doubt in the American people, they hoped to create an outcry against the American leaders and keep them from joining in the war.

Indeed, the United States came to the Second World War a little late to the party, but once the atrocities of the Nazis were seen in the light of day, the people of America and the Allied nations rallied behind their own leaders, their own cause, and their own propaganda machine, which didn't have to exaggerate the sins of the Nazis too much. The Final Solution of the Nazi Party—the genocide of the Jewish people—served to embolden the Nazis

The Final Solution of the Nazi Party—the genocide of the Jewish people—served to embolden the Nazis and to enrage and empower the Allied Nations.

and to enrage and empower the Allied Nations. Symbols like the swastika and the arm salute became representations of evil and destruction and went viral.

The Associated Press (AP) cooperated with the Nazis to downplay their atrocities, according to Philip Oltermann in the article "Revealed: How Associated Press Cooperated with the Nazis," published in the *Guardian* on March 30, 2016. Oltermann reported that the AP, based in New York, entered into formal agreement with the Nazi regime in the 1930s to supply American newspapers with materials selected and produced by the Nazi propaganda ministry. According to archived materials examined by Oltermann, the Nazis wanted to bring the international press in line, and the only Western news agency that stayed open in Hitler's Germany was the Associated Press. It remained there until 1941 and became the prime channel for news reports and photos out of the totalitarian state.

The AP promised not to publish anything "calculated to weaken the strength of the Reich abroad or at home," and it agreed to hire reporters from the Nazi Party's propaganda division. The AP provided the Nazis with its photo archives of anti-Semitic propaganda literature. Some historians say this deal allowed U.S. AP reporters a look inside the Nazi's inner workings, which it most certainly did, but it also served to hide the Nazis' atrocities from public view. This served, as historian Harriet Scharnberg claimed, to disguise the true character of the war led by the Germans. "Which events were made visible and which remained invisible in AP's supply of pictures followed German interests and the German narrative of the war," said Scharnberg, quoted by Oltermann.

World war propaganda served its purpose. In both wars, it helped rally the troops on both sides, encouraged enlistment of young and patriotic men, and created divisions based on race, nationality, and loyalty. Propaganda remains as much a part of modern warfare as bombs and drones.

AIRBORNE LEAFLET DROPS—PROPAGANDA FROM THE SKY

During the world wars and into the Cold War era, one of the most controversial forms of propaganda was the dropping of leaflets from planes and jets. The goal was to have those living in enemy territories, civilians and soldiers alike, read the propaganda and be turned against their own governments or leaders, or be informed as to where they could get food and water and other resources to make those dropping the leaflets look like the good guys. There were six types of air drop leafleting:

An American soldier is shown putting leaflets into a cluster bomb during the Korean War. Spreading leaflets over enemy territory was designed to damage morale, promote the "good guys," warn civilians of impending attacks, and so on.

- Warnings of the areas to be targeted by bombs and attacks. These leaflets were meant to warn civilians in those areas so they could find shelter, and also to encourage enemy soldiers to leave their posts out of fear of attacks.
- Assistance and rewards leaflets were meant to provide assistance with the hope that some people in enemy territories would defect.
- Surrender instructions were included in leaflets to encourage enemy soldiers and civilians to desert their posts and surrender.
- Disinformation and counterinformation were meant to lessen the morale of the enemy, counter news and information by letting people know which radio frequencies to tune to for "real" information, and spread disinformation that made enemy leaders look bad to their own civilians.
- Leaflets meant to teach the enemy about the ideology of the "good guys" in hopes of defections.
- Humanitarian aid with instructions about where food and water drops would be, and when, again to make the good guys look like the real saviors to the enemy soldiers and civilians.

Aerial leafletting was used by both parties during World War I and II. During World War II, special leaflet bombs were loaded onto planes to drop into enemy territories. The British used hydrogen balloons to drop leaflets in German territory. The Germans had their own cardboard tubes filled with leaflets loaded into the tails of V-1 missiles, which were ejected by a small gunpowder charge in midair.

The effectiveness of littering the ground with propaganda leaflets was evident during the lowest points of the war when a morale boost was needed, but many scholars questioned the ongoing use of them once the novelty wore off and people realized they were being manipulated and that the truth was often missing from the messages. Some examples of leaflets that proved at least somewhat effective include an image used by the Allies of a mass grave of dead Germans in an open field, with the distinct message to the enemy that they could end up a part of the scenery. Another popular leaflet used by the Germans featured a man and woman kissing and the text "Farewell. Remember her last kiss ... ?" on one side and, on the other, a reminder to the soldiers that most of their fellow combatants were already dead. By playing on their emotions and desires to get back home to loved ones, American troops were more inclined to wonder how much longer the war would rage on around them.

But this kind of propaganda would only work on any troop or civilian willing to pick it up and read it with a receptive mind, and then act on it. It worked best when directed at the side that had lower morale and was in a losing position, and thus was more willing to take action on what they were being told or persuaded to do.

Leaflet bombs have not been used as widely since the world wars, although tens of millions were dropped during the wars in Korea, Vietnam, and Iraq.

Leaflet bombs have not been used as widely since the world wars, although tens of millions were dropped during the wars in Korea, Vietnam, and Iraq. Revolutionary groups favored leafletting, but they mainly did it on campuses and via handouts on the ground rather than dropped from the air during the 1960s and 1970s. Air-dropped leaflets were instrumental in getting Iraqi troops to stand down and stop fighting during the Gulf War, during which over 87,000 troops eventually surrendered in 1991.

With modern technology, the printed word holds a little less power and influence in today's ongoing war campaigns, and they require enough literacy among the target population to make a difference. They also require aircraft that fly at low altitudes, which puts them in jeopardy of being shot down, and the weather is a significant factor in the successful delivery of leaflet bombs. But they remain an option for spreading information and disinformation into allied and enemy territories, depending on the message and intent, and also for spreading information among like minds during a political revolution or uprising, such as the widespread leaflet bombs during leftist revolutionary movements throughout Latin American nations in the 1980s and 1990s. These

A Wartime Advertising Campaign
That Saved an Entire Industry

During World War II, the word came down from the U.S. government that certain products would be rationed, including petroleum products, gasoline, rubber, metal, and of course foodstuffs like meat, butter, sugar, and cheese. People were not going to movies but instead were staying home, afraid to go out. They were buying only the necessities, which did not include makeup or cosmetics. The cosmetics industries were on the verge of going bankrupt as they were not considered "essential businesses" worth receiving petroleum and other materials for their products.

Thomas Lyle Williams, the founder of the Maybelline cosmetics company, put out an ad campaign during World War II promoting beauty as a way to boost morale.

But one company used propaganda to assure they had all the petroleum they needed to keep their cosmetics line going strong. Maybelline founder Thomas Lyle Williams was not a person to panic, having brought his company from the brink of failure before. Yet even he was worried when the president ordered that the beauty industry would have its petroleum, a staple in many cosmetics, rationed. Williams brilliantly used his advertising expertise and created a campaign that not only got Maybelline all the petroleum it needed but also the blessing of the U.S. government to continue its cosmetics coup.

Williams did it by creating a line of magazine and publication ads that put the spirit of beauty and patriotism together. He knew about the pin-up girls whose posters soldiers at war had pinned to their huts and bunks. The women wore makeup and looked gorgeous. So he and his business and

---

A Wartime Advertising Campaign
That Saved an Entire Industry (cont.)

life partner, Emery Shaver, created an ad campaign featuring a housewife with her eyes done up in Maybelline mascara and cosmetics, and the accompanying slogan: "They're doing their part by keeping their femininity. That's one of the reasons we are fighting." Another ad featured an elegant young lady with an admiring military officer helping her put on her white stole. That slogan read, "Just as he dreamed her eyes would be."

These campaigns played on the concept of "War, Women, and Maybelline," as the creators put it, and encouraged the morale of both the women at home and the soldiers fighting to return home to them. It was a massive success, and not only was Maybelline permitted all the petroleum it needed, but it helped save the cosmetics industry as a whole from massive bankruptcy.

---

movements also relied on ground dispersal of leaflets and pamphlets when they didn't have the money or luxury to drop them from a plane.

Aside from war, leaflets are an important form of propaganda used by protest groups today at rallies and marches to get people to visit a website and sign a petition or join an organization, and they are also a popular method of spreading the word about a new band playing a gig in a club or a coming art show on the beach or at a park. Giving someone a piece of paper to take home with just enough information to get them to come out to an event is still a great method of securing interest and participation on a local level.

Anyone who hung out on the Sunset Strip in Hollywood in the 1980s to partake of the nightlife there can attest to the power of a band leaflet or flyer to fill a club with screaming fans!

The Cold War Era

"The people who sell the panic, sell the pill."
—Anonymous

The Cold War era spanned the decades between 1947 and 1991 and was defined by an underlying tension between the United States (and its allies) and the Soviet Union (and its allies). Rather than fight each other directly, the two superpowers gave aid to other countries (including for military conflicts) in an attempt to win allies, and the world was largely divided into the Western Bloc and the Eastern Bloc. After World War II, therefore, rather than one great war, there were several smaller ones, including the Korean and Vietnam conflicts, which left their mark on the psyche of global history. There were also propaganda campaigns that created paranoia and ruined lives. Ask anyone who lived through the 1950s about McCarthyism (more on that later), and they are sure to tell you how, to this day, the same tactics at work then are used now in racial and social propaganda campaigns.

This was a time of heightened "us versus them" fear and paranoia, and it was easy to show the American people why they should be afraid of the Soviet Union. Americans now had the power of print, radio, movies, and television to make their case, as did the Soviets, escalating the already incendiary situation to a near breaking point. By this time, there were intelligence agencies in place to spy on the enemy and formulate the at-home propaganda campaigns to make sure the populace knew who they were supposed to hate and fear.

The Soviet Union was attacking the United States on all fronts in terms of propaganda, but none was more critical than radio. It took a while before the United States caught up and responded by changing its international Voice of America broadcasts from all music and straight news to more blatant counterattacks on the Soviets. It also began broadcasting programs in Russian to influence citizens in the Soviet Union with some good old-fashioned American ideals.

Moscow would retaliate in 1949 with a campaign to jam American programs and devoted approximately 1,000 broadcasting stations to assist. This prompted the U.S. government to protest the jamming via the International Telecommunications Union and the United Nations Sub-Commission on Freedom of Information and of the Press. The United States claimed the Soviets were violating internationally accepted principles related to freedom of information. A resolution was adopted in 1950 by the Economic and Social Council General Assembly asking all members to refrain from radio broadcast jamming.

A Soviet-era poster paints a negative image of religions, using images that suggest it leads to social illnesses such as drunkenness and domestic violence.

In 1950, Radio Free Europe (RFE) began to broadcast its own propaganda into Eastern Europe, along with the BBC Radio and Voice of America. RFE sought to counterpoint Eastern Europe's Communist news media with its own. RFE believed Communist news was like the fake news of today, and it set out to expose lies and disinformation, of course giving its broadcasts its own bias and spin.

The Other Side of the Coin was one such program, broadcast in both Polish and Czech languages to expose Communist news media lies by repeating the stories told via the Communist channels, then telling listeners the real facts, urging listeners to automatically assume they were being lied to by the Czech or Polish media. This counterpropaganda broadcasting became a game of "they say, we say" and often bypassed the truth entirely in favor of spin that was meant to influence and mobilize global opinion, starting with the enemy nations.

President Harry S. Truman gave a speech in 1949 in which he labeled the people in enemy nations "captive peoples." He claimed these captive peoples were kept in ignorance by their own government leaders and that they would no doubt wish to be free if they were told the truth. This "campaign of truth" was one of many American propaganda campaigns against the Communist nations overseas in which the Americans, of course, claimed to have nothing but the truth, asserting they were simply providing that truth to those in the world who were captive behind the Iron Curtain (the name given to the boundary between the countries of Eastern and Western Europe). Meanwhile, radio programs and news media in the nations of Eastern Europe countered those claims with their own, stating that their people were not captive at all but were freely engaged in building strong socialist societies.

Each side used radio to spin the news to its favor. Each side thought it was in the right, fair and just in its quest to tell its version of the truth. Each side excused propagandist techniques as necessity to help save the world from "the other guy." Each side found ways to use fear and paranoia to create an atmosphere of distrust among the other nation's peoples and their governing leaders. One example of this was the proliferation of programs on Radio Free Europe scaring people about police informants among them and causing many listeners to take it to heart and flee their countries for fear of informers in their own towns. Many became homeless refugees. This was proof that the propaganda directed at them by the U.S. and British radio worked, and it worked well. RFE pushed the "captive peoples" label hard, hoping to play upon the fears and vulnerabilities of the Eastern European people enough to encourage them first to accept that they were captives and then to rise up and rebel.

Not all of these radio shows were news broadcasts. The use of comedy and drama added to the propaganda wars, with broadcasts of sitcoms and dramatic stories that made it look wonderful to live in capitalist America. These stories celebrated the American spirit, the nuclear family, loyalty, community, and all things deemed good and wholesome. Pro-American values were alive and flourishing in comic books, newspaper cartoons, movies, animated cartoons, television shows, radio shows, and novels. The animated feature film *Make Mine Freedom,* released in 1948, instilled patriotic pride and the love of capitalism. *Meet Joe King* was released in 1949 and encouraged the average worker to be happy with what he had because, golly gosh, he had it better than most others in the world. At least that's what *Ozzie and Harriet, Leave It to Beaver,* and other black-and-white family classics wanted viewers to believe. The culture of the 1950s was all about the joys of being an average American.

Popular actor John Wayne starred in a movie called *Big Jim McLain,* playing a House Un-American Activities Committee investigator sent to Hawaii to sniff out commies on the Big Island. Science fiction films like *Invasion of the Body Snatchers* and *The Blob* played upon the fears and hysteria of the Cold War. The James Bond franchise glamorized the battle between spies, as did television shows like *The Man from U.N.C.L.E.* and *I Spy.* Even sitcoms like *Get Smart,* featuring Don Adams as a resourceful spy, jumped into the fray. Children got exposed to the heroism of Americans against the bad Russians via cartoons like *Rocky and Bullwinkle,* which created stereotypes of the Russians as bumbling spies (in the form of Boris Badenov and his sexy sidekick, Natasha—Boris's name was a play on the name of sixteenth-century Russian tsar Boris Godunov).

THE RED SCARE AND MCCARTHYISM

The rise of Communism in the Soviet Union presented a constant challenge for the Americans and their allies. The "Red Scare" of the Bolshevik Revolution from 1917 to 1920 had set the stage for a growing concern in the United States that a similar Communist revolution would take place on home soil. Watching the social and political uprising across the Russian empire end with the establishment of Bolshevik-style Communism under the leadership of Vladimir Stalin in 1923 and end the civil war between the "reds," the Communists, and the "whites," who were the counterrevolutionaries and factions opposed to the Bolsheviks, America wondered if the same leftist surges could occur at home. In fact, they already were.

Communism in America following the end of World War II created the first American Red Scare as the idealism of the Bolsheviks spread among the more radical left. This was propagated by people like John Reed, a radical journalist whose life story became the 1981 movie *Reds.* The film starred Warren Beatty in the lead role and Diane Keaton as the high-society socialite Louise Bryant, who became one of Reed's most avid supporters, even leaving her husband and shunning the life of the wealthy elite for the Communist gatherings of writers, artists, and activists in New York City's Greenwich Village. Her radicalization through Reed would lead to her becoming a founding force of feminism.

It was Reed's idealism, later explained in his book about the Bolshevik Revolution, *Ten Days That Shook the World*, that was instrumental in bringing a vision of Communism to America. He watched front and center as the revolution played out in Russia, and he got involved in labor strikes of the Communist Labor Party of America. His book was inspired after he became disillusioned with the way the Communist leadership in Russia was behaving and hoped he could inspire a different kind of Communist Party in America. He died of a kidney disorder, leaving his book behind as a testament to his own beliefs.

But not everyone shared his idealistic views of Communism. After World War I, people weren't comfortable with the Communist labor movement or the anarchists who were calling

The 1920 painting *Bolshevik* by Boris Kustodiev depicts the revolution in glorious, patriotic terms.

for the United States' own revolution. Could there be a Bolshevik Revolution on American soil? Newspapers and radio stations across the country stoked the fear and paranoia of the "Reds" especially when labor strikes rose between 1917 to 1919. These involved the steel and iron workers, the railroad workers, even the local law enforcement, but the Red Scare worked hard to portray their strikes and demands as anarchistic, radical, and dangerous to America's way of life, so much so that in 1917 Congress passed the Espionage Act to stop all information about national defense from being used against American forces and to ensure that anyone caught spying for the "enemy" would be guilty of the highest treason.

RED SCARE NUMBER TWO

It was the second Red Scare most people today recall, either through their own experiences or those of their parents and grandparents. In the 1930s, the concept of Communism was popular among the intellectuals and the labor parties, who couldn't have been further apart on the class spectrum. In 1940, the Communist Party of the United States of America (CPUSA) had more than 50,000 members and had taken on the antiwar platform after the end of World War II. Americans assumed the Commies and the Nazis were hand in hand, but when Nazi Germany invaded the Soviet Union, that perception was clouded. The CPUSA then took on a prowar platform and began supporting the United States in the war. CPUSA chair Earl Browder crafted the perfect slogan: "Communism Is Twentieth-Century Americanism." Any opposing groups, such as the Socialist Workers Party, who were against the war and prolabor strikes, were arrested and convicted under the Smith Act, which made it a crime to knowingly or willfully advocate, assist, advise, or in any way support any organization desiring to overthrow the U.S. government. The Smith Act was broad enough to include anyone deemed either a Communist or right-wing threat against the United States. Even being affiliated with someone who fit this description was enough to earn a conviction.

After World War II, tensions increased and loyalties shifted, prompting President Truman to create the Federal Employees Loyalty Program in 1947. This was the first of many so-called witch hunts that demanded that federal employees sign an oath of loyalty to the nation and the government. Anyone who refused or confessed as a spy was fired. This included anyone the committee board decided was displaying un-American behavior. Over 12,000 federal employees resigned or were fired between 1947 and 1956.

Senator Joseph McCarthy (left) talks with his chief legal counsel, Roy Cohn, at the Army–McCarthy hearings involving a legal battle with McCarthy's aggressive investigations into possible communists in the military.

This program led to others, including one that became known as the greatest and most destructive modern-day witch hunt in history—the House Committee on Un-American Activities, or HUAC.

The HUAC, championed by Wisconsin Republican senator Joseph McCarthy, who formed his own committees, overstepped its power and began conducting investigations into the characters and activities of not just government employees but anyone they saw fit, including many in the Hollywood entertainment community. This was a time of growing tension after the formation of the Iron Curtain in 1945 and the first Soviet nuclear weapons test in 1949, along with trials and conviction of Americans Ethel and Julius Rosenberg, who were then put to death for spying for the Soviets and giving them top-secret documents regarding American radar, sonar, and nuclear weapons designs. President Truman had already ordered background information on all government employees after a high-ranking state department official named Alger Hiss was convicted on espionage charges.

Things would go from bad to worse shortly. The savior complex was alive and well in Senator Joseph McCarthy in the 1950s, and he embraced the challenge of trying to save America from the scourge of Communists. Communists in China had won their civil war and became the People's Republic of China, aligning with the North Koreans in the Korean War in the early 1950s. McCarthy provoked deep fear among the citizens of America, stating that the Communists had infiltrated every aspect of American life, and he stood before Senate committee hearings making accusations against dozens of Americans with little to no evidence of their wrongdoing. He was a master at the use of fear to incite paranoia and created such an incendiary atmosphere that he had neighbor turning in neighbor as he and his committee interrogated actors, writers, activists, producers, government employees, and civil employees. Anyone who refused to be interrogated, McCarthy deemed automatically guilty.

Many people alive at the time recall his famous words — "Are you now or have you ever been a member of the Communist Party?"

Many people alive at the time recall his famous words — "Are you now or have you ever been a member of the Communist Party?" Those people also recall how the Constitution of the U.S. forefathers was all but forgotten amidst an atmosphere of fear and paranoia, something the nation would see repeated again later during similar "witch hunts."

President Truman tried to fight back by vetoing a restrictive law called the McCarran Internal Security Act that restricted civil liberties for security, something Benjamin Franklin once warned about in his famous quote, "Those who would give up essential liberty to purchase a little temporary safety deserve neither liberty nor safety." Truman knew it was a slippery slope downward, but his veto was overridden by a Congress caught up in the witch hunt fervor. Even as Hollywood in general was being accused of Communism and its members added to a Black List that prevented them from ever working in the industry again, there were propaganda films being pumped out playing into the fear of the "reds and commies," with prominent themes of subversion, distrust, and even alien invasions as the symbols of the Communist threat.

One blacklisted screenwriter, Dalton Trumbo, became a member of the Hollywood Ten, a group of Hollywood individuals who refused to answer questions about Communist involvement when brought before the HUAC. He later won an Oscar for screenwriting in 1956 under a pen name, Robert Rich, for a movie called *The Brave One*. The Hollywood Ten were sentenced to one year in jail for contempt of Congress.

Ronald Reagan testified to the HUAC in 1947 as president of the Screen Actors Guild. He said, "Sir, I detest, I abhor their philosophy, but I detest more than that their tactics, which are those of the fifth column, and are dishonest, but at the same time I never as a citizen want to see our country become urged, by either fear or resentment of this group, that we ever compromise with any of our democratic principles through that fear or resentment."

In 1954, after Congress on a power trip passed the Communist Control Act making it illegal for anyone in the Communist Party to hold office in a labor organization, Joseph McCarthy finally took it a little too far when he accused known war heroes of being Communists. He quickly lost credibility and power, leading to a formal censure, but even after the era of McCarthyism ended, a similar sentiment reared its ugly head many years later after the terrorist attacks of 2001, and again in 2020 during a viral pandemic. More on those later.

THE DOUBLE RED SLOGAN

After its new Communist Party was reconstituted to include the five additional Soviet republics of Ukraine, Georgia, Belarus, Azerbaijan, and Armenia, the Soviet Union became a formidable power as the newly dubbed Union of the Soviet Socialist Republics, or USSR.

The color red was forever associated with this first Red Scare, and from 1947 to 1957, the span of the second Red Scare, the propagandist motto "Better Dead Than Red" acted as a battle cry for anxious Americans, now paranoid of the infusion of Communist ideals in labor unions, workplaces, and society at large. Citizens were encouraged to be concerned about the proliferation of Communist spies, and it was an era ripe for fear-based propaganda. Americans would rather die than come under control of the evil Communists.

This slogan, attributed to the publication *The Nation* in a 1930 editorial, was a flipped version of the original "Better Red Than Dead," which many attribute to British philosopher Bertrand

The color red was forever associated with this first Red Scare, and ... the propagandist motto "Better Dead Than Red" acted as a battle cry for anxious Americans....

Russell. He wrote in his 1961 *Has Man a Future?*, a work about nuclear war and disarmament, that the slogan came from the "West German friends of peace." "Better Red Than Dead" signified the belief that if there were no alternatives to the Communist domination of the human race, other than extinction, the former choice was considered the "lesser of two evils."

The phrase "lesser of two evils" itself became a propaganda tool in 2016 during the U.S. presidential campaign between Donald Trump and Hillary Clinton, with many voters and news media pundits claiming that both candidates were so unappealing that choosing either one of the candidates meant choosing the lesser of two evils ... depending on one's political stance.

OPERATION MOCKINGBIRD

The U.S. Central Intelligence Agency (CIA) began a propaganda program on a major scale in the early 1950s called Operation Mockingbird. Its intent was the spread of propaganda and disinformation via media channels by manipulating the news.

The Soviet Union was busy with its own campaign to make Americans look bad to their population by influencing public opinion via news and journalism. In 1947, Joseph Stalin had created the Communist Information Bureau, known as Cominform, for the stated purpose of coordinating the work of the Communist parties under Soviet direction. This included writers, artists, professionals, intellectuals, and other groups that could be controlled under one banner organization.

In the United States, the CIA recognized the need to counter the Cominform, and the result was Operation Mockingbird, a concerted effort to recruit and find willing journalists to play the game of working for the "network" via many front groups devoted to spinning and skewing public perception. The result was over 400 journalists working for the CIA over a 25-year period.

Director of the CIA from 1953 to 1961, Allen Dulles was in charge of Operation Mockingbird, which directed American newspapers to publish false and misleading information to counteract Soviet propaganda.

Allen Dulles, the CIA director, was the man in charge, overseeing more than two dozen newspapers and wire services that carried false and misleading stories and reports developed from CIA intelligence. Many of the reporters recruited may not have known what they were participating in, and often these reports had citations and references from recipient reporters that were released to the rest of the media and quoted as viable sources. Media companies included in Operation Mockingbird had pro-American, pro-business, liberal, anti-Soviet leanings and included the likes of William Paley at the CBS broadcasting network, Alfred Friendly at the *Washington Post*, James S. Copley of Copley News Service, Joseph Harrison of the *Christian Science Monitor*, and Henry Luce of *Time* and *Life* magazines, among many others at NBC, ABC, the Associated Press, United Press International, Reuters, Hearst Newspapers, Scripps-Howard, *Newsweek* magazine, the *Miami Herald*, the *Saturday Evening Post*, and the *New York Herald-Tribune*.

Carl Bernstein, the famous *Washington Post* investigative reporter who helped break the Watergate scandal from 1972 to 1974, covered this topic in his seminal cover story for the October 20, 1977, *Rolling Stone* magazine, "The CIA and the Media." In the article, he wrote of the long relationship between the CIA and journalists that literally shaped public perception via the American press. The program's intent, he said, was to use journalists as a productive means of intelligence gathering for the CIA here and abroad. These journalists, as later revealed in CIA documents, would perform tasks from the menial, such as serving as the "eyes and ears" of the CIA while reporting overseas, to the more serious creation of "black propaganda" by bringing American journalists together with foreign spies for the sake of setting up information drops at lunches or hotel rooms to exchange highly sensitive information.

"In the field, journalists were used to help recruit and handle foreigners as agents; to acquire and evaluate information, and to plant false information with officials of foreign governments," Bernstein wrote. "Many signed secrecy agreements, pledging never to divulge anything about their dealings with the Agency."

The way it usually worked was that the highest-level individuals in top management at the newspaper, wire service, or broadcast network worked with a high-level official at the CIA. These special relationships allowed the CIA to get undercover operatives in the form of journalists into foreign capitals. This went on without a hitch for over two decades before the U.S. Congress, coming off the Watergate scandal and hearings, became concerned about the president abusing the CIA for things like domestic surveillance, which led to a series of investigations into CIA activities in 1975 and 1976, during which their many operations were put under a microscope, including Operation Mockingbird.

The CIA expressly stopped the use of "accredited" journalists but did not mention stringers or freelancers....

The CIA had already been moving away from working with journalists even before the 1976 Church Committee completed its final report on the CIA and foreign and domestic media. This report exposed it all, but three years earlier, then-director William Colby of the CIA had already informed the committee that the agency would no longer use journalists and media personnel for clandestine activities. When the Church Committee Report was released in 1976, the CIA claimed all activities had stopped. However, there was one caveat. The CIA expressly stopped the use of "accredited" journalists but did not mention stringers or free-lancers—meaning that, for all we know, Mockingbird could still be alive and well in some form.

USIA: PROPAGANDA AS PUBLIC POLICY

In 1953, the government of the United States instigated an organization devoted to propaganda called the United States Information Agency (USIA). According to the agency: "The United States Information Agency is an independent foreign affairs agency within the executive branch of the U.S. government. USIA explains and supports American foreign policy and promotes U.S. national interests through a wide range of overseas information programs. The agency promotes mutual understanding between the United States and other nations by conducting educational and cultural activities. USIA maintains more than 211 posts in over 147 countries where it is known as USIS, the U.S. Information Service. On April 15, 1993, Dr. Joseph Duffey was nominated by President Bill Clinton to be USIA Director, and was sworn in on June 3, 1993."

With a budget for the fiscal year of 1994 alone set at $1.1 billion, the USIA continued for decades to employ over 8,500 people. One thousand of them were Foreign Service officers who were assigned overseas; more than three thousand were Foreign Service nationals; and 4,300 were employees based in Washington, D.C. According to the USIA description of the U.S. government archives, "The work of USIA is mainly carried out by its Foreign Service officers assigned to American missions overseas. With guidance, support and material from Washington headquarters, they manage cultural and information programs in support of American foreign policy objectives and greater mutual understanding between the U.S. and foreign societies."

According to the American Security Project, the USIA was created "to understand, inform and influence foreign publics in promotion of the national interest, and to broaden the dialogue between Americans and U.S. institutions, and their counterparts abroad. Specifically, this mission is carried out through four distinct functions." The functions are listed as follows:

1. Explain and advocate U.S. policies in terms that are credible and meaningful in foreign cultures
2. Provide information about the official policies of the United States, and about the people, values, and institutions which influence those policies
3. Bring the benefits of international engagement to American citizens and institutions by helping them build strong long-term relationships with their counterparts overseas
4. Advise the President and U.S. government policymakers on the ways in which foreign attitudes will have a direct bearing on the effectiveness of U.S. policies.

The goal of the USIA was clear—to create public policy that served as propaganda in disguise, and to shape public opinion in the process. It ended up being the largest public relations organization in the world, with an annual budget over $500 million in the 1980s, which eclipsed $1 billion in the years directly after the fall of the Berlin Wall. "Information and education are powerful forces in support of peace. Just as war begins in the minds of men, so does peace," President Dwight Eisenhower said about USIA in January 27, 1958.

The most famous director of the USIA was Edward R. Murrow, who was appointed by President John F. Kennedy and

Interestingly enough, famed broadcast journalist Edward R. Murrow was known for his professional integrity and honesty when it came to the news, and yet he was head of the USIA propaganda machine from 1961 to 1964.

presided over the organization from 1961 to 1964. The USIA was formally dissolved in 1999 but not before enacting a string of important legislation involving the use of propaganda in American media. According to the American Security Project, "Upon USIA dissolution, its responsibilities were divided between the Broadcasting Board of Governors (broadcasting function) and the Under Secretary for Public Affairs and Public Diplomacy within the State Department (information and exchange functions)."

SECRET AGENT MAN

During the Cold War era, popular culture was rampant with stories about spies and secret agent heroes like James Bond, fighting off the evil Russians for the British Secret Service. Espionage filled novels by authors such as John le Carré, who was actually David Cornwell, a former employee of M15, a British spy agency. His novel *The Spy Who Came in from the Cold* is a classic thriller, set in East Germany and no doubt mixing real espionage elements in its fictional background. Ian Fleming rose to massive success with his James Bond novel series, many of which were made into equally successful movies. *The Hunt for Red October* by Tom Clancy was released in 1984 and set the stage for Clancy's huge success with more than a dozen other Cold War–era novels featuring espionage, technology, and a lead hero named Jack Ryan. Other such titles included *Patriot Games* and *Clear and Present Danger*. His 1986 *Red Storm Rising* was set against a NATO/Warsaw Pact conventional war.

Frederick Forsyth wrote the best-selling *The Fourth Protocol*, which is a term referring to conventions that, if broken, might lead to nuclear war. In the novel, all conventions were broken except for the final one—the fourth. Perhaps readers could live vicariously through these novels and alleviate some of their fears through the actions of the heroic American and British characters.

The Cold War inspired a wide array of fiction involving super spies such as author Ian Fleming's James Bond character, who worked for the British, often against communist plotters.

One of the most telling and factual-based novels and later films was Richard Condon's 1959 neo-noir psychological thriller, *The Manchurian Candidate,* which made reference to the brainwashing and creation of sleeper assassins later revealed in the CIA-sponsored Project MKUltra experiments of the 1950s through the 1970s. This was a mirror of real life as told in a fictional format, with a movie to follow in 1962 starring Laurence Harvey, Angela Lansbury, and Frank Sinatra and later rebooted with Denzel Washington, Liev Schreiber, and Meryl Streep. The creation of sleeper assassins proved to be a reality when the MKUltra documents were declassified (those that hadn't been destroyed first) after the Church Senate Committee Hearing in 1973, which exposed the horrendous experimentation done during the program's history.

The Cold War era provided novelists a propaganda heyday for writing about patriotism and American heroes battling the foreign forces working against them. Many of these novels became movies or television series, increasing their reach. Fiction is one arena where pop culture often mirrors real life, so these themes were natural to expect in light of the tensions of the times. Labeling it propaganda is more about the fact that it served to influence the thoughts and emotions of the reader just as a romance story would. Whether or not the influence was intentional is known only to the novelists!

Perhaps the most influential novels during this long period were those of George Orwell, and they still have the ring of truth in today's world. *Nineteen Eighty-Four*, published in 1949, was predictive in its look at the future, and many of the things the book predicted have come true, especially in the area of Big Brother technological surveillance. Orwell also wrote of something else we live with in these modern times—perpetual war.

These and other novels and films held the events of the time up to a mirror and reflected them back to society in ways that were more palatable than fact and statistic, which shows the power of fiction and storytelling. The subconscious messages dug deep into the American psyche and created more distrust, more paranoia, and more fear in a way that the plethora of nonfiction books of the era, such as J. Edgar Hoover's *Masters of Deceit*, about the virtues of America over Communism, simply could not achieve.

Television shows like *I Spy* and *The Man from U.N.C.L.E.* and even the comedic *Get Smart* allowed the themes of the Cold War entry into the collective psyche via the "boob tube," sneaking in as entertainment and, to some extent, escapism from the scary realities of the world. Movies such as *Red Dawn* and *Rocky IV* normalized the "us versus them" mentality while introducing new concepts into the collective. In the case of *Red Dawn*, which was released in 1984, the target was youth. Adults knew all about the Soviet threat, but what better way to introduce American youth to the cause than via an entertaining action thriller about a small Colorado town invaded by Soviet soldiers, starring some of the hottest young stars of the time as the rag-tag army that forms to take back their country. Patrick Swayze, Charlie Sheen, Lea Thompson, Jennifer Grey, C. Thomas Howell, and others pitched in along with adult stars Powers Boothe and Harry Dean Stanton to help director John Milius's ode to American patriotism achieve huge success. It was also the first movie in America to earn the newly minted PG-13 rating, which was established after audiences rebelled at the violence of the PG-rated *Indiana Jones and the Temple of Doom* months earlier. *Red Dawn* opened the door for more adult subject matter to appeal to a wider-aged audience. It was rebooted in 2012, only with an invasion by North Korean soldiers to better reflect the current geopolitical threats.

By portraying young people as the heroes, *Red Dawn's* freedom fight between the United States and Soviets embraced a whole new generation. Kids were already being exposed to the Cold War at school via duck-and-cover drills, social behavior and physical hygiene films, and the daily recital of the Pledge of Allegiance, which in 1952 included the introduction of the words "under God." Often the Pledge was followed by singing the first verse of "America (My Country, 'Tis of Thee)," a patriotic song about freedom written by Samuel Francis Smith and sung to the same tune as the United Kingdom's "God Save the Queen." Children were being taught virtues and values about how to be a good American, even as their fear was stoked by weekly nuclear bomb drills and daily nuclear sirens wailing in their neighborhoods as they played outside. (The author of this book grew up hearing the siren every night promptly at 7 p.m.!)

Get Smart (1965–1970) was a TV series that spoofed the secret agent genre and starred Don Adams as Control agent Maxwell Smart. The Bondesque spy gadgets were parodied with such devices as the "shoe phone."

The fourth installation in the *Rocky* movie franchise added a whole new object of American fear: technological superiority. During the Cold War, the United States was in a race for military superiority with the Soviet Union. In the film, released in 1985, Rocky, our streetwise hero, trains as a street hero would—with old farm equipment and knee deep in snow—while his Soviet opponent, Drago, uses the top high-tech equipment, trainers, and steroids to compete. It's a David versus Goliath American dream, with Rocky defending the death of heavyweight champion Apollo Creed, killed by the evil Drago, then going into the ring himself with Drago on Soviet soil, with the Soviet leadership present. Before long, even the Soviet crowd and the Soviet premier stand and cheer for Rocky, having a newfound respect for the relentless underdog who declares that if he can change, anyone can change. It's a happy ending for all, but especially for the American propaganda machine that made turning the Soviet people around to the U.S. way of thinking look like kindergarten kid stuff. Rocky was a hero, a true American story of grit and courage. Audiences ate it up.

The use of entertainment as a method of mass influence worked its magic to portray America as the best country in the world, with amazing freedoms.

The use of entertainment as a method of mass influence worked its magic to portray America as the best country in the world, with amazing freedoms. Historian Daniel Leab once said, "The United States and its allies tried to convince their citizens that they lived in the best possible society. It may not have been as free, democratic, or egalitarian as the propaganda asserted, but it did boast free markets, limited government, the rule of law, individualism, and human rights." He went on to say that despite America's enemies trying to portray it otherwise, this system of propaganda was already entrenched enough to continue to be successful in keeping Americans focused on how great they were, even as the Soviet Union was attempting with its own propaganda to show the cracks in the supposedly perfect system.

Sometimes Americans even pointed out their own cracks, as in the novel *The Ugly American* by William J. Lederer and Eugene Burdick, published in 1958, in which the lead character, an engineer named Homer Atkins, is sent to a fictional nation in Southeast Asia where he comes face to face with the failures of America's foreign policy at the hands of the U.S. diplomatic corps. The book caused controversy upon its release and led to the formation of the Peace Corps. The two authors had both been U.S. Navy men and were disillusioned with America's handling of Southeast Asian politics and civilian interactions. To this day, this book is considered one of the most politically influential novels of all time, proving that the pen can be mightier than the sword.

Edward Bernays wrote in *Propaganda* that American motion pictures were the greatest unconscious carriers of propaganda as distributors of ideas and opinions. "The motion picture can standardize the ideas and habits of a nation," he said. "Because pictures are made to meet market demands, they reflect, emphasize, and even exaggerate broad popular tendencies, rather than stimulate new ideas and opinions." Movies mirrored what was already in vogue, reflecting back the cultural norms to the viewers embedded in entertaining fare.

WAR AND RUMORS OF WAR

Films, novels, television shows, comic books—anything portraying the terrors of Russian invasions, nuclear or conventional war, and associated spy games with the Soviets was fair game in the world of entertainment. Here's a partial list of the war of the superpowers on the big and small screen:

Movies
- *The Third Man*, 1949
- *Invasion, USA*, 1952
- *On the Beach*, 1959
- *Dr. Strangelove or: How I Learned to Stop Worrying and Love the Bomb*, 1964
- *Fail Safe*, 1964
- *The Russians Are Coming, the Russians Are Coming*, 1966
- *Damnation Alley*, 1977
- *Telefon*, 1977
- *World War III*, 1982
- *Firefox*, 1982
- *War Games*, 1983
- *Testament*, 1983
- *The Day After*, 1983
- *Gotcha*, 1985
- *Spies Like Us*, 1985
- *Invasion U.S.A.* (with Chuck Norris), 1985
- *The Falcon and the Snowman*, 1985
- *The Manhattan Project*, 1986
- *Russkies*, 1987
- *Project X*, 1987
- *Miracle Mile*, 1988

Television Series
- *I Spy*
- *Get Smart*
- *Mission: Impossible*
- *The Man from U.N.C.L.E.*
- *Airwolf*
- *MacGyver*
- *The Twilight Zone*

This list doesn't include the various science-fiction alien invasion films that symbolized foreign invaders on American soil and the fear of the enemy/other. These included everything from the radio broadcast and subsequent film *War of the Worlds* to the shlock horror of the 1950s and 1960s. In the later decades of the Cold War, the aliens became more threatening and sinister, thus requiring stronger and more courageous heroes and heroines to fight against them, and then Hollywood decided to add zombies to the list of things symbolic of the "enemy." George A. Romero's 1968 black-and-white classic *Night of the Living Dead* introduced

Zombie movies such as the classic *Night of the Living Dead* (1968) could be consider metaphors for evil, invading forces that must be fought off by good Americans.

audiences to the risen dead—or walking dead by today's standards—as a new representation of invading forces to be fought off by good and decent living Americans.

FLOWER POWER AND THE PEACE MOVEMENT

During the late 1960s into the mid-1970s, the Vietnam War was front and center in American culture. Propaganda was in full swing in the news media to sell to the public a war that was very unpopular, not least because of the draft that sent young men to fight it, like it or not. The streets were filled with protestors using chants, signs, and another very powerful weapon of influence—protest songs. Music became a primary force for influencing public opinion, especially with young people who were either going off to a war they didn't agree with, often against their will, or left at home, unable to help. During the same time period, there were mass marches in the streets in the United States and in England demanding rights for women, an end to nuclear war, and a push for civil rights, all converging into an incendiary historical period of great change in culture and politics.

"Ban the bomb!" signs were everywhere during both anti-nuclear and peace marches. Folk and pop music responded accordingly with songs by artists such as Bob Dylan, Peter, Paul, and Mary, Melanie, the Beatles, and a host of others, including the seminal song "Eve of Destruction" by Barry McGuire in 1965, which went straight to number one on the pop charts. Bob Dylan sang about the "Masters of War" and warned during the Cuban Missile Crisis that "A Hard Rain's Gonna Fall," and that the answer, my friend, was "Blowin' in the Wind." The Byrds sang of the cycles of life in "Turn, Turn, Turn," and John Lennon and Yoko Ono compelled their listeners to seek peace at Christmastime in "Happy Xmas (War Is Over)."

This was a time when the top-ten lists on radio included many songs exclusively devoted to some message of hope, peace, tolerance, equality, and an end to war. "Make love, not war," the signs at protests said, and one way to do that was to promote love and the dawning of a new age—the "Age of Aquarius," as sung by the Fifth Dimension from the Broadway musical *Hair*. Harmony and understanding were in the air, and the hippie "flower power" lifestyle promised the kind of freedom and love for all that the government seemed to oppose. The hippie movement labeled the government "the Man" and "the establishment" and encouraged people to "let it all hang out" and live outside the confines of the box. It was a time of massive and revolutionary countercultural shift.

Some representative songs of this era were:

- "The Sounds of Silence" by Simon and Garfunkel
- "Peace Train" by Cat Stevens
- "For What It's Worth (Stop, Hey What's That Sound)" by Buffalo Springfield
- "Lay Down (Candles in the Rain)" by Melanie
- "Teach Your Children" by Crosby, Stills, and Nash
- "If I Had a Hammer" by Peter, Paul, and Mary
- "Freedom" by Richie Havens
- "War (What Is It Good For)" by Edwin Starr
- "This Land Is Your Land" by Woody Guthrie
- "What's Going On" by Marvin Gaye
- "Mercy Mercy Me (The Ecology)" by Marvin Gaye
- "I Am Woman" by Helen Reddy
- "Say It Loud (I'm Black and I'm Proud)" by James Brown
- "Joe Hill" by Joan Baez
- "Fortunate Son" by Creedence Clearwater Revival
- "Ohio" by Crosby, Stills, Nash & Young

Protest songs would always be an important part of music no matter the era, but this was a time when they became a weapon in and of themselves....

This is just a miniscule sampling of the songs throughout the 1960s and 1970s that spoke of disillusionment and anger, of revolution and change. Protest songs would always be an important part of music no matter the era, but this was a time when they became a weapon in and of themselves and a means for bringing together huge and diverse groups of people for a common cause, such as the 1968 three-day music festival at Woodstock, New York. It was here that many artists sang of war and an end to war, and one of the most memorable came from a group called Country Joe and the Fish. Their song "I-Feel-Like-I'm-Fixin'-to-Die Rag (The Fish Cheer)" became a chant that represented an entire generation and their disgust and anger at politicians who sent young men off to fight their wars for them. "It's one, two, three, four, what are we fighting for? I don't give a damn, next stop is Vietnam."

- "Power to the people"
- "Make love, not war"
- "War is hell"

- "All you need is love"
- "Bread, not bombs"
- "War is bad for your health"
- "Resist the draft"
- "Not our sons"

These and other iconic phrases became messages that could be chanted and sung at protests, rallies, and marches, written on signs and book covers, and they became the counter-propaganda of the peace movement and its affiliated movements when confronted with the terrifying prospect of being drafted, of nuclear war, of gender and racial violence, and of politicians cracking down on dissent and free speech.

JAZZ FOR AMERICA

In its efforts to spread American pride and influence the Soviet youth, the U.S. State Department carried out a program between 1956 and 1979 sending jazz musicians overseas to tour on enemy soil. The State Department later added classical music to the propaganda campaign, supporting many classical music tours and performances sent to the Soviet Union as part of a cultural diplomacy exchange initiative. One such tour of the Howard Hanson Eastman Philharmonia Orchestra represented America as part of an international concert tour with musicians and orchestras from sixteen countries touring Europe, the Middle East, and the Soviet Union.

Spreading musical goodwill was also a great way to show our enemies how wonderful freedom to express oneself through music was in "free countries," and to hopefully incite the young people to become envious of how good life was over here on U.S. soil. It was subtle and powerful at the same time and as part of a mutual cultural exchange, an acceptable form of propaganda for both sides, similar to the performances of Russian ballet and dance troupes in America. Music could be a powerful and effective method of influencing and spreading ideas just as much as cinema, television, and books. It could even start revolutions.

THE 1980s AND 1990s

While punk rock bands sang their own brand of protest songs and Black music decried abusive treatment at the hands of the police, women continued to push for equality, and those who loved animals formed the animal rights movement to fight against vivisection. The Cold War continued, influencing every aspect of American life. Prior to the Gulf War in 1991, American politicians and military officials were priming the public for wars to come via the entertainment industry, action toys and figures, and a wave of patriotism in politics. But culturally, this was a time of movements and revolutions, of large protests and mass marches that seemed in stark contrast to the political push for perpetual wars overseas. At home, in many ways, all hell was breaking loose.

AIDS appeared on the scene, striking terror into the hearts of gay men and those who loved them. The antinuclear movement marched in cities around the globe. So did the women's rights movement, the animal rights movement, and the lesbian, gay, bi-sexual, and transgender (LGBT) movement. Large rallies, protests, and marches continued long past the end of the Vietnam War and other crises of the 1970s as the concept of equality among all liv-ing things, and the protection of the planet from nuclear devasta-tion, moved front and center.

The decade of the 1980s was a contrast between big hair rock music and death on a wide new scale from a disease unlike

Encouraging patriotism can start at a young age through such things as military toys and video games that influence the views of children.

any other. It was a time when the American public was being primed for the ongoing ideologies of the Pentagon (that is, the U.S. Department of Defense) and the war hawks in political office that hoped the young men who cheered watching *Red Dawn* would cheer even more so when the United States engaged in the Gulf War in 1991. David Sirota writes in his March 15, 2011, article for *Salon*, "How the '80s Programmed Us for War," of the concerted effort of the Pentagon players to take advantage of the fact that young men of recruiting age cited movies and television as their primary source of opinions and information about the military. The armed forces loved the idea of using these sources to show America's young the possibilities of becoming the next soldiers. "In the same way adult politics, media, and entertainment in the eighties tried to recast the U.S. military as a yellow-ribbon-worthy underdog helping supposed 'freedom fighters' in Latin America, rescuing POWs from Vietcong, and liberating Kuwait from the supposed Iraq behemoth, *Red Dawn*'s Wolverines are positioned as outgunned insurgents scratching their way to victory against the Russian colossus." The film's director, John Milius, stated that this message was the liberation of the oppressed, even though the oppressed were the Americans—the most powerful military force on Earth!

This film, more than any other, played upon militaristic themes as a form of propaganda to get young men angry and excited and patriotic enough to sign on the dotted line for the next war. The jingoism intended by the film was obvious, and despite the fact that Oklahoma City bomber Timothy McVeigh claimed the movie was a favorite, the studio stood by that jingoistic ideology.

Culture wars were forcing people to take sides and consider new threats to existing traditions and ways of life.

A different type of war was occurring outside the halls of politics and military maneuverings. Culture wars were forcing people to take sides and consider new threats to existing traditions and ways of life. Among the hot-button issues of the 1980s that spilled over into the 1990s and beyond were gun control, animal rights, separation of church and state, privacy rights, an end to censorship, political transparency, equal pay for women, civil rights, abortion, the death penalty, the legal use of marijuana and other recreational drugs, and sexuality and sexual orientation in the new era of AIDS. These issues divided people along party lines in general, with the Republican right pushing for "traditional family values," and the Democratic left pushing for "liberal freedoms." It became a war between the traditionalists and the progressives and even went so far as to pit religion against secularism.

It spilled over into the political elections of the time. The rise of the Christian Coalition in the early 1990s was said to have helped elect Democratic presidential candidate Bill Clinton in 1992 and again in 1996. Clinton's two terms followed George H. W. Bush's one term, from 1989 to 1993, which had brought with it the 1990–91 Gulf War. At the 1988 Republican National Convention, where Bush Sr. accepted the nomination on August 18, the world was regaled with his now iconic six-word phrase, written by speechwriter Peggy Noonan, "Read my lips: no new taxes." It was a fine piece of propaganda repeated in the media and on the lips of citizens over and over ad nauseum, and it helped him win the election. It also became a broken promise when Bush later agreed to raise taxes.

THE GULF WAR

The Gulf War, along with a military operation in Panama under Bush's watch and an economic recession to boot, had left many voters wondering if the United States would ever not be at war with some country in the Middle East or elsewhere. People also wanted more freedom from the religious right and looked to Bill Clinton as a new direction, even though his own administration included an impeachment during which he firmly stated he did not have sex with intern Monica Lewinsky. The mood of the nation shifted again after Clinton served two terms and then gave the torch back to the Bush family and the 43rd president, George W. Bush, in the 2000 election.

The Gulf War, codenamed Operation Desert Shield in its operation stage and Operation Desert Storm in its combat phase, lasted from August 2, 1990, to February 28, 1991, and pitted coalition forces from 35 nations under America's leadership against Iraq in response to Iraq's invasion of Kuwait. It was all about the oil, too, as portrayed in the American mass media, spinning the war as necessary to protect the country's oil interests overseas while also liberating poor Kuwait from Iraqi annexation. The result was the expelling of Iraqi soldiers and presence from Kuwait and independence for the nation, even though much of the country's infrastructure had been destroyed during combat. It has been estimated that the United States and allies lost hundreds of soldiers,

U.S. Air Force fighters fly over destroyed Iraqi oil fields in this 1991 photograph. The quick and decisive victory boosted American patriotism.

but the Iraqis lost upward of 50,000, and the Kuwaitis over 4,000. The United Nations quickly slapped Iraq with sanctions and established a no-fly zone in the northern part of the country.

The Gulf War served as a perfect foundation for another war against Iraq that was to come within the next ten years. It also led to additional loss of life due to the Gulf War syndrome, a mysterious illness reported upon the return of soldiers from overseas. Controversy erupted when it was revealed via a U.S. Senate Committee report titled "U.S. Chemical and Biological Warfare-Related Duel Use Exports to Iraq and Their Possible Impact on the Health Consequences of the Gulf War" in 1994 that the soldiers could have been exposed to chemical or biological warfare with weapons the United States had supplied in the previous decade to Iraqi president Saddam Hussein. There was also evidence of the use of depleted uranium by the U.S. military in the area also contributing to major illnesses and health problems in returning veterans.

American and allied POWs were shown in the news as prisoners of the Iraqis, tortured and abused and, in the case of Royal Air Force crewman John Nichol and John Peters, forced to make on-air statements against the war. This was powerful media to incite anger and patriotism among the American and allied public. The entire war was broadcast widely, with live pictures of bombs and missiles hitting targets and reporters close to the front lines. This nonstop coverage proved a boon for the CNN network, which skyrocketed in ratings during the war for its landmark coverage and audio reports live from a hotel in Baghdad. When other networks couldn't get live coverage, CNN came through. However, what the public saw on television was restricted and censored by the policies of a Pentagon briefing called Annex Foxtrot, which was organized by the military and instructed key journalists to conduct interviews with soldiers on the front lines, always in the presence of officers.

All interviews and reports had to be approved by the military for broadcasting. The military claimed this was to protect sensitive security information....

All interviews and reports had to be approved by the military for broadcasting. The military claimed this was to protect sensitive security information, but many cried full-on censorship and claimed the public was being spoon-fed "spin" and manufactured news, most likely to avoid the kind of public outcry and opposition seen during the Vietnam War's more open media coverage. But about halfway through the duration of the war, the Iraqi government and military agreed to allow live satellite coverage of the war, and soon the footage being broadcast was more immediate, only this time censored by Iraqi interests.

The only real opposition information was coming from alternative news media and sources such as Deep Dish television and the Gulf Crisis TV Project, which served not only to give more uncensored coverage of the war but also to expose the ongoing censorship of information and news and the mass media's complicity in promoting only one side of the war narrative. An organization called Fairness and Accuracy in Reporting (FAIR) began to analyze media coverage of the Gulf War via written materials and books, pointing out the propaganda and spin in mainstream news. It wasn't the first time a war was censored and spun, and it wouldn't be the last.

Pop culture was soon to follow with video games, movies, and television shows depicting the war and soldiers coming back home to deal with the aftereffects. One movie stood out, 2005's *Jarhead*, which was based on the memoirs of a U.S. Marine named Anthony Swofford.

TOWARD THE END OF A CENTURY

Americans had lived through the scandal and embarrassment of Watergate in the early 1970s that led to the shameful resignation of President Richard M. Nixon. They had survived the Reaganomic "trickle-down economics" years and the Bush war years. In the 1990s, it was all about the Clinton sex scandal that led to his impeachment, although he did serve two terms and was considered by many a popular establishment Democratic president. America went from the "peace and love" generation to the patriotic generation to the "me" generation and volleyed from one end of the political and cultural spectrum to another.

And then it was time for Y2K, or the end of the world as we knew it. As the clock ticked ever closer to the end of the millennium, panic set in as people speculated about what would happen when the year—or, more to the point, computers—turned over at midnight from 1999 to 2000. The news media was consumed by it, as were advertisers and the entertainment industry, taking advantage of both the fear and the humor surrounding the mysterious situation. With the proliferation of computers and technology at unprecedented levels, there were fears the world would somehow cease to function, as if some powerful entity were about to pull the plug on the global technological grid. People made bumper stickers and T-shirts, and companies banked on products with Y2K logos. Software companies sold millions of dollars in protective programs to keep computers from frying, and New Year's Eve plans included stocking up on survivalist gear and extra food and water should the grid go down and plunge the world back into the Stone Age. Fear sells, and everyone was buying.

In the end, it was a nonevent, and the year 2000 did not end much of anything, except maybe naïveté toward the way computers worked. One year later, everything would change.

9/11 and
Weapons of Mass Distraction

"The greatest tyrannies are always perpetrated in the name of the noblest causes." —Thomas Paine

This is just in. You are looking at obviously a very disturbing live shot there. That is the World Trade Center, and we have unconfirmed reports this morning that a plane has crashed into the towers of the World Trade Center. CNN Center right now is just beginning to work on this story, obviously calling our sources and trying to figure out exactly what happened. (CNN Anchor Carol Lin, 8:49:50 a.m., 9/11/01)

For anyone who was old enough to watch a television in September of 2001, this was the news that changed everything. When the terrorist attacks occurred on the morning of September 11, an event that became known as 9/11, millions watched in horror as four passenger planes crashed into the World Trade Center, the Pentagon, and a field in Pennsylvania. Loss of life quickly approached 3,000 with over 25,000 injured, and by the end of the day, the world was watching as a terrorist group called Al-Qaeda was deemed responsible and the war on terror began.

As the world watched the buildings burn and the heroics of first responders trying to save people from the destruction, the news also showed joyous anti-American celebrations in the terrorist nations believed involved, stoking anger and rage among U.S. citizens and widespread support for an invasion of Afghanistan to go after the Al-Qaeda stronghold.

Within just one day, the powerful symbolism of the empty section of the New York City skyline where the Twin Towers once stood, contrasted with scenes of anti-American protestors cheering the act, set the stage for a war of battling ideologies that still resonates. Osama bin Laden, a founder of Al-Qaeda and mastermind behind the attacks, was public enemy number one. President George W. Bush was pushed into the spotlight he later admitted he never wanted. Soon, the news was filled with phrases like "terror attacks," "a new Axis of Evil" (Iran, Iraq, and North Korea), "Islamic extremists," and "Ground Zero," and these became as seared into the collective U.S. memory as the images of the planes flying into the towers.

Bush named the invasion of Afghanistan "Operation Enduring Freedom." This name was chosen for its emphasis on the spread of freedom on a global scale as the goal of the U.S. and allied military. It sounded good and indicated a long-lasting fight for loyalty to the nation and its goals. The names of all military actions were carefully chosen propaganda with a great deal of strategic thought behind them. They were not random or trivial. It was a lot easier to sell a war or two when you could imply to the public the purpose and meaning behind it as something positive and beneficial for all involved, and make them proud to be Americans as well.

Americans watched in horror as New York City's Twin Towers were destroyed by terrorists who deliberately piloted two airplanes into the skyscrapers on September 11, 2001.

The U.S. media became the means of spinning the war on terror always in favor of the United States, with stories censored or shaped to portray whatever U.S. government or military leaders needed the public to believe at the time. But propaganda has always been as available to one side as to the other. According to Daisy Ramirez in an article titled "Protecting Ourselves from Media Manipulation: The Use of Alternative Media as an Information Source," the Pentagon could not always control the information the public received. Ramirez writes:

> During the War in Afghanistan, the Pentagon [was] less successful at limiting the information that has made its way to the public. While the Bush administration attempted to control the information being expressed in American media sources, the Taliban also attempted to control the information being expressed in Afghanistan media. This was when Al Jazeera television network was able to emerge as an alternative source of information from behind.

> Immediately after the September 11th attacks, Al Jazeera began to work on images they could provide the American media explaining the unfolding of events in Afghanistan. The images being produced began to form a larger impact on the dynamics between the media and decision-makers in the United States.

No longer was American media in total control of the perceptions and perspectives of the war. The more outlets available to provide news, the more chance there is never going to be one narrative everybody accepts.

The more outlets available to provide news, the more chance there is never going to be one narrative everybody accepts.

The mainstream media also had to deal with this little thing called the internet and the ability of stories and news reports to suddenly go viral on alternative and foreign news services in a matter of minutes, not to mention the many news sources questioning the rush to war and the immediate narrative of the official story. Ramirez went on to point out the natural progression of the "rally 'round the flag" sentiments in the news media and public:

> In order to understand why the American public began to feel that all Arab countries were anti-American it is important to examine the media tactics pro-

vided by U.S. media sources and the not-so-heard-of alternative media attempts in the Middle East. It is also important to wonder if the American media was able to contextualize the news reports presented by this non-Western source and what consequences this had for the range of information available at the time.

Clearly it was all about the context in which information was framed and presented via the media, and that context was no doubt shaped by the motives and agendas of either side in the war, just as in any prior war. It was a lot like advertising, where each party promotes its product and shows why it is superior to that of the competitors. Whoever controlled the media outlet controlled the narrative. And by the implementation of different tools and techniques such as framing stories or priming the public with inciting language and rhetoric, such as the use of the term "evil-doers," the United States could call upon patriotic fervor again and again when needed to keep support for the war on terror fresh and strong.

With enough repetition, just about every American became familiar with the enemy as "the Taliban" and "Al-Qaeda" without necessarily understanding who these groups were or what they stood for. It didn't matter. Labeling them as "evil-doers" was enough to keep pesky reporters and "truthers" at bay and to ensure that the war on terror was worth the number of lives lost and the rising financial burden.

In 2003 President Bush launched an all-out war on Islamic terrorists and any nation that ostensibly supported or financially sponsored them. This time the war was in Iraq, which had nothing to do with the 9/11 attacks whatsoever, nor did its leader Saddam Hussein. But the United Stated had always wanted an excuse for regime change in Iraq, and here was the perfect opening. Bush talked about a stash of weapons of mass destruction, or WMDs, that were biological, chemical, and nuclear in nature and kept somewhere in Iraq, and asserted that the United States had to find those weapons or they might be used against the country or its allies. In March, Bush launched Operation Iraqi Freedom, and within three weeks, American troops took control of Baghdad and knocked down the massive statue of Saddam Hussein in a symbolic image that would be shown on every form of news media for weeks.

Americans were still angry over the 2001 attacks, and because the attacks had been perpetrated by brown-skinned Muslims, many white Americans now lived in fear of their brown-skinned neighbors. Attacking Iraq over nothing more than its inclusion as part of a potentially dangerous broad terrorist network that may or may not have WMDs (later it was revealed they did not) raised few eyebrows at the time. They reportedly hated Americans? Attack them! It was a mentality echoed throughout much of the public thanks to the mainstream media's headlines of deadly WMDs and the remote possibility of terrorists blowing up grocery stores or football stadiums. If it bled, it led, and if fear was being sold, Americans were lining up to buy it.

The news media promoted fear of Muslims and portrayed the "Islamic" enemy as negative enough to cause a wave of anti-Muslim violence and sentiment among whites in the United States. Forget the fact that like any other religion, Islam had a tiny element of extremism, and most Muslims were peaceful people. That acknowledgment didn't sell newspapers or make good media ratings. Not to mention the additional paranoia induced with the "see something, say something" policies of snitching on neighbors engaging in anything that might remotely be attributed to terrorism or terrorist activity. As with the McCarthyism of the 1950s, the country had returned to the concept of fear as a weapon to be abused, and many people squealed on other

An image like in this photograph of a happy Muslim family enjoying a meal together is not something you would see in the American media, especially during the time of 9/11. Muslims were (and often still are) portrayed as violent terrorists.

human beings for the most trivial things, simply because they were scared—and because they were told to. It was patriotic!

Using the public's fear and complacency, the government passed a far-reaching anti-terrorism bill called the USA Patriot Act in October, right after the attacks. The acronym stood for the Uniting and Strengthening America by Providing Appropriate Tools Required to Intercept and Obstruct Terrorism, but soon it became evident that this was a massive crackdown on civil liberties and an invasion of privacy unlike any other. Because it was used as a tool for fighting "scary" terrorists, the public accepted it with little pushback. Eventually critics shed light on the darkest corners of the act and how it changed the public's illusions of freedom to this day.

The TIA, Total Information Awareness program, was initiated by the U.S. Information Awareness Office in February of 2003. It was then renamed the Terrorism Information Awareness program and was a form of predictive policing where citizens were encouraged to contribute information to create a detailed database of activity and possibly prevent the next big terrorist attack. Senator Ron Wyden of Oregon called it the biggest surveillance program in U.S. history. It drew such ire and criticism that it was officially suspended in late 2003, but elements of the program continued under various codenames, such as "topsail" and "basketball."

In the time immediately following the 9/11 attacks, radio stations played patriotic songs by country artists. Flags sold out at stores. "God Bless the USA" signs filled yards, and bumper stickers with some patriotic phrase or another adorned cars and trucks. Citizens declared that they were "proud to be an American," as one song proclaimed, and let their love of country be known as never before. Someone had attacked the comfort of Americans—their safety and security—and destroyed buildings symbolic of industry and military might. Innocent people had died. What happened at Ground Zero had created a rebirth in the zest and zeal for the American way. This happened on a global scale, too. After the attacks, patriotism spread even in countries that were allies of the United States, who proclaimed they, too, were Americans. The French newspaper *Le Monde* went so far as to

In the time immediately following the 9/11 attacks, radio stations played patriotic songs by country artists. Flags sold out at stores. "God Bless the USA" signs filled yards....

feature a headline reading "We are all Americans now." Citizens in Iran held vigils for the Americans. Europeans flew U.S. flags and cheered on the "American war on terror."

But cracks in the official story, the rush to war with Iraq, the lack of WMDs, and Bush's 9/11 Commission report placing blame on the CIA's lack of communication and insight, among other factors, began to stoke a fire of conspiracy theories. A massive truth movement sprung forth right after 2004. Before then, the media, whether mainstream or alternative, mainly reported the official story line, despite some reporters claiming there had been warning signs of terrorist activity before the attacks, and others claiming they had heard an explosion at the Twin Towers site before the planes struck. These were just whispers but eventually as more people saw inconsistencies and asked more questions, the cracks got bigger and bigger.

A shift in language emerged. Reporters who had been on the scene and had interviewed first responders could be heard yelling and shouting about an "explosion" when the South Tower fell. This included a live broadcast by N. J. Burkett, an ABC news correspondent who was about a block away from the Towers that morning. He interrupted his commentary by shouting "A huge explosion now—raining debris on all of us! We'd better get out of the way!" Many early reports used the word "explosion," but by the evening news broadcasts, all mentions of "explosions" were now replaced with "collapse."

Amy Goodman of the news program *Democracy Now!* interviewed author David Ray Griffin on May 26, 2004, to talk about his book *The New Pearl Harbor.* Their discussion revolved around Griffin's evidence that the event was an inside job and even questioned whether it was a plane or a missile that hit the Pentagon. This was one of the first times a media outlet gave the mic to an alternative viewpoint, and the floodgates opened wide. Soon, the 9/11 truth movement was born, and it grew quickly with each new revelation about the attacks and about the Afghanistan and Iraq wars. The media became filled with reporters and stories asking questions, seeking clarifications, positing theories, and pointing out inconsistencies.

PATRIOTIC PROPAGANDA

During the administration of George W. Bush, Karen Hughes, the public diplomacy chief, created the Digital Outreach

Team. Its job was to defend the United States in online chat rooms, much as trolls do today on social media. Hughes also worked with Disney to produce a patriotic, feel-good film called *Portraits of America*, which was shown in all U.S. embassies and in many national airports.

On the other side, Osama bin Laden created live videos from various remote hiding places giving lectures to his supporters. TV network Al Jazeera, headquartered in Doha, Qatar, aired these messages for a global audience. Al Jazeera was the first English-language news channel headquartered in the Middle East. It claims to be editorially independent and to be funded by loans and grants.

Right after the 9/11 attacks, jingoism had invaded all aspects of culture, including movies and television shows. There was a new sensitivity to violence and terrorism on the big and small screen, and many shows and movies edited out scenes depicting plane crashes, bombings, the Twin Towers, and the destruction of cities, including *Lilo and Stitch*, a children's movie that had featured a scene of Stitch on a 747 flying amidst tall buildings. The *Power Rangers* and *Pokémon* series had episodes removed from broadcast schedules because of scenes of cities being destroyed. Adult television shows like *Sex in the City* and *The Sopranos* removed the World Trade Center from opening credits. Movies such as *Zoolander*, *Serendipity*, *The Time Machine*, and *Men in Black II* removed shots of the Twin Towers. Movies featuring terrorists, like the popular *Die Hard* and *Air Force One*, focused more on the Russians as the enemy and avoided Middle East references.

Other shows didn't shy away at all and promoted blatant jingoism and even mass panic, such as the boisterous and clearly patriotic *Independence Day* and the reboot of *War of the Worlds* with Tom Cruise. Only later, after 2008, would movies dare show the more serious side of the war on terrorism with *The Hurt Locker* and *Zero Dark Thirty*, both of which portrayed the dark aspects of war and even torture, even as they promoted them as a necessity in the ongoing "war on terror."

An example of the power of patriotism occurred when France suddenly became ostracized for its position on the war. Suddenly, French fries were boycotted in the United States and replaced on some restaurant menus with "freedom fries" as a slap in the face to a nation that was simply questioning the narrative. Of course, as time passed, this was all forgotten, and restaurants returned to calling them French fries again on their menus.

By the year 2014, both the United States and a militant group known as the Islamic State (also called ISIS, for the Islamic State of Iraq and Syria, or ISIL, for the Islamic State of Iraq and the Levant) would become adept at using social media as a propaganda tool. The United States would shift its focus from showing the evils of Al-Qaeda to the Islamic State as the enemy, while the Islamic State would report on news interspersed with gruesome videos of beheadings as a warning to its enemies. Alternative media was becoming too powerful to ignore, with websites and publications questioning the narrative. This new media was hard for governments to control or contain, as most of the journalists operated entirely independent of political bias or corporate influence. News organizations such as Media Workers against the War, Democracy Now!, IndyMedia, Common Sense, and a number of "underground" news sites on the internet provided other voices and interviews with soldiers and citizens in the United States and abroad who often painted a completely different picture from the one portrayed on MSM—mainstream media.

A restaurant in North Carolina announces it is serving "freedom fries" not French fries as a protest against France's political policies.

It was an ongoing war between the United States constantly seeking to counter and discredit the ideology of militant Islam, and the Islamic State trying to spread that same ideology to any potential new members who might be watching or listening. In 2016, it was revealed that the Pentagon had employed a British PR company called Bell Pottinger, paying it over $540 million to produce fake terrorist videos and news articles for Arab news channels and media outlets. The money came from the U.S. Department of Defense (DOD) and was funneled into contracts between 2007 and 2011 to create the fake media and report back to the CIA, the DOD, and the National Security Council. Pentagon officials were also meeting with various news analysts to sway them to spread favorable information about the Iraq War. The analysts would be financially rewarded or given special classified information, lavish trips, or lucrative contracts.

All of this was meant to mold public opinion, including among Democrats and liberals not known for their support of war or foreign invasions, much of which occurred in the "bully pulpit" in Congress and from the White House under Bush. As for the public, the manipulation of the mainstream media worked to create

Iraq's leader, Saddam Hussein, at the time of the 9/11 terrorist attacks. America's propaganda machine placed the blame on Hussein despite any solid evidence.

and support the false belief that there was a link between Saddam Hussein and Al-Qaeda. With enough repetition and spin, the public was soon falling for such an alliance hook, line, and sinker, without a shred of actual evidence of any alliance between Saddam and Al-Qaeda to back those claims. The obvious lie didn't matter because the war machine had one hell of a sales team behind it, and ten years after the war in Iraq began, polls reflected that at least a third of those questioned believed that Iraq was directly involved in the 9/11 attacks.

According to the article "The Iraq War and the Power of Propaganda" by Paul R. Pillar, which appeared in the *National Interest*, "The belief was cultivated by repeatedly uttering 'Iraq' and '9/11' and 'war on terror' in the same breath. The cultivation was so successful that by the peak of the war-promoters' sales campaign in late 2002 a majority of Americans believed that Saddam Hussein not only was allied with Al-Qaeda but also had been directly involved in the 9/11 attacks." The article describes how long after the war this belief persisted due to "officially instigated ignorance." The damage was done, thanks to the work of the administration to manipulate truth and falsehood. "The substantial lingering misconceptions among the public make for broader damage," according to Pillar. "The persistent mistaken beliefs among more than a third of Americans about Iraq and Al-Qaeda greatly inhibit public understanding about terrorism, about the Middle East, and about how their own government has operated."

SHARED VALUES

Propaganda campaigns are public relations campaigns. The Shared Values Initiative was run by a famous Madison Avenue PR and advertising executive, Charlotte Beers. Launched shortly after the 9/11 attacks and funded by the U.S. Department of State via a front group called the Council of American Muslims for Understanding (CAMU), its goal was to dispel current myths about the treatment and status of Muslims by portraying them as happy, successful, and free in the United States. The goal was to sway Muslims abroad into seeing the United States as a place where they could come to live free from religious persecution and pursue the American dream.

The $15 million PR campaign consisted of different phases that utilized the production of videos and documentaries for television, radio, and print media. These films showed that Muslims and non-Muslims shared the same values, and they featured Muslim Americans and their personal histories and lifestyles in America. A website and speaking tours also promoted the vision of freedom to Muslims, and each ad or film ended with the line "Presented by the Council of American Muslims for Understanding, and the American People." It all sounded and felt so warm and fuzzy, but it failed miserably, and after about a month, it was shuttered and Beers resigned.

Not all propaganda works, and no matter how convincing or compelling it may be at first, all propaganda has a shelf life.

Not all propaganda works, and no matter how convincing or compelling it may be at first, all propaganda has a shelf life. It is all but impossible, especially with the internet and the free flow of information at everyone's fingertips, to keep an official story from ever being questioned or even dismantled. Often, by using fear and other tools and techniques, the powers behind the official story can make it last a long time and revive it when it appears to be fading from public memory and focus. But they cannot make it last forever. Why? Because once humans are no longer immobilized with fear or so angry at some enemy that they cannot see straight, they begin to move again. They begin to see straighter. They get curious. They begin to open their eyes. They start to question what they're being told. It's natural human behavior.

Sadly, such an awakening happened only after the public had agreed to the Iraq invasion, although protestors turned out in larger numbers than they had for the invasion into Afghanistan. Perhaps that invasion occurred while America still slept in its fearful slumber, before citizens woke up and expressed their confusion over who the real enemy was (Osama, Saddam, Al-Qaeda, the Taliban, all of the above?), who was truly responsible for 9/11 (especially after more evidence of direct Saudi involvement came to light), and whether the country's real reason for fighting overseas was for ideology, revenge, or oil. Many Americans wondered

Journalistic Spin

Sometimes those asking questions are the journalists covering the event. One of these was MSNBC's Peter Arnett, who was fired by both the network and *National Geographic* in 2003 after he was interviewed by the Iraqi information ministry and claimed the "shock and awe" strategy of the Americans had been a failure and that the Americans had underestimated the determination and willingness of the Iraqi soldiers to fight for their country. Arnett also reported on civilian deaths in Baghdad, which helped fuel the antiwar movement's ammunition against the Bush war machine.

Pulitzer Prize-winning journalist Peter Arnett got in hot water in 2003 when he granted an impromptu interview with Iraqi television in which he said America's military strategy against the Iraqis was not effective.

Other journalists would attempt to tell a more rounded story of what was happening on both sides, but they often met with resistance from both American and Iraqi media because of influence by the Pentagon. Iraqi media outlets, whether television, radio, or print, often had their own spin based upon religious and political backers and their particular motives and agendas. Finding comprehensive, factual news was difficult on both sides of the war. Noted journalist Bill Moyers was one of the lone voices of truth speaking out about the war and the propaganda machines behind it in his "Buying the War" program, part of the *Bill Moyers Journal* on PBS. It featured interviews with journalists from *Meet the Press*, *60 Minutes*, and major news outlets discussing the role of the media in buying into the Bush war machine.

if their own government, working with the Saudis, pulled off the biggest false flag event in the nation's history as an excuse to pass the draconian Patriot Act and put U.S. citizens under the thumbs of constant and widespread surveillance and control. Alternative press writers wondered if the architects behind 9/11 were the same as the ones behind the Patriot Act.

Whether one likes to call these "conspiracy theories," which we explore in a later chapter, or something else, it matters not because in many cases, we can easily see how the media works with those in power to create a specific narrative to feed to the public, and that narrative is often a mixture of truth and untruth. Sometimes it's filled with so many holes in the form of lies, misinformation, or disinformation that it crumbles completely to an entirely new narrative. The mainstream media won't ask questions of the official story at first. They will attack any challenges to the official story. But once one brave network or outlet points out that the emperor has no clothes, often the media is quick to jump on board the bandwagon. Fickle, they are.

The mainstream media won't ask questions of the official story at first. They will attack any challenges to the official story.

One of the first milestones of this shift occurs in the form of language. This is something we see again and again, past and present, when propaganda is involved. The power of words to influence the public must adapt to new information and facts, or else it loses its power to hold sway over the minds it was meant to control.

Throughout the duration of the war on terror, critics lamented the death of democracy. While President Bush was equating it with a modern-day Crusade, the pundits and public were wondering where their freedoms were disappearing to. Propaganda was the mark of authoritarianism and should have had no place in a democratic society. The use of secrecy, control of press, and censorship of dissenting voices were counter to democratic values, yet in a crisis such values seemed to vanish under the heavy cloak of authoritarianism. Freedom of speech and protest were all but obliterated. The trend after 9/11 moved further and further away from transparency of government and truth in reporting to something akin to a secret society running the country with their own rules and ideals.

Those who dared question this rise of authoritarianism were quickly silenced and called the enemy or at least complicit with the goals and motives of the enemy. Only the enemy used propaganda, U.S. authority figures insisted. They and they alone were telling the truth. But dare question that truth and you could be thrown in jail or a detention facility. Flag burning, a symbol of free speech during the hippie years, was briefly punishable by jail time, although the U.S. Supreme Court would rule that it was a form of free speech. And speaking of prisons, what was happening to Iraqi prisoners in the United States' top-secret military prison at Guantanamo Bay in Cuba was nothing short of illegal torture, and as photos were leaked to the press, the public began to turn on Bush and the war, and more and more people demanded we "bring the troops home" sooner rather than later. Meanwhile, the Bush administration excused the torture as a necessity of the war on terror.

Protestors in the Black Lives Matter movement burn an American flag during a 2020 demonstration in Raleigh, North Carolina.

The idea of a "new normal" after 9/11 in which the American people accepted things they never would have before the terrorist attacks occurred—things like total surveillance, snitching on the neighbors, allowing the torture of prisoners with no due process, and living in fear enough to never question authority or the official narrative courtesy of the mass media—sounds eerily similar to another campaign pushing a "new normal," one that involves a virus called COVID-19.

Twenty-First-Century Propaganda: Pundit Wars, Memes, and the Power of the Hashtag

"Those who manipulate this unseen mechanism of society constitute an invisible government which is the true ruling power of our country. We are governed, our minds are molded, our tastes formed, our ideas suggested, largely by men we have never heard of."
—Edward Bernays

The messages of the first two decades of the twenty-first century are embedded in our minds and seared into our memories, thanks to the nonstop talking heads on news outlets, the memes and hashtags scattered over our social media accounts, the sponsored and fake news, and the personalized ads, all giving rise to a creepy realization that we are being both targeted and monitored 24/7 by the technology we have embraced.

Short and catchy soundbites and phrases seem to sum up the political and social angst of the current times. Everywhere we turn, someone is trying to influence us, sell something to us, tell us we're wrong, shut us down, lift us up, or push us to accept something or reject something. Mostly they are trying to make money from us.

The years from 2010 to 2020 were a propagandist's dream. With the advent of social media, a whole new avenue of influence, manipulation, and control opened up. Leaders have new ways to keep the citizenry under their thumbs. Corporations have new ways to get consumers to surrender their credit card numbers and buy things, often things they were only a few minutes beforehand thinking or talking about. Friends and family have unprecedented access to each other on websites where they can post their thoughts and responses to each other's personal opinions.

The more connected we are to the world and to each other, the more we open ourselves to manipulative tactics meant to sway our opinions, change our minds, open our wallets, and get us to fall in line with the "normal" and official narrative everyone else is accepting. Don't rock the boat or you'll get left behind. Don't step out of line or you might suffer #FOMO (fear of missing out) or, worse, be punished for your individuality and unique perspective. Don't speak out of turn or you will be chastised by people you've never met and wouldn't care about you if you had.

Propaganda in the new century is everywhere. It's just gotten really good at hiding behind things like trending hashtags, likes, and follows.

THE OBAMA YEARS

The election of the United States' first Black president was a time for celebration and hope. Barack Hussein Obama, a former lawyer who served as a U.S. senator from Illinois from 2005 to 2008 after several years in the Illinois state senate, became the 44th U.S. president and served two consecutive terms from 2009 to 2017. The nation, at least half of it, celebrated this milestone with parties and marches. The word most associated with Obama's election was "hope," and it was plastered all over television ads, signage, and T-shirts. The other word was "change," and for people of color and women, his winning campaign served as a promise for more diversity in the White House to come.

President Obama's public reach included a host of politically driven media outlets and the proliferation of social media sources such as Facebook and Twitter, which would be both the benefit and the curse of every political candidate and movement to follow. Obama was masterful at speaking in public, and he was able to use these outlets to spread his messages of hope and change even as his enemies attacked him for his race and questioned the Hawaiian-born politician's country of origin.

A gifted public speaker, President Barack Obama knew how to use television and social media to get his message out to the public.

Yet all presidents are a mix of the good, the bad, and the ugly, and a Democratic president's negative policies are often brushed aside thanks to a very powerful propaganda machine behind him. With President Obama, this included a rising liberal-centrist media consisting of CNN, MSNBC, and CBS to counter the right-wing influences of Fox News (which in turn defends or ignores the bad policies of a Republican president), and alliances with the owners of social media giants like Facebook and Twitter. The dividing line between right and left, conservative and liberal, became increasingly obvious and undeniable as both sides engaged in a battle of words and wits to push agendas that were at times almost identical and included wars abroad, fighting Al-Qaeda and the war on terror, and courting lobbyists and Wall Street. The differences—which included gun control, abortion rights, and food programs and other aid for the poor—were the focus of the media wars for dominance in the public eye. The key was to focus so much on the bad the other side was doing, while repeating over and over the good your own side was doing, that people would be too distracted to see the bad on your side.

These diversion and distraction tactics worked like a charm until alternative media sources once again raised questions that weren't being answered and pointed to issues that were not being addressed on both sides of the political coin. They were often quickly censored or drowned out with more posturing and positioning on the right and the left. But even in the mainstream media, you could still find some balanced discourse and debate, if you knew where to look for it.

In 2012, President Obama signed into law an amendment to the National Defense Authorization Act for the fiscal year of 2013. This amendment allowed the United States to create and distribute propaganda that was pro-American within the nation's own borders for the purpose of squashing attempts by Al-Qaeda to turn the world against Western ideals. This amendment updated an older Smith-Mundt Act of 1948 and the later Foreign Relations Authorization Act of 1987 to clarify the kinds of propaganda that would be allowed. For many decades, the United States had engaged in propaganda efforts at home and abroad mainly under the guise of "foreign diplomacy" and for the purpose of encouraging foreign support for American-backed war efforts. But domestically, propaganda had always been banned, at least officially.

The signing of this bipartisan amendment ... served to lift that ban and open the floodgates to domestic propaganda....

The signing of this bipartisan amendment, sponsored by representatives Mac Thornberry of Texas and Adam Smith of Washington State, served to lift that ban and open the floodgates to domestic propaganda, and with the growing popularity of cable news networks and social media, the range was much broader and the reach much larger. It would give sweeping powers to the government to utilize mass media via television, radio, newspapers, and social media to push its agenda on the public. It would not be required to push real, factual news at all. In fact, the information could be partially false or entirely false. Fake news.

At the time, many congresspersons spoke out against the amendment, pointing to how it would neutralize the Smith-Mundt and Foreign Relations Authorization Acts that once protected Americans from government misinformation and disinformation campaigns.

Those in support of the bill pointed to how effective propaganda was overseas when used on foreign audiences and how beneficial it would be stateside if not for those pesky restrictions. Pentagon insiders suggested that propaganda used domestically could garner more support for unpopular wars in Iraq and Afghanistan. In 2012, the Pentagon had already spent almost $4 billion to sway public opinion, and the Department of Defense threw in an additional $202 million on what they called "information operations" in Iraq and Afghanistan. But clearly these agencies wanted even more control of media to push their message within U.S. borders.

This decision would have a major effect not only on what constituted news but also on the journalists trying to report it. Censorship, as we discuss later, was already being exercised on the rogue reporters who dared to write truths the powers that be would have preferred to keep secret. Now, with propaganda to contend with in reporting on issues at home and abroad, some journalists were feeling a new kind of heat. In one example, related by John Hudson in his article "U.S. Repeals Propaganda Ban, Spreads Government-Made News to Americans" in the July 13, 2012, issue of *Foreign Policy*, domestic propaganda efforts ensnared two *USA Today* journalists in 2012 when they reported on millions of dollars in back taxes owed by the Pentagon's propaganda contractor in Afghanistan. "Eventually, one of the co-owners of the firm confessed to creating phony websites and Twitter accounts to smear the journalists anonymously. Additionally, ... the *Washington Post* exposed a counter-propaganda program by the Pentagon that recommended posting comments on a U.S. website run by a Somali expat with readers opposing al-Shabab," a militant group based in Somalia. Such manipulation could impede journalists seeking truth, and with the added focus on social media, it allowed the military to post material and images without even claiming ownership of them. They could attack anonymously.

President Obama signed the bill into law on January 2, 2013, as HR 4310, the Smith-Mundt Modernization Act of 2012. It was part of the National Defense Authorization Act (NDAA) and reversed a long-standing policy, thus allowing fake news, misinformation, and disinformation to be used at home on American soil in all media formats. This bill received almost no attention at the time because most of the country was caught up in another part of the NDAA involving the detention of U.S. citizens without trial. This is one way that bills citizens don't want become laws they don't want. The signing nullified the earlier Smith-Mundt Act and made it legal to use psychological operations, or psyops, and other forms of propaganda on U.S. citizens. It was like signing into law a new kind of mind wars, and the battle was for control of the narratives chosen by the government.

According to Michael B. Kelley in an article for *Business Insider* dated May 21, 2012, Lieutenant Colonel Daniel Davis had released a report critical of the distortion of truth by senior military

This bill received almost no attention at the time because most of the country was caught up in another part of the NDAA involving the detention of U.S. citizens without trial.

officials in Iraq and Afghanistan, and he had openly written about the information operations (IO) used after Operation Desert Storm to spread "the integrated employment of electronic warfare (EW), computer network operations (CNO), psychological operations (PSYOPS), military deception (MILDEC), and operations security (OPSEC), in concert with specified supporting and related capabilities, to influence, disrupt, corrupt, or usurp adversarial human and automated decision making while protecting our own."

IO was originally intended for use overseas to manipulate foreign audiences, but now, with this bill and amendment, it allowed the "direct deployment of these tactics on the American public."

The result? From that point on, it was open season on the truth. Today news consumers often have no idea what is really news, what is opinion, and what is manufactured information or outright propaganda to gain their consent and approval.

On December 23, 2016, President Obama signed another propaganda bill into law. This time it was the Countering Foreign Propaganda and Disinformation Act, a bipartisan bill introduced by senators Rob Portman of Ohio and Chris Murphy of Connecticut. Like the 2013 bill, it was included as a part of the National Defense Authorization Act for the fiscal year of 2017 and was introduced as a result of the 2016 presidential election, when there were growing concerns of foreign influence in U.S. political elections, namely from Russia. The bill would serve to counter any Russian disinformation and covert influence on American politics and political campaigns. Former secretary of state Hillary Clinton was all for it, having just lost the presidential election (despite winning the popular vote) to a man nobody expected to win the White House, and her campaign was adamant that Russian influence was behind the political upset, although her opponents pointed to haphazard campaigning and the influences of candidate Bernie Sanders, senator from Vermont, and his wave of popularity as the real reason.

RUSSIA, RUSSIA, RUSSIA

After the 2016 presidential campaign, the word "Russia" was on everyone's lips, and the Countering Foreign Propaganda and Disinformation Act was passed easily to protect the public and private sectors from foreign influence. This act would allow the U.S. secretary of state to collaborate with the secretary of defense and other federal agencies to create a Global Engagement Center to fight foreign propaganda and to make public attempts by foreign entities to use propaganda and disinformation against the United States. Of course, no one asked Clinton and other politicians who voted for the bill about the money and influence they themselves had received from foreign entities, notably Saudi Arabia. And no one asked about the bill signed just a few years prior practically alerting the American public to the fact that they would be lied to and deceived at every possible turn when their own government saw fit. Propaganda was always easily justified when it was to be used against "the other guy," a lot like censorship … until you became "the other guy."

The point was, the election of 2016 had become a controversy of incendiary proportions, and someone was to blame. For the next four years, the word "Russia" would become a hugely popular hashtag and meme fodder on both sides of the political spectrum. Suddenly, the guy President George W. Bush once called a good friend, and who had met several times with both Obama and Hillary Clinton, was public enemy number one. The name of Vladimir Putin, president of Russia, was suddenly widely reviled. The reason revolved around allegations that he had somehow helped sway the presidential contest between Hillary Clinton and Donald Trump with monetary donations and massive bot trolling of social media. Yet there was also plenty of proof that the Saudis and Israel had given far more in financial contributions to their candidates of choice and of the United States' own repeated interference in foreign elections when it suited U.S. needs. This was rarely discussed in mainstream media, however.

Obama's legacy of hope and change allowed many of his less popular involvements in wars abroad and a drone program responsible for untold civilian casualties in Syria and other nations to be brushed under the rug. He was popular and loved by half the country, and probably could have won another election had he not reached the two-term limit.

A push for diversity in the White House ended when the woman most people thought would win and break perhaps the biggest gender barrier in the country lost to a man who up until then had no political experience. A man who was roundly criticized by Democrats for being very undiplomatic and crass in his speaking

President Vladimir Putin of Russia was accused by many Americans of tampering with the U.S. elections of 2016 so that Republican nominee Donald Trump would gain more votes than the Democrats' Hillary Clinton.

style. A reality-show celebrity and businessman named Donald Trump.

Who would have thought it could happen?

The Trump years would be unlike any other, with propaganda coming out of the mouths of politicians on both sides at unprecedented rates, fake news galore, spin so dizzying it confused even those doing the spin, and a whole lot more.

PROPAGANDA ON A PIN: SELLING A PRESIDENT TO THE PUBLIC

Presidential campaign slogans have been printed on signs, buttons, bumper stickers, and other items and are an artform of propaganda meant to rally support for a particular candidate. They are short, popular, easily remembered phrases that become a brand or trademark of the candidate in question. Today, they are often translated to social media hashtags. Here's a list of several slogans from 1960 to today:

Hashtag Wars

In 2007, an American blogger and product consultant posted the following tweet on Twitter. He could have had no idea how his simple tweet would change the world forever.

While old school political promotions like bumper stickers are still in use today, social media and the hashtag wars have gained prominence.

How do you feel about using # (pound) for groups. As in #barcamp [msg]?

—Chris Messina's original Tweet proposing hashtag usage, August 23, 2007

The hashtag, or number symbol, was a metadata tag used on social media networks such as Twitter. According to Wikipedia, "It lets users apply dynamic, user-generated tagging that helps other users easily find messages with a specific theme or content. Users create and use hashtags by placing a hash symbol in front of a word or unspaced phrase in a message. The hashtag may contain letters, digits, and underscores. Searching for that hashtag yields each message that someone has tagged with it. A hashtag archive is consequently collected into a single stream under the same hashtag." The reaction from Twitter was that this was a tool for nerds, but it eventually caught on and has now become a fixture on social media—so much so that people even use the word in casual conversation. "Oh, that party is going to be hashtag lame!" or "That guy is hashtag losing it!"

With the rise of social media as a ubiquitous form of communication, we now converse in hashtags to indicate our political preferences, the foods we like, the celebrities we support, our favorite sports teams, the things we hate, the things we love, and our current emotions, among other things. Hashtags (along with emojis, cute images that convey emotions and activities) have replaced the short, catchy sound bites of old such as "Read my lips: no new taxes" and "Ask not what your country can do for you, but what you can do for your country." This applies not just to politics but to every aspect of our lives, as made transparent on social media. We communicate our lives through hashtags, and as always, they can be used as a form of propaganda to push an idea, product, person, or agenda. Here are just a few hashtags that have gone viral:

With the rise of social media as a ubiquitous form of communication, we now converse in hashtags to indicate our political preferences....

- #MAGA
- #Imwithher
- #BernieBros
- #votebluenomatterwho
- #KAG
- #itsstillherturn
- #WWG1WGA
- #metoo
- #blacklivesmatter
- #believeallwomen
- #lockherup
- #berniefuckingsanders
- #notmeus

Pandemic Propaganda

In December 2019 a new and extremely contagious coronavirus was identified in China that caused a disease that became known as COVID-19. Within a few months, the virus had swept the world, filling hospitals and closing countries. With the onset of the COVID-19 pandemic, the hashtags started immediately, encouraging people to comply with government orders to stay at home and follow the official safe-distancing orders. The goal was to "flatten the curve" of the spread—a phrase referring to a widely reproduced graph projecting infection rates—to make it easier for hospitals and medical centers to deal with the flood of patients. At first, the hashtags mirrored the seriousness of the pandemic, how critical it was to fully support medical personnel, and the importance of staying home to keep the virus from spreading. On the television, viewers were bombarded with public service announcements and commercials with somber piano music and wordless messages of support and hope.

Sometimes the PSAs would feature the faces of nurses and doctors looking exhausted from their days helping the sick. Other times, they would feature families and couples at home finding the "new normal"—or #newnormal—of lockdowns, quarantines, and social distancing measures.

Before long, people got restless and began asking questions and finding inconsistencies with the reports of deaths, the dates of the initial spread, and the advice given. People were advised first not to use masks to reduce the contagion (because too few were available even for medical personnel, and because the virus was thought to be spread mainly by contact and not through the air) and then to always wear masks in public (once handmade ones became available and research began to confirm the likelihood of airborne spread). In some states, certain businesses were ordered closed, office workers were instructed to work from home, schools were closed, hospital and nursing home visits were curtailed or prohibited, and unemployment benefits were extended, while other states carried on largely as usual. Such apparent inconsistencies led people to become curious as to why different doctors or medical organizations said different things, and why citizens were being asked to give up their freedom to work, shop, or attend school as usual while politicians continued to receive their paychecks and keep their health insurance. With any propaganda, even the kind that is meant to help save lives, people get curious about the repeated narrative. Some groups of people did not believe COVID-19 was a serious illness, and they felt they were being shamed into staying home for no good reason.

Public service announcement about COVID-19 bombarded the public all through 2020, but at times people found the messages confusing, especially during the early months when there was a shortage of masks and people were actually asked not to wear them so that there would be enough for medical personnel.

People also became frustrated over losing their livelihoods and businesses and being told to shut up and do what was right #for thegreatergood, and the hashtags began to reflect the growing unrest of those suffering the economic consequences and wondering why their freedoms were being compromised or ignored. Among the hashtags prevalent during the 2020 pandemic were:

- #stayinsidesavelives
- #alonetogether
- #flattenthecurve
- #thenewnormal
- #saferathome
- #socialdistancing
- #forthegreatergood
- #slowthespread
- #wearamask
- #openthecountry
- #fightback
- #knowyourrights
- #letuswork
- #endthelockdown

It became easy to tell where someone stood just by the hashtags they used or followed on Instagram, Twitter, and Facebook. As the pandemic progressed, people responded, wearing their emotions not on their sleeves but via their hashtags. Watching the entire pandemic unfold was a great firsthand lesson in identifying propaganda, whether it be from the president, a political party, the U.S. Centers for Disease Control and Prevention (CDC), the World Health Organization (WHO), a billionaire like Bill Gates, the media, state governors, or anyone else with an opinion to offer. The country became divided between those who wanted to stay quarantined to slow the viral spread and protect the weak, and those who demanded they be allowed to reopen their businesses or get outside and get back to normal. Caught in the middle were those people deemed essential workers who had no choice but to face the public (and thus, potential exposure to the coronavirus) every day, like it or not, such as workers in hospitals or supermarkets. Those who expressed one viewpoint over another were cheered by the choir they preached to and vilified by those who had different viewpoints. Compromise and working together seemed out of reach for a while, until cooler heads could prevail and operate from common sense. New words and phrases entered into the arguments, such as "social distancing" and "flat-

President Donald Trump became famous (and infamous) for his frequent use of Twitter during his time in office.

tening the curve," and people discussed virology and epidemiology as instant experts, repeatedly quoting and posting what they'd heard on mainstream news and or read on social media.

Those familiar with Twitter already knew the power of a tweet and how a short selection of words could convey volumes on the social media site. Once limited to 160 characters, tweets were later expanded to 240 to allow more expression. People tweeted their beliefs, their ideas, their values, and their political identities, and the creation of the hashtag added a whole new element to the spread of viral information. Former presidents tweeted using hashtags. Senators and celebrities did, too. President Trump became a Twitter celebrity, tweeting daily with hashtags. Soon, they were showing up more on Facebook and Instagram as another way to track and promote a message and watch it spread further on the virtual global stage.

One of the most powerful aspects of hashtags is the ability to bypass censorship. Social media blocks hashtags that promote violence, pornography, drug use, and, increasingly, anything that doesn't correspond with the narrative being pushed by mainstream media and government. Some examples have included hashtags with antivaccination messages, alternative health cures for COVID-19, conspiracy theories, and other such subjects, but people found ways to create hashtags to go around the ban. Twitter and Instagram banned overly generic hashtags, too, that they claimed were too vague and did not fill a particular purpose. What is banned is entirely up to the social media platform, but new hashtag phrases are invariably created that bypass those bans. An example would be banning #naturalcuresforcancer. The way around it would be changing it to #cancercuredbyscience or something that removes the "alternative" suggestion. Another example, addressing a ban on #picture for being too generic, might use #coolpicturesofthings instead. Pretty simple, and it easily follows the content policies of social media while bending the rules to get the messages and memes across.

In July and August of 2020, Twitter went on a banning rampage, hiding certain posts or removing the pages of white supremacists, conspiracy theorists, people who promoted QAnon theories (information drops via a mysterious entity called Q via a website called 8Chan), those opposing vaccines, those in favor of natural health, proponents of COVID-19 cures that did not involve vaccines or pharmaceuticals, some Trump supporters, and certain far-right conservatives, from radio and podcast hosts to organizations supporting those running for office. The move involved mainly so-called alt-right conservatives along with Trump supporters in general, resulting in the removal of thousands of sites, some with millions of followers—according to some, not because they were supporting violence or riots but because they went against the narrative supported by mainstream media. While some onlookers from both the political right and left found that such censorship loomed terrifying as a threat of things to come, others welcomed the curtailing of misinformation and of what they considered hate speech.

The move involved mainly so-called alt-right conservatives along with Trump supporters in general, resulting in the removal of thousands of sites....

Twitter's official policy, according to Bernard Meyer in an article for *Cybernews* titled "Is There Censorship on Twitter?," states that "to be banned, users need to meet certain criteria, and Twitter is fairly open about what these comprise." Meyer outlined those criteria as spamming, hacking, fake accounts, linking to malware, revealing private information about other users (doxing), and tweeting abuse or hateful content. About the last item, Meyer explained, "This is often the most controversial aspect of Twitter's banning policy. What constitutes a threat or insult can be subjective. But as Twitter explains, most speech is protected. Promoting violence against other users, racial abuse, or targeted harassment are all prohibited, as is encouraging others to commit suicide."

Twitter made use of these rules to permanently ban President Trump's account in 2021 for allegedly inciting a riot at the Capitol.

An additional category not mentioned by Meyer, but appearing on Twitter's own "Twitter Rules" page, is "civic integrity." Twitter describes the rule as follows: "You may not use Twitter's services for the purpose of manipulating or interfering in elections or other civic processes. This includes posting or sharing content that may suppress participation or mislead people about when, where, or how to participate in a civic process."

Meme Power
The days of propaganda posters and political cartoons in newspapers and magazines have given way to a new form of

pushing ideas and ideologies, a virtual "sound-bite" called a "meme." The word "meme" was coined in 1976 by the British scientist Richard Dawkins to refer to "a unit of cultural transmission." It was meant to resemble the word "gene," which is a unit of genetic transmission. In social media, a meme is an easily recognized and widely disseminated image or video. As the meme is spread, those who share it may change the caption or the image slightly to convey a new idea.

The Merriam-Webster Dictionary online offers the following quote from writer Anastasia Thrift to illustrate the nature of a meme: "The grumpy cat meme frowned its way onto the Internet in September 2012 and never turned its dissatisfied head back. Since then, the image of the cranky cat has grown more and more popular in direct proportion to appearing less and less impressed by fame."

Dictionary.com describes a meme as "a cultural item that is transmitted by repetition and replication in a manner analogous to the biological transmission of genes" or "a cultural item in the form of an image, video, phrase, etc., that is spread via the internet and often altered in a creative or humorous way." Memes can be drawings, text, cartoons, photographs, images, videos, modes of dress or behavior, or anything else that is conveyable via imagery and has a discernable meaning culturally, socially, politically, or emotionally, and for the new generations growing up with technology and social media as a fundamental part of their culture, they may be all that is needed to say what needs to be said when it needs to be said. Why not speed up the work of putting thoughts into words and just make a meme? It's fun, and easy, and chances are, all your friends will laugh and relate.

Brithish evolutionary biologist and ethologist Richard Dawkins coined the term "meme" to mean "a unit of cultural transmission." Social media adopted the word to refer to an image or video that is widely shared.

The word comes from the ancient Greek *mimeisthai*, meaning "to imitate." Dawkins first used the word in his 1976 book *The Selfish Gene*. The book was an examination of human evolution, and Dawkins coined the word "meme" to describe a so-called cultural replicator—an idea or behavior that spreads across people in a culture. In the same way genes replicate, ideas do. The study of memes is called memetics, a discipline that looks at these cultural units of information and the mechanisms behind how they replicate and spread—or in today's jargon, "go viral"—throughout a population. Dawkins found that the same drivers in genetics were found in the behaviors and characteristics of memes and ideas.

Though the word has been around for decades, it wasn't until social media became all the rage that anyone gave it much thought, at which point it was reinvented as a whole new method of communication, one that could reach a large population in a matter of minutes.

The word "meme" is not intended to describe just any image that is put up on the internet. The proper term for that would be "image macro." If it goes viral and spreads across a culture or population, then it becomes a bona fide meme. But today many people label everything in image form that people post on social media a meme, whether two people see it or two million.

Some image macros are memes, but not all memes are image macros. By that same design, just making an image macro and sharing it doesn't make it an automatic meme. It has to spread, and it has to have a meaning or purpose for doing so. Confused? Nowadays, it's a meme because that label has become a part of the everyday dialog that we all understand. And "meme" just sounds cooler than "image macro."

Memes can be used to add humor to a Facebook post or to put forth a political message without having to go out on a limb and write something textual. Memes are also used to shame, ridicule, and make fun of others under the guise of humor. Even presidents and politicians, former and current, use memes to poke fun at or attack their opponents or a news story they disagree with. And when you want to argue with someone over politics—or anything else, for that matter—you can now engage in a meme war, an escalating online "tennis match" where people lob memes back and forth to get their points and opinions across. Politicians and media personalities have attacked memes that made them look bad while using memes to make themselves look good or to try to sway the public to the opinions they preferred.

During the Trump presidency, memes of the "bad orange man" were everywhere, with his toupee blowing in the wind, courtesy of those leaning left. Those who leaned right spread memes of Trump as a patriotic warrior. Unflattering memes of Hillary Clinton and Barack Obama peppered social media courtesy of those leaning right. Those leaning left portrayed them as heroes. See how that works? Both the liberal left and the conservative right enjoyed the use of meme power when it served their purposes and agendas, and rarely did memes make the "other side" look good or positive.

Both the liberal left and the conservative right enjoyed the use of meme power when it served their purposes and agendas....

Often memes are caricatures of public figures, including celebrities and athletes, used to perhaps knock them off their pedestals or cut them down to size by portraying them in cartoonish fashion. They can also be used to spread awareness of someone's agenda, as during the COVID-19 meme attacks against billionaire Bill Gates and his alleged plans to force vaccinations and supposed associations with eugenicists and population control advocates. Gates and Dr. Anthony Fauci, director of the National Institute of Allergy and Infectious Diseases, were popular subjects of memes during the pandemic, as were Trump and Speaker of the House Nancy Pelosi, portrayed as heroes or villains depending on the political bent of the meme-makers.

The pandemic opened the door to a meme war between those who believed in closing businesses and schools for months (and using governmental funds to compensate businesses and employees for their income losses) to reduce the spread of the coronavirus, and those who wanted to keep businesses open (and limit compensation for shutdowns or lost work) regardless of the virus's spread. It was also a war against which political party was showing more leadership. It was politics via pictures, with a good laugh to boot. In a presidential election year, memes proved cheaper than hiring political campaign consultants and were probably way more effective at shaping the voting preferences of the younger generations.

Everyone is fair game in the meme wars, including nonpoliticians. Business magnate Elon Musk has often been the butt of meme jokes for smoking pot on the Joe Rogan radio podcast. Macho actor Chuck Norris is featured in many a meme celebrating his bad-ass-ness. Internet users sent actor Keanu Reeves and his film *The Matrix* to the meme stratosphere as more and more people sought to "take the red pill," a phrase from the movie signifying the acceptance of a harsh truth. Athletes were lambasted by fans when they lost major games. Actors who said or did something dumb in public ended up on hundreds of memes on social media pages and posts all over the world. You couldn't make a wrong move without risking getting "memed" for it.

Ordinary people were lambasted and skewered via memes portraying them as nosy, intrusive, virtue-signaling "Karens" and whatever the male equivalent is to that person we all know and cannot stand who snitches on everyone, will not mind their own business, and gets offended at the drop of a hat when someone offers a conflicting opinion or fact. In the late 2010s the name "Karen" itself became synonymous with such a negative person, much to the chagrin of people actually named Karen. Some of the most popular Karen memes included a blond woman screeching over some offense (actually a woman named Taylor Armstrong on the set of *The Real Housewives of Beverly Hills*), and a cat sitting at the dining table commenting in return. Funny and cute as they were, they allowed the meme-maker to say some otherwise controversial things in the guise of a good laugh and a readily recognizable viral image.

When it comes to the queen of all memes, though, a grumpy-faced cat takes the crown. Grumpy Cat was a female cat named Tardar Sauce who became a massive internet sensation appearing on thousands of memes world-wide thanks to her strange downturned frown. Grumpy Cat, who died in May of 2019 to the collective mourning of millions, and other unlikely meme stars proved that social media could be utilized to convey everything from products for sale to politics to push and reach huge numbers of people doing it, if it was done right.

It seems that memes are fair game to spread rumor, innuendo, ideology, rhetoric, misinformation, libel, accusations, disinformation, conspiracies, lies by public officials, stupid celebrity quotes, and all kinds of stuff that the poor subject of the meme would rather not have viral. Yet because it is in the guise of humor, it is allowable.

Tardar Sauce (2012–2019) was a cat used in many internet memes in which he was nicknamed "Grumpy Cat" and would say a variety of grouchy things.

Memes can also spread positive quotes and motivational affirmations; they don't always focus on the negative. All a meme has to accomplish to be successful is to appeal to enough people who get what the image is trying to say, and when accompanied by a hashtag or two, it can go around the world in a matter of minutes—"go viral"—via social media posts and reposts. The more the meme can make people laugh, the better it spreads, as humor is a powerful form of communication. Many memes are neutral and merely mirroring something in society, such as a popular television show, a dance, a song, or a strange new fashion trend. Memes don't have to be destructive or constructive. They serve, as pop culture does, to simply mirror back to us what we collectively are talking and thinking about, and in some cases, arguing about.

Memes and images allow those who cannot communicate well via the written word to converse and debate with the best of them, and one day in the far future, an alien civilization that looks into the past of humanity will define us by our communication styles. They'll excavate our cities and reboot our ancient computers and cell phones and look at our memes to determine that we modern humans, like primitive humans, liked to put art up on walls.

Spin, Sponsored News, Fake News, and the "Lamestream" Media

"The basic tool for the manipulation of reality is the manipulation of words. If you can control the meaning of words, you can control the people who must use the words."
—*Philip K. Dick*

In November 1963, when U.S. president John F. Kennedy was assassinated, the coverage was carried on the three major news networks at that time: ABC, NBC, and CBS. Reporters gave the facts, mostly, and investigative journalism was permitted in the coming decades on nightly news specials that went beyond the daily news reportage. Over time, more channels and networks entered the mass media fray, including CNN (Cable News Network), MSNBC (created from a merger between Microsoft and NBC), and Fox, along with many local affiliates and smaller cable outlets. You might have thought with more channels to choose from, it would be easier to get real, factual news, but sides were being taken, mergers were being executed, and the news media was given the freedom to report just about anything they wanted to thanks to a lift on the ban of domestic propaganda.

All of this went into the pot to create the perfect stew of what we call news today—a seemingly chaotic mess of occasional fact, a ton of opinion, political spin based on who owns the network and their political leanings, and outright fake news designed to spread a particular, agreed-upon narrative. Fake news works by creating a slow drip of misinformation, disinformation, and propaganda to cast doubt on the facts and create a "wilderness of mirrors," as it is called in the counterintelligence world—an illusory mix of truth, half-truth, and outright lies that makes it incredibly difficult for anyone to know what is really going on.

President Donald Trump often tweeted about the "lamestream media" attacking his every move and was considered immature for his constant whining, but many believed he had a point. He was a natural target for the liberal media and liberal social media outlets, just as Democratic presidents had always been the natural target of right-wing media. Mainstream media, meanwhile, attempts to report the facts about both sides and to hold representatives of both sides accountable to the truth. Although he was certainly good fodder for opinion pieces and talking heads, reports on his activities were confusing to follow as the mainstream media had become diluted with far-right and far-left news sources.

President Donald Trump often complained about the "lamestream" media and its "fake news." While many considered his rants childish, others made the point that modern-day media is often very biased and do not report facts objectively.

Once President Obama lifted the domestic propaganda restrictions in 2013, the news media became flooded with questionable governmental information and began reporting more spin, more opinion, and more sponsored information, and the broadcast network news channels became overshadowed by three cable news giants—CNN, MSNBC, and Fox News. Fox News and its affiliates were known for their right-leaning position, and CNN and MSNBC began moving further left.

Viewers on the right used Fox News to shore up their beliefs and political identity, and those on the left used CNN and MSNBC as their holy grails of news, and neither side tends to consider that they might only have half the truth ... if that much. When President Obama allowed the use of propaganda during his presidency, it was motivated mainly by the desire to keep people on board the war in Iraq. But once the floodgates were open, both sides of the political chess game took every advantage to use it. And their viewers clung to every word as if truth, never bothering to ask how the "other side" had a completely different truth to tell.

Mainstream media groups are the children of corporate ownership and advertising dollars and the politicians, world leaders, and billionaires who most align with the corporate agendas—the two forces that drive the direction of the news reported on each network. In decades past, it was much harder to control every single story that broke in the news in time to create a desired narrative to present to the public. For one thing, there were many more local news sources, uncontrolled by corporate interests. But even larger news magazines, newspapers, and radio and television broadcasts were more likely to offer multiple viewpoints in their news stories, whereas today, a fixed narrative is often presented that is unquestionable and rigid, again depending on the political agenda of who is broadcasting it. The old adage "if it bleeds, it leads" (that is, bad news sells better than good news) applies today more than ever, with stories of violence, death, scandal, and ruin splattered across the headlines to keep readers engaged—often measured by the number of links they click online. Ever notice how as soon as one shocking story dominating the headlines begins to fade, there is often another waiting in the wings? The media needs something to hype to its followers, to keep ratings and popularity and clicks high so that they can charge more to advertisers. Happy, gentle stories of love and compassion don't usually cut it.

Nowadays, if a story breaks and someone posits a different theory other than the mainstream media narrative, they are vilified, called a conspiracy theorist, or censored outright. The media has changed drastically, making it all but impossible to discern real news from manufactured and doctored propaganda. Jim Marrs, in his 2015 book *Population Control: How Corporate Owners Are Killing Us*, says, "Critics today … view television news as quick and cheap programming that is repetitive, simplistic, and insulting. Cable TV news is viewed as predominately unqualified talking heads, and newspaper reporting as mostly rewritten press releases full of unnamed sources. Many see news stories today as no more than opinion pieces that reflect the zealotry and intolerance of advocates."

In 2020, six major players owned 90 percent of the media and entertainment outlets, including radio stations, television sta-

The Comcast Center building in Philadelphia headquarters one of the five large media companies in the United States. The other four are Disney, AT&T, ViacomCBS, and Fox Corporation.

tions, cable outlets, magazines, newspapers, and publishing companies. Over 227 million Americans rely on these six corporate giants for their news and information. Even if you watch smaller outlets, they are most likely owned by one of the Big Six (at the time of the writing of this book; new mergers can change things quickly): Time Warner, Viacom, News Corp, Disney, CBS, and Comcast. (Sony is often included on this list but is as of this point not so much a news media outlet.) Because of constant sales and purchases of subsidiary companies, it's hard to keep up with what these outlets own and operate.

Marrs went on to equate the shoddy news reporting of today with an age of conformity, as in the 1950s. Certainly, ample accusations have been made about mass media manipulation of the public, who are portrayed as "sheeple" who follow it without question or concern. This is evident in the loyal viewership of the Big Three—the liberal-biased CNN and MSNBC, and the conservative-biased Fox. Even smaller outlets may have their own political bent toward the left or the right, including Vox, Buzzfeed, Huffington Post, Politico, RT, Epoch Times, OANN, and Newsmax (more on this later in the book). Not that this is something they wish to hide; most outlets are quite up front about whether they offer readers and viewers a more liberal angle or a more conservative one.

There is nothing wrong with news outlets being honest about their projected audiences; in fact, it is the proper way to do things. Although they may still spin stories in one direction or another, outlets that announce their biases are not as manipulative as the mainstream media outlets that pretend to be reporting "the truth, the whole truth, and nothing but the truth." It rarely is.

CORPORATE CLUSTERS

It's easy to see how well propaganda proliferates when most of the media today falls under the ownership of a handful of major corporate conglomerates that dictate everything we see, hear, and believe via news and other forms of entertainment. In addition to the Big Six listed above, other major players are

Google, Apple, Sony, Facebook, Twitter, Cox, Charter, and the German publishing giant Bertelsmann, although mergers and maneuverings change this basic lineup now and then. With such a small group of corporations owning the media and all we watch on cable and network channels, and considering the hundreds of political officials affiliated with each corporation, some sitting on their board of directors, and the power of the lobbyists from mainstream media in the halls of Congress, it's no wonder we are no longer being told the truth. We are being told *their* truths.

Such monopolization of media has resulted in an ongoing war over deregulation, with those in favor saying that removing government rules and blocks will allow more diverse media ownership. Those against deregulation claim it will open the door to global companies buying out American media and will reduce the diversity of programming and opinions allowed. Now social media giants and Amazon are entering the news market, promoting certain stories and narratives over others, depending of course on the political ideals of the main owners, the stockholders, or the amount of advertising dollars they receive from any given industry (such as pharmaceuticals).

Even websites like Yahoo and AT&T offer slanted news stories that reflect their politics and advertising support. Yahoo has "sponsored news" stories on its front page. These are stories that have a corporate sponsor or advertising company that pays to have front page space. These stories must be labeled as "sponsored," but no doubt many alleged news sites don't bother to point that out to their readers, who then believe the stories are real news from real sources.

ANONYMOUS CONTENT

With the rise of fake and spun news and the lack of diversity in media ownership, journalism suffered a severe blow. No longer were reporters doing their best to fully investigate all angles of a story; instead they presented the story they were told to present by their superiors, meaning the owners and stockholders of

When it was allowed on the Big Three of CNN, Fox, and MSNBC, stories were often censored or cut off the air if they went too far from the repetitive narrative.

the corporate entity that owned them. Investigative reporting was only to be found on more independent news sources. When it was allowed on the Big Three of CNN, Fox, and MSNBC, stories were often censored or cut off the air if they went too far from the repetitive narrative.

Reporters do use whistleblowers and unnamed sources on occasion, but the new age of spin allowed for anyone to claim they had some "anonymous source" without providing any backup or additional facts or data. How easy it had become to get on the air in front of the country or even the world, attribute any information to an "unnamed source," and not have it questioned except by the news channel belonging to the political polar opposite.

The tenets of journalism and reporting the news had become weak, almost nondescript, replaced by phony facts and inflated figures, anonymous sources and third-party input, and opinion dressed in news, worn by a panel of talking heads that all parroted whatever lines their masters approved.

LOCAL NEWS

After the rise of cable conglomerates, it was often easier to find out real news from local affiliates, which were inclined to make their reporters work to give a story a local angle. Finding out what happened in your own neighborhood could be a lot more accurate than finding out what was going on in the world at large, as national reporters often read stories right off the wire and didn't have the time or the permission to ask questions or present alternate viewpoints as they did with local stories. Still, local news channels could be a bit laxer when covering the official national narrative, as this author found when watching a variety of local affiliates in comparison with the national news and cable news. The general spin remained; it was just more subtle.

Local news channels didn't have the time to feature panels of talking heads blathering on about their opinions, either. They had an hour in the morning, maybe an hour at noon, and one at dinner time before a late-night recap to talk about what was happening not only locally but also nationally and globally. The faster pace and shorter airtime meant less opportunity to confuse the audience with five people yelling over each other to be heard as they spewed their opinions about everything from who the current presidential candidates were to the handling of a global pandemic. Twenty-four-hour news channels had to fill all those hours with content. Often, that content was opinion, spin, and pure propaganda.

ADVERTISING AND CORPORATE INFLUENCE

True journalism and objective news reporting had also fallen prey to the almighty advertising dollar. Following the sources to the money behind the sources offers an incredibly enlightening view into who pulls many of the puppet strings of society. The masterminds behind corporate propaganda look at the public as nothing more than dollars in the bank or sheep to be herded and led to slaughter. The slaughter isn't literal. It means getting them to go out and buy something. Many people are convinced that the true power elite in the world are not government, military, or religious leaders, but corporate CEOs and billionaires—the one per-centers who sit atop a very disproportionate pyramid. These people own the media we watch, hear, and read. They own most of the stock in the companies that dictate public policy, social media, and the flow of information.

Edward L. Bernays (1891–1995), the nephew of psychoan-alyst Sigmund Freud, a mastermind at public relations propa-ganda, long considered the "father of spin," and the patron saint of mass manipulation, is an idol to corpo-rate propagandists. Bernays had a long his-tory of involvement in propaganda during World War I and even coined the slogan "Let's Make the World Safe for Democracy" before he became a master PR person. The same techniques he helped perfect to sell a war to the public worked on selling anything else to the public.

With just a handful of corporations owning most of our news media and enter-tainment companies, everything we are told is news, fact, or worthy of our belief and hard-earned dollars comes from the ideo-logies behind these corporations. The tools they use to manipulate us are all the same regardless of whether the company makes movies, drugs, or toilet paper. Michael Eis-ner, former CEO of the Walt Disney Co., was once quoted as saying, "We have no obli-gation to make history. We have no obliga-

Known as the American "father of prop-aganda," Edward Bernays (1891–1995) was a master of the art, famously cre-ating a campaign to convince women to smoke by calling cigarettes "Torches of Freedom."

tion to make art. We have no obligation to make a statement. To make money is our only objective."

Nowhere is this more obvious than in the advertising world, where the consumer is not the king but the pawn of nonstop prodding to choose product A over product B, buy this thingie instead of that thingie, and believe they need the thingie in the first place. Creating a need where there wasn't one before is crucial in a world where the public has a limited amount of money to spend on a limited number of things.

Watching just a few hours of a particular cable news channel is enlightening if you want to learn who has the most to win or lose from the narratives. Just take a look at what kinds of commercials dominate any given time period. Chances are, it will be pharmaceutical ads, car manufacturer ads, and food and drink ads. In the first two decades of the twenty-first century, the pharmaceutical industry has poured more advertising dollars into cable channels than any other industry. Not just news networks, but cable channels such as TV Land, HGTV, and Hallmark are riddled with ads for new drugs you should "ask your doctor about," despite lengthy lists of horrific side effects.

If you think for one moment these companies have no influence over programming, you are sadly mistaken. Advertising dollars speak volumes, and when it comes to news channels, they even influence the angles of stories you are exposed to. "Big Pharma"—the pharmaceutical industry—pumps billions of dollars into advertising new drugs and vaccines, leading to a pro-pharmaceutical and anti-natural medicine spin in the vast majority of medical news stories on CNN, Fox, and MSNBC. These networks are beholden to those who pay the bills and therefore will lean heavily toward narratives that promote those products in stories about pandemics, flu cures, general health, medicine, research, and more. Health insurance companies also pour incredible amounts of money into advertising and have a huge say in dictating the types of medical and scientific research the public sees. The field of public health has become increasingly focused on the profits of the pharmaceutical industry. The collapse of public health is due to the pharmaceutical industry's control of the field and how much money drug companies can make. They buy up advertising, oversee the writing and editing of textbooks, write or sponsor public health policies, support politicians agreeable to their agenda, and decide who gets funding and for what research. Honesty and science have taken a back seat to propaganda and profit.

The collapse of public health is due to the pharmaceutical industry's control of the field and how much money drug companies can make.

In their book *Toxic Sludge Is Good for You: Lies, Damn Lies, and the Public Relations Industry*, PR experts John Stauber and Sheldon Rampton, who also wrote *Trust Us, We're Experts*, looked at how PR agencies are employed to make industries with awful pollution records look good, and how the media instills and perpetuates favorable public perceptions of corporations and their products. The authors point out a few examples of implanted conventional wisdom, or propaganda, used by the health care field and Big Pharma:

- Pharmaceuticals restore health.
- Hospitals are safe and clean.
- All drugs are thoroughly tested for safety before they go on the market.
- Chemotherapy and radiation are effective cures for cancer.

These and other generalized claims of the health care field have all but demonized any evidence, research, and ideas to the contrary and are considered acceptable corporate spin throughout the medical field, backed up by billions of dollars in advertising money. Maybe that's why it's so hard to spot any commercials, news stories, or opinion pieces that challenge those generalizations and suppositions anywhere on mainstream media. Look who pays their bills.

During the COVID-19 pandemic, organizations such as the U.S. Centers for Disease Control and Prevention (CDC), a federal agency that owns dozens of vaccine patents, worked to give specific information to the public via mainstream media and specifically encouraged research for and adoption of a coronavirus vaccine. Anything that challenged CDC information, even from reputable doctors and researchers, was deemed "fake news," "misinformation," and "conspiracy theory" and blocked on social media outlets and YouTube. Alternative cures and theories were given zero airtime, no matter who the expert voices were behind them, because they did not fit into the narrative driven by Big Pharma, mainstream media, and the corporate and political entities aligned with that narrative. Those who question vaccine ingredients, safety, and efficacy are called terrorists despite

The CDC headquarters in Atlanta, Georgia, is one of many large campuses across the United States. The CDC owns many vaccine patents and has recently used mainstream media to campaign for COVID-19 research.

hundreds, if not thousands, of doctors and researchers asking the questions. (The Department of Health and Human Services lost a lawsuit for failing to file vaccine safety record reports for 32 years when it had been required by law to do so every two years.) People died because of poor choices made in handling COVID-19, and possible cures were kept from the public in order to protect a delicate facade of power and control. Those who even dared ask questions that might expose it were called the propagandists in a perfect example of projection, where the guilty project their "sins" onto those accusing them.

Until the day comes when the masses stop believing everything they are told by corporate media spin doctors, they remain puppets to the richest puppet masters on earth. Social, economic, and environmental agendas are being written by wealthy and powerful corporations who make billions off hard-working people with their products and services. Most people rely on the mainstream media for news, but when it comes to the products being sold via commercials, the mindset to overcome is thinking that just because you see more commercials touting a particular drug or product, that doesn't mean it's better than its competitors or something you need to have.

We are constantly being sold something, whether it's a headline news story, a new pill to lower our blood pressure, or a mattress that conforms to our body, even when we aren't yet ready to buy.

CORPORATE MONEY TALKS

In large part, the economy is controlled by a handful of billionaires who own much of the mainstream media and use it to push their particular narratives. These include Rupert Murdoch, Michael Bloomberg, Brian Roberts, and others. Murdoch was famous as the former CEO of 21st Century Fox and the chair of News Corp. Fox News became the right-leaning monster media source thanks to Murdoch. News Corp also owns the *Wall Street Journal*, a conservative outlet, and controlled more than 120 newspapers in five countries in 2020.

Michael Bloomberg, a former 2020 presidential candidate, is considered the media world's richest man, with his Bloomberg LP and Bloomberg Media. Donald and Samuel Newhouse inherited Advance Publications, which controls print media, news channels, and outlets including the *New Yorker* and *Wired* magazine. Jeff Bezos, the richest man in the world and founder of Amazon.com, bought the *Washington Post* in 2013. Billionaire Sheldon Adelson, who made his money in the casino world, owns the *Las Vegas Review-Journal*. John Henry, Red Sox baseball team owner, owns the *Boston Globe*. The second largest shareholder of the Tribune Publishing Company, which owns the *L.A. Times*, is pharmaceutical billionaire Patrick Soon-Shiong. Warren Buffett, the CEO of Berkshire Hathaway, owns about 70 regional daily newspapers.

George Soros—Hungarian-born American billionaire, hedge fund manager, and philanthropist—is considered one of the most powerful and influential figures affecting mass media, especially when it comes to pushing an agenda. His contributions to the left-leaning watchdog media group Media Matters for America were said to influence the group to work with establishment journalists to push a corporate media agenda to counteract alternative and conservative media outlets. In fact, groups from the left and the right targeted alternative news media sources to stop them from questioning the official stories being promoted in mainstream media, which continued to fill airtime with, as Jim Marrs puts it in his book *Population Control*, "such a constant stream of disconnected and unproved reports that it paints a false, even grotesque picture of the world that herds viewers into conformity."

It is no longer really necessary to ban or censor news when the constant repetition of pure drivel is enough to make most viewers believe they are well-informed on a certain story or topic. Alain de Botton writes in his 2014 book *The News: A User's Manual* that the constant flow of random-sounding news bulletins, often repeated without any context at all, within an agenda that changes without any continued relevance to the initial issue, is enough to "undermine most people's capacity to grasp political reality—as well as any resolve they might otherwise have summoned to alter it." It's a form of brainwashing and mind control. The controllers? The ones who benefit from the

Billionaire George Soros has contributed money to left-leaning media companies and his foundation, the Open Society Foundations, to push his liberal and progressive agenda.

political agenda behind the story, the ones who pay for the promotion of said story, and the ones who have the money not only to create news but to shape it to their specifications knowing few people will ever admit that the emperor is wearing no clothes when he parades down the street.

Money talks when it comes to the political and social slants and spins of the media. Sadly, for the public, it means being spoon-fed less-than-accurate information with little or no alternatives to choose from should they want to know more. Add to that the censoring and spin of social media's Twitter, owned by internet entrepreneur Jack Dorsey; Facebook and Instagram, owned by Mark Zuckerberg; and YouTube, owned by Google (more on it later), and you can see how the rich and powerful influence everything we see, hear, and come to believe. Sure, there may be shareholders involved, and that means more money-driven influence deciding exactly what it is you will be exposed to.

Watching the news is not the best way to get the news. In the year 2007, the Project for Excellence in Journalism said, "MSNBC is moving to make politics a brand, with a large dose of opinion and personality." That statement alone sums up the state of American mass media and the manipulative propaganda it pushes as part of its brand. That brand might be liberal. It might be conservative. Sometimes it features opposition talking heads just for the sake of saying it's balanced, but careful viewing reveals its true intent. It's to direct news in a certain direction, and usually not down the objective, fact-based center of things.

Fox News and its affiliates will continue to be the "news of the right," putting forth a positive spin on every politician with an (R) after their name; and CNN and MSNBC and their affiliates will do likewise with the "news of the left" and their respective politicians (D). The viewers lose out because all of these outlets lean one way or another and engage in the same identity politics, confirmation bias, spin, propaganda, and fake news they accuse their opponents of. The result is an increasingly sad, inaccurate, and downright manipulative state of media that leads the average viewer astray unless he or she has the time, energy, and wherewithal to look for the truth on his or her own.

LOBBY DOLLARS

Lobbying adds another layer to the propaganda machine. In the halls of Congress, the lobbyist offers promises of money to support a campaign, among other gifts. Organizations and groups send their best salespeople to lobby congresspersons in hopes of securing a yes or no vote on an important issue. Big Pharma is one of the biggest lobbying groups, giving millions of dollars each year to lawmakers to push forward their agenda, whether that means funding research for a new vaccine or getting a new drug quickly to market. In the August 26, 2019, *USA Today* article "Pharma Cash Donations Target 'Vulnerable' Lawmakers as Industry Tries to Defend Itself," by Emmarie Huetteman, Jay Hancock, and Elizabeth Lucas of Kaiser Health News, the reporters stated that in just the first six months of 2019 alone, pharmaceutical political action committees (PACs) gave more than $845,000 to 30 senators running for reelection. "The number of big contributions and the lawmakers receiving them signal the industry is building loyalty as voters push candidates to talk about drug prices in the 2020 elections."

Big money donations from the pharmaceutical industry alone amount to huge donations to Democrats and Republicans and directly influence the laws that are passed involving new drug testing, safety issues, the price of medications, and more. The two biggest beneficiaries of money from Big Pharma in early 2019 were Delaware Democrat Chris Coons and North Carolina Republican Thom Tillis. Coons received $103,000, and Tillis took in $102,000. It's no coincidence that Tillis and Coons led the Senate subcommittee on intellectual property and were working on legislation to overhaul the patent system that drug makers use to keep their prices and profits as high as possible.

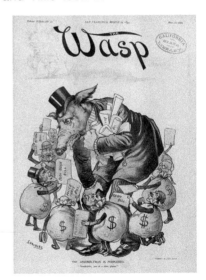

The House also saw a rise in donations from Big Pharma during this time period. Both political parties took part in the money bonanza, and both parties thus became obligated to promote and support whatever Big Pharma asked of them. In the last ten years alone, over $81 million has gone into the pockets of U.S. lawmakers from 68 pharma PACs run by employees of companies that make drugs and of industry trade groups.

As this 1891 political cartoon illustrates, lobbying for influence in local and federal governments has long been a practice criticized by Americans for causing corruption.

That's an awful lot of influence. Now consider that Big Pharma is only one of dozens of lobbying groups pushing U.S.

lawmakers to do their bidding. With many of these same groups financing corporate media with advertising dollars, it becomes clear that those who have the money can buy votes, laws, media exposure, and, as the end game, control over the public.

CREATIVE ARTS AND DIGITAL DICTATORSHIPS

World events often suffer from a mainstream tunnel-vision narrative, despite some pushback coming from artists, writers, documentarians, and filmmakers. Think of director Oliver Stone's film *JFK*, which raised questions anew about the official story behind the assassination of JFK, or political documentarian Michael Moore's *Fahrenheit 9/11,* which questioned the draconian Patriot Act crackdown on civil liberties and constitutional rights after the 9/11 terrorist attacks. Moore also dared question the comfort zone of mass media after the horrific 1999 Columbine High School massacre with his 2002 documentary *Bowling for Columbine*. Pop culture and independent media often mirror or question the official stories presented by government, organizations, or corporations or in mainstream news sources.

Using film, art, writing, music, and other means of expression, in addition to alternative news sources, allows creators and viewers to explore events in ways other than the way they were presented. Unless they are actively censored, these forms of expression act as a form of alternative news media in and of themselves. Just as comedians can speak about things that never would be permitted in a civil society, disguised in a laugh or a joke, creative arts offers the opportunity to put forth different theories and question narratives that would never be allowed on mainstream television or cable outlets.

Documentary filmmaker Michael Moore makes movies that criticize everything from the greed of large corporations (*Roger and Me*) to society's ills (*Bowling for Columbine*) and questions about government plots (*Fahrenheit 9/11*).

Documentaries specifically have taken on a wide range of topics in the world of politics, war, mass murders, the media, assassinations, corporate crimes, secrecy, and more without being censored in what they can say. The censorship comes later when they try to find viewing outlets, as seen in 2020 with a host of natural health documentaries and those that questioned the official story of the COVID-19 pandemic being removed from Facebook, YouTube, and Vimeo. They went viral anyway and were seen by millions who simply wanted the chance to ask questions, even if they didn't necessarily lead to answers, or if they led to answers outside the narrative being repeated by the media.

Censorship ran amok on all fronts in 2020 when COVID-19 struck and became the topic of countless news stories. Suddenly, it was all but impossible to post about the benefits of vitamin D without being blocked or banned on Instagram. People posting about naturopathic medicine or cures for the flu and other viruses were particularly censored, despite many of their claims having the backing of research studies, scientists, or doctors. Fake news was everywhere, but those who called out the fake news were being removed from social media outlets by the hundreds. Twitter did a sweep of thousands of accounts it claimed were Russian bots simply because they promoted conservative ideals. Facebook removed hundreds of sites pushing natural foods, breastfeeding, vaccine injury information, and natural cures for COVID-19 and labeled them "misinformation" despite the page owners often featuring real doctors, scientists, and research backing up their claims.

Those with the power and the money choose the narrative. And they employ an army of propagandists to help them spread it, including engaging in their own fake news campaigns. Why? To push an agenda, perhaps. But more often, to make money. Advertisers pay the bills for these media corporations, and the more people they can reach, the more chance they have to sell whatever it is they are advertising. On social media, people often share stories without even reading them, and this makes the stories travel even faster and further, reach more readers, and hopefully create more profit in return.

Those with the power and the money choose the narrative. And they employ an army of propagandists to help them spread it, including engaging in their own fake news campaigns.

Social media spreads propaganda and fake news at a speed mainstream media can only dream of. This is not lost on our politicians, governments, and corporations, who utilize social media as a way to manipulate and engineer certain responses from users. It's all about influencing public opinion, and hopefully encouraging them to buy, buy, buy, whether that means buying a product being advertised or buying an agenda being constructed and spread.

Many people point to the spread of Russian election propaganda on social media platforms during the 2016 presidential campaign, but these same tactics were also being used by other countries such as Saudi Arabia, Israel, Australia, and Italy. Even the United States was engaging in election-related propaganda against its own people and against people in other countries the U.S. government wished to influence. Yes, influencing elections happens all the time, and America is as guilty as the next country!

Even as people like Mark Zuckerberg, cofounder and CEO of Facebook, pronounced that free speech was critical to Facebook's success, the site was busy blocking and censoring accounts that ran counter to the national and official stories that most benefited the company. Freedom House, a U.S. government–funded nongovernmental organization (NGO) that conducts research into human rights and freedoms, reported a nine-year decline in internet freedoms worldwide after consulting with over 70 analysts and researchers. Internet freedoms and net neutrality continue to be challenged every single day, and during the COVID-19 pandemic, some of the same sites promising to protect freedom of expression were locking down anyone who expressed their freedom to question authority and counter the mainstream media's repeated sound bites.

In 2020, Facebook hired what it called an oversight board to basically censor posts. This 20-person board was made up of diverse individuals who all had similar political leanings and opinions. The heavily partisan board specifically targeted conservative and pro-Trump accounts and removed content from both Facebook and Instagram that the board felt violated its "deep commitment to advancing human rights and freedom of expression." Sadly, that freedom was biased from the start, as many people found out when they tried to post a variety of subjects such as alternative health cures, vitamin therapies, vaccination concerns, conservative values, progressive Democratic values, support for Bernie Sanders, conspiracy theories, the QAnon movement, and news stories that exposed corruption across the political divide. They heavily targeted anything and anyone that questioned pharmaceutical corporations, and mandatory vaccines, even when those

Facebook CEO Mark Zuckerberg has been criticized both for having his social media website allow too much free speech (allowing fake news and propaganda) and for censoring and banning certain accounts for not supporting Facebook's positions.

doing the questioning were legitimate doctors and researchers. So much for free speech.

Twitter, cofounded and run by professed liberal Jack Dorsey, was actively flagging posts, deleting posts, and shutting down pages by the hundreds. It began tagging some posts with a fact-check notice, indicated by an exclamation mark and a brief phrase to click for more information, to indicate the folks at Twitter felt the post was inaccurate, even when those being tagged could prove otherwise. The platform really got on the radar for censorship when it began tagging and fact-checking President Trump's tweets, and then in January 2021 banned the former president's account permanently. In May 2020, after Twitter flagged as inaccurate two of the president's posts about the potential of mail-in ballots to lead to election fraud (which the *Wall Street Journal* later backed up with factual evidence), Trump counter-tweeted his outrage. He then took further action by signing an executive order targeting companies that had been granted liability protection through Section 230 of the Communications Decency Act. This section holds that internet service providers and social media platforms cannot be sued or held liable for the content posted by others on their sites, effectively ensuring that people and entities may use the platforms to publish content, including propaganda, without the providers of platforms being held responsible for the content of that propaganda. In short, the service providers could not be sued for what people, posted using their services. The section also allowed the platforms limited "good faith" abilities to censor untrue or potentially dangerous content.

Trump's executive order rescinded some of the legal protections granted to the service providers and platforms, citing Twitter specifically. It stated that fact-checking was an "editorial" act, which was not permitted under the law for a "platform." Once a social media site editorializes, according to the executive order, it becomes a publisher and should be held to a different set of rules. Trump's action proved hugely popular to all those people and groups being banned and tagged were condemned roundly by the mainstream media and by establishment politicians on both sides of the aisle.

People felt Trump was retaliating for the attacks on his posts and a bruised ego, and a few days later, Twitter flagged an

Trump's executive order rescinded some of the legal protections granted to the service providers and platforms, citing Twitter specifically.

incendiary post Trump made about calling in the National Guard to help quell the violence in Minneapolis after a black citizen was killed by a police officer. Trump tweeted that "when the looting starts, the shooting starts." The media took it as a threat of violence, and Twitter promptly placed the tweets from Trump's account and the White House behind a content notification, so users would have to click on the notification to read the tweet. The next day, Trump tweeted again and explained what he meant by the statement, claiming that usually shootings happen as a result of lootings, but it was too late for backtracking. (Many politicians fall prey to tweeting in the moment, then backtracking their tweets, proving that thinking before acting is probably a good idea.) The country was already divided, with those on the left assuming he meant the National Guard would start shooting everyone, those on the right stating he meant shooting only rioters and not peaceful protestors, and many people appalled that anybody at all should be shot. It was business, and politics, as usual, with people on either side refusing to listen to the other side and insisting censorship was okay, as long as it wasn't them being censored.

One week later, Twitter stated it was merely labeling tweets to provide "context" and not fact-checking them, the latter of which would be an editorial act and thus establish Twitter as a publisher under the new executive order. Dorsey shared Twitter's principles in a tweet (one of which was to increase diverse perspectives, something it had been accused of doing the opposite of) as a way to clarify that it was providing context and nothing more. Trump supporters countered that Twitter was trying to avoid being slapped with the new and undesired label of "publisher" and losing its much-needed liability protection.

Sadly, the "Twitter wars" between Jack Dorsey and Donald Trump overshadowed a growing wave of years of tweet wars between people with opposing views on a variety of subjects, which included the outright banning and censorship of alternative thought and voices across social media platforms that didn't line up behind the current narrative being pushed by mainstream media. They also exposed to the public the fact that even larger social media outlets lean politically one way or the other, and it's up to people to demand they allow all forms of expression that do not lead to illegal activities or inciting violence, or stop calling themselves a platform and take the consequences that go with being a publisher. It's also up to the people to seek out social media sites that do not allow censorship of free expression.

The deeper problem here wasn't, and isn't, an often-buffoonish president bloviating on Twitter. Trump had become known for his arrogant and boisterous tweets, which often incurred the wrath of citizens and media alike. The bigger and scarier issue here was, and is, the ongoing and increasing blocking, banning, and shutting down of any page, person, or site that goes against the chosen narrative backed by the owners of said media sites and their political and corporate affiliations—who are themselves beholden to certain laws, rules, and regulations they seem to ignore in favor of pushing their own political, social, or economic agendas. If they continue to censor, they cannot play by the rules of free speech forums, which social media platforms fall under. They become something else—in this case, they act more like publishers. They lose their liability protections, and rightfully so. Freedom of speech should never be censored by anyone, right, left, or in between, especially on a platform that promises freedom of speech. That is a slippery slope to slide down.

Meanwhile, conservatives were leaving Twitter in droves to join up on a new social media site called Parler that promised no censorship and was becoming a home to more conservative voices. More on Parler later.

When censorship doesn't work, there is always another tactic to manipulating the social narratives. According to Wendy Schiller, a political science professor at Brown University, interviewed in "How Social Media Brought Political Propaganda into the Twenty-First Century" for *Marketplace*, propaganda works by creating a funnel of information. "They persuade people to go to one source. If you can get over that one hurdle, it's much easier to persuade or brainwash people, because they are only listening to that source that they deem most credible. Then you simply repeat, repeat, repeat." And what better way than to click "share" on social media and make something go viral in a matter of minutes. It doesn't even require you to think about what you are posting. Someone has done all the thinking for you.

Never mind whether the story you are taking viral is true or not. Remember that Hitler himself said if you repeat something often enough, people will believe it. He was living proof. The public has proven that if

Adolf Hitler, who was a persuasive orator to say the least, asserted that repeating the same statements over and over will convince your audience that they are true, whether or not that is so.

you say something enough, and if they hear it enough, they will accept it as truth. Clickbait news stories meant to entice you to click on the headlines only to be taken to an advertising site are spread like wildfire before anyone ever bothers to see if they are accurate. It's propaganda on steroids, thanks to social media and instant access to information, misinformation, and disinformation. And when it has the honor of becoming a trending hashtag, people just assume it's both important and true.

WHO FACT-CHECKS THE FACT-CHECKERS?

In the attempts of social media groups and online media sites to censor anything that didn't fit their narrative, they often turned to fact-checkers to ban, label, tag, or chastise posts and pages that were promoting "fake news." Though fact-checking is a tenet of good journalism, it has become something entirely different in the social media age, with fact-checkers beholden to certain political slants, agendas, and of course whomever paid their salaries. Thus, much of the fact-checking itself needed to be fact-checked for further accuracy.

Because most people don't have the time, energy, or wherewithal to do research when they see or hear something in any media format, fact-checkers were elevated to a position of trust with the public. You did not question the fact-checkers. Except you should have.

Cherry-picking, spin, and confirmation bias occur all the time, but the possibility tends to be ignored when information aligns with a person's already entrenched political identity and socially accepted narratives. For example, if you want some facts about the virus that causes COVID-19, you might go to a mainstream medical website. There, you will find "fact-checked" information about the virus from the perspective of the medical community that owns the site. Now, they could indeed be providing you facts and truth, but what happens when you go to an alternative, natural health news site and see "fact-checked" information to the contrary? Does that mean one side is lying and the other isn't? Not at all.

The cherry-picking of news, facts, and information lies at the heart of media manipulation, disinformation, and misinformation. The fact-checkers will always align their facts and statistics with the narratives being pushed by their preferred media outlet. Always. This is why people who watch Fox News can insist they have the facts, and those who watch CNN can insist likewise. The fact-checkers on both sides of the political spectrum are cherry-picking only the facts and information that align with the political viewpoints of the outlet in question. So they are not lying. They are simply deceiving by omission. Sadly, this happens all over media, mainstream and otherwise, and it ends up being the responsibility of the viewer to discern truth and fact from the mess left behind. If you turn to conservative media for the facts, you may well get them, but you will not get the whole story. If you turn to liberal media, same thing, but the facts will support a different spin or agenda. This has been going on all along, and it is not new, folks. Propaganda is alive and well in all media in the form of picking and choosing exactly what is conveyed to the viewer and pushed as truth.

The cherry-picking of news, facts, and information lies at the heart of media manipulation, disinformation, and misinformation.

Why do you think it's so impossible at times to reconcile everyone to the same truth? The same facts? The same information? Perception is not fact, no matter how many people want to believe otherwise, yet the majority of people evaluate the news based on their perception, not objectively. Here's an example:

A man walks to the mailbox in his underwear to get his mail. He grabs it, walks back, cusses out loud, and goes inside.

Liberal media spin: Slovenly pig with no respect for his neighbors, cussing out loud, in his underwear because he has no morals or ethics, must be a conservative.

Conservative media spin: Lazy liberal with no job cusses because he has to pay bills and socialist government welfare won't help him.

Does that sound familiar? The facts are simply these:

A man walks to his mailbox in his underwear to get the mail. He grabs it, walks back, cusses out loud, and goes inside.

Unless we know the man and understand why he had to get mail in his underwear and why something caused him to cuss out loud, at which point we most likely will form more interpretations and perceptions based on our existing beliefs and biases, we don't know the truth! He could have rushed out in excitement to get the bonus check he's been waiting for to help pay for his wife's cancer surgery and just plain forgot to put on his pants, then stepped on a sharp object, at which point he cussed. But not knowing this, we create our own facts and truths and conjecture, then tell others, who then spread it like wildfire, adding their own perceptions and beliefs on top of it, and so on, and so on. Trying to fact-check a story requires going back to the original source of the story and examining the bare basics of journalism—who, what, when, where, why, and how. But it has to be bare-bones facts and no spin. Is that possible for any human to accomplish, no matter how objective or bipartisan they claim to be?

On May 25, 2020, a Black man named George Floyd was killed on camera by a white cop named Derek Chauvin of the Minneapolis Police Department. Floyd, 46, died from Chauvin pressing his knee to Floyd's neck for approximately nine minutes. Floyd was pinned to the ground and could not breathe.

Those facts led to huge protests against ongoing police brutality, and some of those protests turned violent. A few devel-

Protestors march in Miami, Florida, in May 2020, angered by the death of George Floyd at the hands of police. Protests often turned to violent riots, and leaders on both the left and the right were blamed by media despite the lack of facts available.

oped into riots, and more people died in those. Buildings were vandalized—some reportedly by protesters, others reportedly by people posing as protesters to cast them in a bad light. Watching the events unfold via media sources was a circus of spin, perception, propaganda, and outright political twisting and turning to vilify either the right or the left, depending on the media source. Trump was blamed for this, and Joe Biden, the Democratic presidential candidate at the time, was blamed for that. Everyone blamed everyone, and soon it was all but impossible to find factual information that wasn't tainted in spin. Meanwhile, fact-checkers on social media were somehow deciding that certain political perceptions should be banned and tagged, and not others. Fact-checkers who didn't yet have the facts were reporting "the truth" about stories in the news that even their mainstream media masters hadn't figured out yet.

It was a major lesson in the sheer size and power of the propaganda machine on all fronts, and incredibly irresponsible. Fact-checkers sometimes check facts even when there aren't any available to check. When this happens, it can indicate a hidden agenda to keep a particular narrative alive or active. But not always. Do your homework.

Some of the key fact-checking sites that operate independent of a mainstream news outlet have been put under a microscope to assure they are not politically biased. Snopes came under fire in 2016 as the internal workings were exposed when the two founders, David and Barbara Mikkelson, filed for divorce. Snopes is one of the oldest well-known fact-checking companies. It began to fact-check urban legends, online myths, and misinformation, but it came under fire when it began debunking rumors and reports showing President Barack Obama in a negative light, leading to accusations of a liberal agenda.

Snopes fought back, showing its dedication to transparency and objectivity, and stating it did not hire anyone with a political bent of any nature. Other fact-checking groups like Truthorfiction, FactCheck.org, and About.com did their own research and cleared Snopes of any leanings or agendas. But the divorce and David's secrecy about the details, as well as his suggestions that his wife did not contribute anywhere near the amount of content she claimed she did, raised questions about the company's workings. The *Daily Mail* did its own digging, which Kalev Leetaru reported on in "The *Daily Mail* Snopes Story and Fact Checking the Fact Checkers" for *Forbes* on December 22, 2016. Leetaru reported that when he reached out to David for comments, he was not met with a reply in Snopes's "trademark point-by-point format, fully refuting each and every one of the claims in the *Daily Mail* article and writing the entire article off as 'fake news.'" Instead, Leetaru was told by David, "I'd be happy to speak with you, but I can only address some aspects in general because I'm precluded by the terms of a binding settlement agreement from discussing details of my divorce."

Leetaru expressed his disbelief that Mikkelson, owner of one of the world's most respected fact-checking organizations and the soon-to-be official fact-checker of Facebook, couldn't respond to a fact-checking inquiry because of a legal agreement. This and other accusations from alternative and conservative media sources of a liberal bias hurt Snopes's stellar record, especially after Mikkelson admitted that his staff may have included someone who ran for political office, meaning they might have had a particular political bent. Leetaru stated that when he asked colleagues if this made them suspicious of political bias, they unanimously agreed that "people with strong self-declared political leanings on either side should not be a part of a fact checking organization." Like many people, these reporters and journalists had assumed Snopes felt the same way and would have a policy against hiring partisan people on their staff.

Attempts to fact-check older Snopes stories about George Bush, Sarah Palin, and Barack Obama proved Snopes's work highly accurate.

Still, Barbara was Canadian, and there was no proven record of any political leanings. David had been a registered Republican in 2000 but was shown to have not contributed to any particular political campaign since then, and as of 2008 he had no party affiliation. Snopes has continued to fend off accusations of a liberal bias or associations with George Soros, the billionaire liberal business magnate. Attempts to fact-check older Snopes stories about George Bush, Sarah Palin, and Barack Obama proved Snopes's work highly accurate. But do keep in mind when researching that you are leaving the checking of important facts in the hands of human beings who always have a bias, acknowledged or not.

Another fact-checking organization accused in the past of liberal leanings is PolitiFact, which uses a Truth-O-Meter to discern fact from fiction. PolitiFact is owned by the *Tampa Bay Times*, which some have labeled as "liberal media." The company received a Pulitzer Prize and has been commended for tracking both political parties, stating it uses original reports to glean its facts rather than news stories, and it claims to verify all facts and interview impartial experts (if such a thing exists).

NewsGuard is a self-appointed internet watchdog that rates websites on various criteria of credibility and transparency, but it has direct ties to the pharmaceutical industry, which brings up a potential conflict of interest. The company received much of its startup funding from Publicis Groupe, which has a health subsidiary with many large pharmaceutical companies as clients, including Eli Lilly, Roche, Amgen, and Gilead Sciences. One of its biggest clients is GlaxoSmithKline, the pharma giant among giants. NewsGuard has been accused of restricting access to natural health websites, vaccine information and injury sites, and alternative health and science sites while favoring pro-pharma and industry sites that promote the chemical, drug, and food industries, according to Dr. Joseph Mercola's article "New Thought Police: NewsGuard Is Owned by Big Pharma." NewsGuard is not very transparent when asked about its funding, declining to disclose the size of its revenue to the U.S. Securities and Exchange Commission. The sheer fact it is so beholden to the pharmaceutical industry raises the question of accuracy and lack of bias in its quest to fact-check those who are not beneficial to the pharma bottom line. Even when it comes to fact-checkers, follow the source to the money and the money to the source.

FactCheck.org also claims to be nonpartisan. Funded by the Annenberg Public Policy Center of the University of Pennsylvania, it, too, was accused in the past of a liberal bent, when it was revealed in March of 2007 that Wallis Annenberg personally donated $25,000 to the Democratic National Committee. It was later revealed Annenberg donated to numerous Republican campaigns, too. The center's charter stipulates nonpartisanship of all staff.

The Media Research Center is a media watchdog group that is open about its lean to the right. Run by founder Brent Bozell, the center claims to "regularly provide intellectual ammunition to conservative activists, arming them with the weapons to fight leftist media." At least the group is transparent about its slant, so you know going in who its sources are and what its agenda is.

Sometimes you have to get on the organization's website to see who its supporters, funders, and sources are to determine if there is a bias. Again, bias in either direction doesn't mean these organizations are not great at what they do or that they are lying

Brent Bozell is a conservative writer and founder of the Media Research Center, CNSNews.com, and the Parents Television Council, for which he also once served as president. He has served on the board of the American Conservative Union and the Catholic League for Religious and Civil Rights.

or promoting fake news, but if you are looking for objectivity, it helps to be forewarned. The News Literacy Project (NLP) works to educate students and educators on how to spot propaganda and fake news. Its goal is to empower students to learn to identify misinformation and disinformation, utilizing its Checkology program, a browser-based platform for students in grades 6 through 12. It's a great idea to educate young people to identify media manipulation, and the NLP has many projects and helpful tips and resources. A look at the media sources used by the NLP shows it leans to the left, with only one or two of over a dozen considered conservative.

You can also find, on the more transparent sites, a list of the financial backers, sponsors, and supporters to see who is putting their money into these organizations. Many even post their tax documents and papers of incorporation, seeking to be as open as possible with their users. Do your research if you seek pure objectivity, or whatever comes close to it. Keep in mind that the name of a fact-checking group or media watchdog group can be misleading or so general and generic that it might sound and look as though it is more objective than it really is.

The Reporter's Lab at Duke University keeps a database of more than 100 fact-checking organizations worldwide that claim to be nonpartisan. These organizations must meet specific criteria to be included in the database, including how they reach conclusions to claims, how transparent they are with sources and methods, whether they disclose funding sources and affiliations, and whether their primary mission is news and information or something else. But there are also fact-checking bodies now associated with major news media outlets, social media platforms, and print publications. That's a lot of fact-checkers.

Carole Fader wrote in her article "Fact Check: So Who's Checking the Fact-Finders? We Are" for the September 28, 2012, *Jacksonville.com/Florida Times-Union* that the best thing people could do when trying to find the truth was to confirm accuracy through multiple sources and original reports. She quoted David

Emery, a fact-checker for About.com, as saying, "In the thorny search for truth, there's no substitute for doing one's own research and applying one's own considered judgment before thinking oneself informed."

The more pressure people can put on these organizations, the better, because it will help the public find out the facts instead of merely a perception of the facts.

The more pressure people can put on these organizations, the better, because it will help the public find out the facts instead of merely a perception of the facts. In June of 2020, the *National Pulse* took Facebook to task over an article titled "Black Lives Matter Website, 'Defund the Police' Donations Go to 'Act Blue,' the 'Biden for President' Campaign's Top Source of Donations." The article, published by the *National Pulse* and posted on Facebook, was marked as "partly false" and given a warning screen on Facebook. The fact-checking was in fact accurate, as the headline should have read "Donations Go *through* 'Act Blue'" and not "Go *to* …" because this is true. Act Blue is a payment processor for Democratic campaigns. The *National Pulse* changed its headline to make it more accurate, but it never got a retraction, and the article continued to be flagged despite the bulk of it being factual.

As a result, some researchers decided to look a bit deeper into the fact-checking service used by Facebook, called Lead Stories, and found a conflict of interest amongst the staff. It was found that many staff members, including Lead Stories founder Perry Sanders, had donated to the Democratic Party and its candidates over the years. Was this bias showing in Facebook's decisions to ban certain stories over others? Do people's past or present political leanings prevent them from being objective when it comes to facts and accuracy?

Facebook responded to this and other accusations by stating that Lead Stories was an independent fact-checking service certified by the Poynter Institute's International Face-Checking Network, a company with ties to George Soros and his Open Society Foundations, which support liberal causes.

Is it possible for humans to separate their ideologies from their jobs? Can there truly be media outlets and fact-checking services made up of individuals who are miraculously able to set aside their own personal feelings and beliefs to put forth totally objective information and results? Maybe we need to accept that human nature limits that objectivity, and we need to know going in who we are dealing with and what their beliefs are before we take anything at face value.

The responsibility to fact-check anything you see on the internet or the nightly news should not be the responsibility of people you don't know, have never met, and have no clue what motivates them. The best way to fact-check is to check the facts yourself as objectively as your level of consciousness and awareness of your limitations to accept information that contradicts what you currently believe will allow.

WIKIPEDIA

Another hotbed of propaganda, false information, and misinformation is Wikipedia. The site can be valuable for finding basic information, and although it does supply sources to many entries and has a system of quality control, because it is generated by the public and anyone can add or change content, it is not considered a trustworthy source of information. One recent example was released before it happened via leaked documents stating the energy corporation Chevron planned to rewrite Wikipedia pages to attack environmentalists and environmental lawyers. Wi-

Lago Agrio in Ecuador was polluted thanks to oil fields owned by the Chevron Corporation. To counter bad publicity, Chevron hired people to write false Wikipedia entries about the issue.

kipedia proved that Chevron did just that when it was revealed that Chevron consultant Sam Singer was hired to ghostwrite fake Wikipedia pages attacking human rights defenders fighting against pollution disasters in Ecuador. Chevron also submitted these ghostwritten stories, slanted in its favor, to Amazon Watch and other outlets.

Wikipedia is full of great information and sources to back up that information, but user beware: just in the course of researching this book, this author spotted plenty of political spin, misinformation, disinformation, and propaganda. When you know what to look for, you begin to see it everywhere.

It's also critical to always follow the money to the source and the source to the money—or in this case, follow the information to the source and to the hidden agenda that source has in rewriting and altering facts to their benefit. Often there is no hidden agenda, and the sources are legitimate, unbiased, and accurate. But other times you can track an entry via its sources and readily spot how it leans toward a particular mindset or ideology.

Facts over feelings works best when doing research and hoping to find unbiased sources.

YELLOW JOURNALISM: SENSATIONALISM SELLS

There was a time when sensationalistic reporting was mainly the stuff of grocery store checkout tabloids that screamed ridiculous headlines and bizarre stories to tempt bored shoppers waiting in line into a last-minute purchase. Sensationalism has a long history in the news media, and it has seeped into even the more mainstream outlets with the rise of so-called fake news and domestic propaganda. It's becoming harder to tell the utterly fantastical from the factual when tabloid-style journalism has infiltrated the norm.

The term "yellow journalism" was coined in the mid-1890s to label sensationalism, in particular a battle between the *New York World* owned by Joseph Pulitzer and the *New York Journal* owned by William Randolph Hearst. The term relates to a cartoon character called "the yellow kid" in a comic strip that ran first in the *World* and then in the *Journal*. In the competition to increase circulation and readership and come out number one, each paper resorted to sensationalism alongside more serious reporting. Because a lot of these sensational stories involved murder and vio-

A cartoon by Louis Glackens shows William Randolph Hearst publishing and tossing about irresponsibly sensationalistic stories from his newspaper to gain readership.

lence, the expression "if it bleeds, it leads" became the battlecry of news outlets to increase profits.

Much of this yellow journalism revolved around the headlines, which were written to inflame, incite, terrify, anger, and worry. Such appeals to the baser emotions made newspapers sell. Readers soaked up the violence, the scandal, the crime, and the rumors, whether or not factual information backed up the headlines. Propaganda had been used earlier to flame the fires of wars and political uprisings, and now it worked under any circumstance. As Michael Scandling wrote in the February 27, 2018, article "If It Bleeds, It Leads. No Matter Whose Blood It Is," on the website of STAND: Scientologists Taking Action against Discrimination, yellow journalism is about using fear, scandal, violence, and sex to sell. "Why print such drivel? Simple: appealing to the base human instincts was an easy way to sell papers—far easier than appealing to intellect," Scandling pointed out. "Selling papers was necessary to sell advertising. Selling advertising brought in revenue." It's all about profit.

American historian and Pulitzer Prize–winning journalist Frank Luther Mott wrote in his 1941 book *American Journalism* that yellow journalism has five key characteristics:

1. Scare headlines, often misleading, in large print, often of minor news stories
2. Lavish use of pictures or imaginary drawings
3. Fake interviews, pseudoscientific claims, and false learning from so-called experts
4. Appearance in full-color supplements, usually with comic strips
5. A sympathetic viewpoint favoring the underdog fighting against the system

With the advent of television, the phenomenon only got worse, with local and national news stations fighting to get the best ratings and using the adage "if it bleeds, it leads" as their method of operations, only now they had cameras to videotape the blood, violence, and chaos. Audiences ate it up, and today with the internet, social media, and the rise of "clickbait" headlines using the same sensationalist principles to entice people to click and read advertisement-heavy stories with little or no substance, we are swimming in a sea of yellow journalism.

As Scandling wrote, "That's not to say there isn't some well-researched, well-written, deeply probing news and information from independent websites—there is—but these are small beacons of integrity in a huge sea of noise." Freedom of the press, he states, is owned by those who own the press. Today, those owners make sure their media outlets promote specific agendas and turn the best profits they can. Fear, sex, and scandal always sell better than charming tales of humans helping other humans. "Of course, after the lead, the newsroom has to deliver the story, and if you're looking for blood and tears—and sometimes sweat— local TV news doesn't disappoint."

Local and national news, including talking-head cable channels, love the close-up shots of the dead and bloodied, the car accidents, the plane crashes, and grieving families.

Local and national news, including talking-head cable channels, love the close-up shots of the dead and bloodied, the car accidents, the plane crashes, and grieving families. Not that they shouldn't report on this news, but have you noticed how these stories lead? Later in the newscast you might see a "human interest" story about a local kid who made his own business empire, or a woman who has fed 10,000 homeless people. The first impressions on the eye and the mind are violent, fear-based, and meant to keep you coming back for more, the same way a good horror movie would. Scandling suggests one small and simple move to counter yellow journalism and its mental and emotional effects and to keep media moguls and corporations from getting rich off of your emotions—turn off the TV, the radio, and the computer.

DEEP FAKE: THE ULTIMATE FAKE NEWS

Imagine the horror of seeing your face and hearing your voice on a viral video you know you never made. Imagine "you" saying and doing things in that video that you would never say or do. Welcome to the world of "deepfake." Thanks to the development of cutting-edge artificial intelligence (AI) and video- and audio-editing software, people now have the ability to take your image and voice and create original footage and images without your consent or knowledge, including pornography. It's a whole new way of influencing and sending messages with ample room for incredible abuse. Imagine a "deepfake" video of a politician having sex with a minor, or a celebrity abusing a child; although these videos would not be real, the damage they could inflict across social media would be immediate and in many cases, inalterable, even after the truth was made known.

In April of 2020, State Farm Insurance debuted a television commercial during a showing of ESPN's documentary series *The Last Dance*. The commercial featured footage from 1998 of an ESPN analyst making accurate predictions about things that would occur in 2020. Problem was, it was not real. It was AI-generated deepfake technology that alerted many viewers to a whole new concern about privacy, overreach, and the potential to destroy another human being.

The term, allegedly first used in a Reddit forum about the topic, combines the phrases "deep learning" with "fake" and first hit the internet around 2017, albeit in a crude fashion. It was part of a deep learning method called GANs, or generative adversarial networks, a form of synthetic media that takes an existing image or video and replaces it with another person's likeness. The powerful AI behind this technology manipulates those images and videos to the point where they become indistinguishable from the real thing, opening the door to complete deception when posted on social media or sent to news outlets. While once the stuff of online communities and individual users, in January of 2018 a proprietary desktop application called FakeApp was introduced

Computer technology was used to manipulate the face of one man to look like several other people. This is called a "deepfake" alteration. The technology can be frightening because it makes it even more difficult to tell what images are real and which are lies.

and allowed anyone to make deepfakes and share them with other users.

Similar apps were soon developed, and companies began using the technology in both video and audio clips. They also created apps that could distinguish deepfakes from the real thing. In March of 2020 a mobile deepfake app called Impressions was launched and allowed users to create celebrity deepfakes from their cell phones.

Soon it was reported that users were making revenge porn deepfakes of ex-lovers, and before long, politicians were targeted in deepfake videos, including Argentine president Mauricio Macri, whose face was deepfaked into Adolf Hitler; Barack Obama, using Jordan Peele's voice as part of a public service announcement; and President Trump in the Oval Office, making fun of his own fake tan. Facebook's Mark Zuckerberg was deepfaked into claiming he started the social media platform to exploit its users. President Obama was again deepfaked into using a cuss word to describe President Trump.

All it takes to make a deepfake video or audio is to have a computer and a little tech savvy, and you can make it look like real people are saying and doing things they aren't—and so convincingly it will fool even the sharpest eyes. You can make a political opponent look like a rapist or turn your ex-girlfriend into a porn star. You might even start a war. The concerns were enough to spark a U.S. House Intelligence Committee hearing in June of 2019 on the potential malicious use of deepfakes to influence the 2020 presidential election.

In the *Forbes* article "Deepfakes Are Going to Wreak Havoc on Society. We Are Not Prepared," dated May 25, 2020, writer Rob Toews quotes U.S. senator Marco Rubio as saying, "In the old days, if you wanted to threaten the United States, you needed 10 aircraft carriers, and nuclear weapons, and long-range missiles. Today … all you need is the ability to produce a very realistic fake video that could undermine our elections, that could throw our country into tremendous crisis internally and weakens us deeply."

The problem now is whether you can truly trust anything you see in the news or on social media. Is it real? Is it deepfake? We have opened a Pandora's Box that just might take us all down with it. Toews writes, "Even more insidiously, the mere possibility that a video could be a deepfake can stir confusion and facilitate political deception regardless of whether deepfake technology has actually been used." He cites the small African nation of Gabon where, in 2018, the president Ali Bongo Ondimba, known popularly as Ali Bongo, had been missing from public view for months, sparking rumors of his demise, when his administration announced that Bongo would give a televised speech on New Year's Day.

Bongo appeared on camera and looked, to many, stiff, stilted, and unnatural, with weird facial mannerisms. This caused many to suspect the government was deceiving the public with a deepfake. Bongo's political opponents seized on the confusion and launched a coup, the first in that country since 1964. The coup wasn't successful as eventually Bongo did appear in public and retook control, but the event caused a great deal of destabilization and distrust.

Now imagine a deepfake of a world leader declaring war on another country. Missiles are launched and nuclear devastation is imminent, and all because of a manipulated, manufactured piece of video or audio. This is the new propaganda, and it's the next best thing to being real.

In our post-truth world of fake news, deceptive and manipulative media, and spin, adding another element to confuse

Bongo appeared on camera and looked, to many, stiff, stilted, and unnatural, with weird facial mannerisms. This caused many to suspect the government was deceiving the public with a deepfake.

people and try to influence their beliefs and emotions makes it even harder for them to grasp reality and truth. There are challenges to the use of deepfake, but they can be at odds with censorship and freedom of speech laws. In January of 2020, the House Ethics Committee released a memo with a strong warning to its members to be careful not to post deepfake photos or videos to their social media accounts, especially leading up to the November election. Facebook followed with a statement that it would ban all deepfakes.

In the world of advertising, deepfakes are already used as a creative tool to sell products, as long as the audience is told upfront they are not real and the advertiser exercises some level of responsibility to use them constructively and transparently.

Time will tell as to just how much of a threat deepfakes will be to our collective and individual realities.

INFOTAINMENT AND INFOMERCIALS

Cable television created a new form of news program called "infotainment" that blended information with entertainment, offering news and gossip in an entertaining format. This blending of the lines between factual reporting and rumor often fell under the category of "current affairs" and usually featured just as much scuttlebutt on celebrities as it did headline news. The term "infotainment" was coined in 1974 at the Intercollegiate Broadcasting System's college radio stations convention on bridging the worlds of information and entertainment. One wonders if the convention attendees had any idea of how extensively this new brand of television programming would become the junk food of media.

With a focus on gossip, crime stories, scandals, and human-interest stories, infotainment was more about presentation than substance. That presentation was flashy, noisy, and fast-paced, with the hottest live hosts and cutting-edge music. It consisted of consumer-driven, advertising-heavy sensationalism in the guise of real information the audiences needed to know. *En-*

tertainment Tonight remains one of the most popular infotainment television shows on the air today.

As the internet and cable news began competing with more traditional media outlets, the need to up the ante and outsell the competition gave birth to this new way of selling news. Most mainstream media news outlets remained the purveyors of hard news and talking-head analysis, but the channels and shows that focused on so-called soft news could combine the serious news with catchy and titillating gossip and attract audiences who tired of hearing only breaking news disasters. Soft news such as info-tainment was more personal and eventually included a plethora of talk shows and soft news shows such as *Oprah*, *Ellen*, *Larry King Live*, *Extra*, and *Access Hollywood*, and then morphed into pundit shows featuring hosts like Rachel Maddow, Sean Hannity, and other political mouthpieces of the right and the left, including those in radio like Rush Limbaugh.

In 2020 the hugely popular comedian and mixed martial arts commentator-turned-talk-show-host Joe Rogan left a lucra-tive position podcasting his *Joe Rogan Experience* on YouTube and inked a $100 million deal to broadcast on Spotify to avoid the censorship attempts of YouTube. Rogan is but one of hundreds of popular podcasters, video channel hosts, and online radio show hosts offering the latest infotainment via the "interwebs."

Even though shows like *The Colbert Report* and *The Daily Show* are meant to editorialize or satirize the news, many Americans feel these days that they get more factual news from infotainers like Stephen Colbert than from mainstream news channels.

News magazine shows such as *20/20*, *Dateline*, and *60 Minutes* touched on infotainment, even though they were more focused on presenting investigative report-ing and digging into real and important stories of the times. *The Daily Show*, *The Colbert Report*, and various other "news and culture" programs, often featuring a healthy dose of comedy and satire, also fall within the realm of infotainment. These shows often delivered hard news amidst the gossip and laughs, but they did so in an en-tertaining style and format that was quite different from straight local and national news. The hosts would also interject their own opinions, potentially making it difficult for viewers to discern truth and fact from near-truth and personal perspective.

Not all critics agree that infotainment is even informational, and various infotainment shows have received plenty of backlash about cultural biases, political leanings, and a blurry division of fact and fiction, as well as the overuse of anonymous sources often cited in these shows. Even the shows featuring news of the entertainment world alluded to interviews about celebrities with "family and friends" or "anonymous sources," making it hard to discern what really happened and to whom. Serious journalism is secondary to getting the ratings for such programs, which focus more on flash than fact, confusing consumers. Journalistic accountability can be rare on these shows, with accusations and gossip freely thrown out as fact and, when proven wrong, rarely corrected or acknowledged.

But in a world where sex, violence, and scandal sell, infotainment offers all three and then some, with a touch of important need-to-know information thrown in for good measure. Sadly, that important information takes a back seat to who is sleeping with whom, what the latest scandal involving a famous figure is, and speculations about crimes and who committed them with little regard for the victims or the falsely accused. While hard news focuses on serious subjects and timely events, soft news and infotainment focus on the least serious subjects and may or may not be timely. There is even a category of hosts of these shows called "infotainers," many of them with journalism backgrounds but some hired just for their charm and appeal. Barbara Walters, the former host of *20/20* and many special news shows, is considered the queen of infotainers, and perhaps Geraldo Rivera could be considered the king for his now defunct talk show/news show that featured some pretty sensationalistic and outlandish guests and subject matter. Rivera practically created the "sleazy talk show" that became hugely popular, spawning a slew of daytime "anything goes" shows featuring the dregs of humanity and tabloid subject matter.

Similar to infotainment are informative commercials that are meant to look like news programs. Infomercials blend sales tactics with sets designed to look like a newsroom or talk show, often featuring alleged experts and scientists to back up the product claims. For the viewer not inclined to do their own research into the product and the alleged experts selling it, it becomes easy to part with hard-earned money, believing the products are vetted by those in the know. Often it requires reading the tiny fine print running along the bottom of the screen, where it might say the doctors, scientists, and experts are merely actors and the statistics presented are not true for everyone.

Infomercials blend sales tactics with sets designed to look like a newsroom or talk show, often featuring alleged experts and scientists to back up the product claims.

Infomercials tend to run throughout the night when there is less original programming to fill the time slots on broadcast and cable channels. They might be described as a cross between a home shopping network, like QVC, and a feature on a local news channel about a local business product or new invention. Except in this case, the end result will cost you $49.99 plus shipping and handling, and if you buy within the next hour, you'll get a second one free.

The presentation of what is newsworthy, what is pure entertainment, and what is for sale often blurs the lines between what people perceive as real and what is embellished and fictionalized. It's another way to sway the viewer.

MANUFACTURED CONTENT

If you want to sell a product to a person, or sell a war to a population, by all means go ahead and fake it till you make it. Manufactured news stories to gain the consent of a person or a group is as much a part of propaganda as anything. Lying, distorting, and creating news that isn't accurate are the means to an end and have been used to attempt to win over the public in every war, political election, foreign invasion, or political coup throughout history. When done in the name of "official sources," you can get almost anyone to consent to almost anything because, sadly, most people don't question what they see or hear in the media, and they question authority even less.

Usually, it's the wealthy and powerful elite, the corporations and politicians, and the billionaires and royalty who have the most to invest in manufactured media and news. Why? Because they have the most to lose, and if the truth about an event or situation might bring about such a loss, or even paint the powers that be in a bad light, it will rarely make it to the public without alterations and fabrications. The advent of the internet has made this more difficult, no doubt, as people have more methods to record for themselves, research, and question what they see in the mainstream media, but manufactured content still works to influence people, and now it has an even bigger, broader reach … thanks to the same internet.

In their classic and important book *Manufacturing Consent: The Political Economy of the Mass Media*, published in 1988, Edward S. Herman and Noam Chomsky examined a number of case studies involving what they call the "propaganda model" used by media. The authors state that despite the image of the news media as obstinate seekers of truth and justice, the more accurate picture is that of defenders of the economic, social, and political agendas of the privileged groups in domestic and global society. The media is a mouthpiece for and a slave to the whims of the elite, to the detriment of the public, which is often left in the dark when it comes to real, accurate news.

The public has no choice but to watch what these elites choose for mass viewing. "The public is not sovereign over the media—the owners and managers, seeking ads, decide what is to be offered and the public must choose among these. People watch and read in good part on the basis of what is readily available and intensively promoted," Herman and Chomsky write. Corporate ownership of media, driven by profits and sales, drives the choices of the so-called "free press" that we, the viewers and readers, are left with. It's not very free at all. When those corporate entities align with government and political entities, the waters are further muddied. Whatever is at stake politically and economically will be reflected in the news that makes it in the papers and on the air.

This is why so much of the news reporting on foreign affairs, political coups abroad, genocide, mass protests and movements, and foreign elections is handpicked by those who have an agenda they wish to benefit from. Mainstream news plays that agenda 24/7, and few people realize they are being misled or outright duped. The media always favors the client "paying the bills," so to speak, and not the higher moral goal of reporting important information you, the viewer, needs to know. Journalism goes out the door as the money walks in. Even the portrayal of victims of wars and coups will be skewed toward the bias of the buyer. If the U.S. government

Philosopher, scientist, social critic, and linquist Noam Chomsky (pictured) and economist and social critic Edward S. Herman posited that the media are not noble truth seekers but rather promote social, political, and economic messages that benefit society's elite.

can benefit from overthrowing a political leader elsewhere in the world, all news will portray that leader's victims as brutalized, abused, and in danger if we don't do something to stop their abuser. Likewise, if the U.S. government likes a particular leader, it will be sure to ignore the abuses and victims and show that leader only in a positive light. It's all optics, meant to put on a show for the audience. It's the man behind the curtain praying he won't be exposed.

Optics is the way an event or situation is presented to the public to get them to buy into it, whether it is true or not. It is also a method of presenting material or information visually to influence public thought. An example would be mainstream media calling an election for a presidential candidate they support to convince the public this person won, long before the electoral process was official. This often leads to *coups d'etat* and color revolutions, which are designed to overthrow a candidate the establishment does not want or is fearful will expose their crimes. This happens both at home here in the United States and abroad. Optics can also be used by Big Pharma or other corporate interests (banking, agribusiness, social media) to push a particular agenda that benefits them, often using fear and division.

The symbiotic relationship between media and government is also to blame. According to Herman and Chomsky, "The radio-TV companies and networks all require government licenses and franchises and are thus potentially subject to government control or harassment. This technical legal dependency has been used as a club to discipline the media, and media policies that stray too often from an establishment orientation could activate this threat." So under the threat of being censored, shut down, or fined, media outlets rarely say no to the demands of the government. Media companies also depend on the government for support such as pro-business policies and taxes, reforms and regulations that benefit them (as opposed to those that benefit the public), and the enforcement (or nonenforcement) of antitrust laws. This is a relationship neither party can walk away from. There is no breaking up with each other, because without the government's support, the media ceases to compete and exist. Without the media's support, the government can't sway and manipulate the public to gain that much-needed consent, especially when it comes to, for example, a presidential election or an overseas military action they want the American people to get on board with.

A perfect example of the web of manufactured consent might be a city grappling with the decision to allow a nuclear power plant to be built on the shores of its local beach. The nuclear industry would work with the city and state government to promote the financial and economic benefits of the power plant. Then, when they are all in agreement, the research safety reports and environmental studies would be conducted by pro-industry researchers and released to the media. Meanwhile, any public dissent would be squashed or countered with dozens of positive studies showing there would be no threat to human health. Research showing negative effects of a power plant on a beach would be ignored, suppressed, and censored.

So under the threat of being censored, shut down, or fined, media outlets rarely say no to the demands of the government.

We saw manufactured consent in 1991 during Operation Desert Storm and again after the 9/11 attacks with the 2003 invasion of Iraq. Story after story portrayed the evil enemy as violent terrorists worthy of going to war with no matter the cost because of what they had done to the United States (even if they hadn't engaged in the action the country was ostensibly punishing them for), and the poor citizens of said countries being invaded and bombed were portrayed as victims of brutal regimes who welcomed American help, even begged for it. Of course, later, the real facts trickled out, and it turned out the United States invaded more for its own territorial and resource benefits than a moral desire for justice. That's the key to manufactured consent. Once you have it, who cares how things end up down the road? You got your war, your coup, your end game.

News stories to the contrary of both wars were often labeled as conspiracy theory or junk news, and journalists were called un-American, unpatriotic, or even traitors for not going along with the plan. Consent may be manufactured, but it isn't always foolproof. Some percentage of the population will be able to see the cracks in the facade of truth. The result might be a powerful form of "flak," the negative responses to an event, media statement, or program, that result in protests, letters, demands for new laws, calls for Congressional actions, and petitions against the responsible parties. This flak is uncomfortable for the media it if gets big enough, such as a nationwide boycott, especially if it threatens to derail profits and shed light on unsavory news reporting. Enough flak might cause advertisers to pull out or certain politicians to back away from supporting the station.

But savvy media outlets know to give the flak just enough lip service to make it appear to the public as if they care or are taking some action, even when they have no intention of doing so. This might mean offering the opposing side an opinion piece or an invitation to be on a talking-head panel. Just enough to make the opposition feel heard and acknowledged.

Sometimes, the power of alternative and citizen-driven media calls the media out on their lies, distortions, and subservience to the elite. Herman and Chomsky state that changing this situation of elite media control and ownership requires a movement toward a more democratic and decentralized media with independent funding sources, such as nonprofit, community-based broadcasting stations, internet media outlets, and independent media outlets that are not beholden to government or corporate agendas.

But savvy media outlets know to give the flak just enough lip service to make it appear to the public as if they care or are taking some action, even when they have no intention of doing so.

The authors identified five filters of editorial bias to include in their propaganda model for how news is reported in mass media:

1. Size, ownership, profit orientation—Dominant mass media outlets are the largest profit-based organizations and must cater to the financial interests of the corporate owners and investors. A media outlet's size is consequential to the amount of investment monies behind it to enable the outlet to reach a mass audience.

2. The advertising license to do business—Media outlets cannot operate without advertising backing and support and therefore must cater to the political agendas and ideologies of the advertisers.

3. Sourcing news—The powerful bureaucracies that subsidize mass media and get special access to the news do so by their contributions to the outlet to reduce operating costs. "Editorial distortion," the authors claim, "is aggravated by the news media's dependence upon private and government news sources." Therefore, it behooves the media outlet to never encourage disfavor with the sources of the news and to favor government and corporate policies so they can stay in business.

4. Flak and enforcers—Flak, or negative responses to a news story or media statement, can cost the outlet viewers. Controlling the flak is paramount and expensive. It is easier for a media outlet to avoid broadcasting news that might entice flak and negative responses.

5. Anticommunism, antiterror, etc.—Depending on where we are at in history, this filter is focused on the major social control mechanisms operating at the time. Today, that might be antiracism.

The more people understand how mass media works and grasp the symbiotic relationship between politics and media, and the more they can step away from the mainstream media once they do understand it, the closer they might get to the true stories going on in the world around them. It seems ironic that the only way to save real journalism is to stop engaging in the media. For now.

SEARCH THIS, NOT THAT

Aside from mainstream news and social media, simply searching for news and information has become a land mine of censorship, spin, and outright propaganda. The main search engine, Google, has been embroiled in controversy after several news stories broke revealing data-mining practices, invasions of privacy, and the secretive and clandestine involvement of Google with the National Security Agency (NSA) and Central Intelligence Agency (CIA). Google has also reached a level of power and authority that is mind-boggling in its reach, and its reach is spreading like the arms of a gigantic octopus.

Think about how many times a day you use a search engine to look something up. It might be a correct spelling of a word or the origin of a phrase. A recipe. A list of side effects of a medication. The height and weight of your favorite celebrity. Imagine each time you search, you are directed not to what you are looking for, but to what the "powers that be" think you should be looking for. You won't even know the difference, because the powers that be will make that choice instantaneously, giving you a plethora of websites and articles to pick from to cast the illusion of choice. But whose choice?

Search engines such as Google, Bing, Baidu, and Yahoo might *seem* free, but you actually pay by having your personal data mined and then sold. Such activities have drawn the attention of the CIA and NSA.

"The powers that be" mostly means Google. For most people, the stories of Google's clandestine operations and relationships began in 2013 when a CIA employee and subcontractor named Edward Joseph Snowden turned whistleblower by revealing copies of highly classified documents showing the mass domestic surveillance tactics of the NSA. Later revelations of privacy violations and surveillance tactics of cell phone carriers, Facebook, and Amazon were exposed, but Google stood out as the beast among beasts when it came to spying on Americans and abusing the private information of civilians.

Snowden revealed information and insight about a program called Prism that showed Americans were having their personal data collected by the U.S. government and allies. He fled the country and was given asylum in Russia for opening our collective eyes to the ways our favorite and most-used search engine was using its technology to spy not only on terrorists but also on people who had yet to ever break any laws. Worse still, Google had the backing of the most powerful people and corporations on the planet, many of whom made deals with the tech giant to spy on people and attempt to influence them.

Nobody was policing Google and these other entities. Google started out as the enterprise of two Stanford University postgraduate students, Larry Page and Sergey Brin, in September 1998. It has a long history of growth, adding numerous products and services, merging and partnering with other entities, and becoming the leading subsidiary of another major corporation, Alphabet, of which Page is still the CEO. Over time, Google spawned Google Docs, Google Maps, Google Drive, Google Calendar, Google Earth, and a dozen other applications and services that solidified it as a giant among tech giants. Google.com is still the most visited website in the world, and it remains the most used search engine of all time.

While an employee of the CIA, Edward Snowden decided to leak information about the National Security Agency's massive, secret surveillance program of Americans. Snowden had to flee the country as a result and now lives in Russia.

There are many accusations that Google has worked with the CIA and NSA to become a powerful, Big Brother–like company that can control information and even shape thought. Researchers and whistleblowers like Julian Assange, founder of WikiLeaks, claimed Google was not all it seemed on the surface and that it had ties to the U.S. Department of Defense's Defense Advanced Research Projects Agency (DARPA), the CIA, the NSA, and the Pentagon, who would surely all desire to make use of its technology capabilities. Emails released and published by the media outlet Al Jazeera America in 2014 showed communications between Google chair Eric Schmidt and cofounder Sergey Brin and then-NSA director Keith Alexander going back to 2011. One of the emails described a meeting between these individuals in San Jose, California, where "a classified briefing for the CEOs of key companies" was discussed, according to Alexis Kleinman in the May 6, 2014, "Tech" section of *Huffington Post*.

In September of 2019, 50 state attorneys general launched an antitrust investigation into Google, focusing on its advertising, and then added the search engine and other business applications to the investigation. Antitrust abuses and monopoly concerns followed Google's announcement that it would expand into the world of banking and the push from technology giants to protect themselves from foreign regulations. At the time, the Communications Decency Act's Section 230 served to provide internet "platforms" liability protection from user-generated content (as discussed in the section above called "Creative Arts and Digital Dictatorships"), assuring freedom of speech, but also allowing some censoring and filtering of content. This applied as well to Facebook, Instagram, Twitter, and YouTube. Lawmakers began to question whether Google and other tech giants should be allowed to keep those legal protections from offensive and violent content carried by their sites and not have to take responsibility for it. The tech companies argued that the law allowed them to post user content and then deal with what is offensive later once they caught it, in effect policing their own sites.

But who polices the police, and what happens when these platforms "choose the news"? Or at least the news they decide to let you see? Google search engine algorithms place particular stories and information above others due to a variety of reasons, often popularity, branding, ad sales, known mainstream media news sources, and so on, but criticisms and accusations about censorship, lack of search neutrality, and social engineering have opened the crack in the facade and revealed how Google controls the actual results of your searches. It engages in direct censorship by manipulating the results to assure you don't see anything that goes against the mainstream narrative.

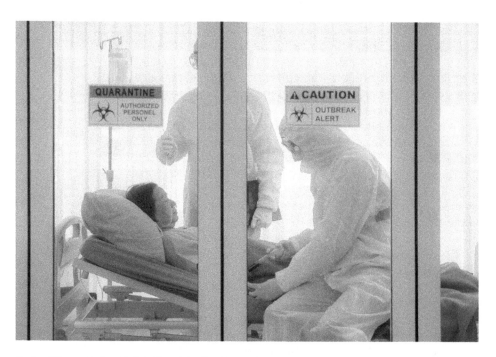

During "Pizzagate," a glitch in Google's algorithms allowed people to type any three-digit number and get news stories from cities all over America reporting that this random number was the reported number of COVID-19 cases in a list of cities.

In April of 2020, for just a few days, there was a bizarre breach in the Google algorithms that allowed searches into subject matter usually censored, including conspiracy theories and photographs involving allegations of pedophiles in Hollywood and the highest levels of government (a conspiracy that came to be known as "Pizzagate"), scientific studies showing the dangers of vaccines and pharmaceuticals, and articles and news items otherwise suppressed that countered the accusations of Russian collusion in the 2016 elections. For just those few days, people took screenshots and copied links before things went back to normal and it was all but impossible to find the same information once again. Was that hidden information accurate? Possibly. Possibly not. The real question to ask was, "Why was it hidden in the first place?" Is Google policing what it thinks people should see, and according to whom?

In June of the same year, Google was slammed yet again for algorithms that allowed anyone to search for any three digit number and the term "new cases" and turn up a list of cities where the count of new COVID-19 cases matched the three digits. In other words, if you searched for "439 new cases," the search results would pull up stories of city after city with 439 new cases reported. Type in "666 new cases," and the result would show city after city with 666 new cases. This included cities all over the world. Any three-digit number worked, and each one pulled up an article that stated the new number of cases were identified. People on Twitter posted hundreds of screenshots, wondering how there could be an article for every single number combination they tried. It seemed uncanny and highly suspect. At the time this book was written, Google had not commented on the "glitch in the Matrix."

In no way does your Google search guarantee you are getting the most accurate news or information—not by a long shot. You're getting the most widely accepted and agreed-upon information, which often is accurate and true. But not always. You're getting the most beneficial information that aligns with the desires and agendas of the corporate and government backers of Google. You're getting the official establishment story, and if you want the counterinformation or opposing viewpoints, you'll have to do your search elsewhere.

WHAT YOU GET IS WHAT YOU SEE?

In June of 2020, Google announced that it would fact-check images for Google searches. When looking for a particular image, you may get a "fact-check" label under the thumbnail of an image. Click on the image and it pulls up a summary of the fact-check that appears on the linked web page that carries that image. The fact-checking might apply to the image, to the article, or both.

Google of course claimed it was doing this not to censor things it didn't agree with but to provide users with critical context for the images and the accompanying articles they searched for. Google claimed this new service wouldn't effect a search ranking but then countered that by saying its search results offered the most relevant, reliable information first on the ranking list, including from sources that it fact-checks.

Of course the question remains: Who is behind the choices of which images get the stamp of approval and which get the other stamp? What is Google's agenda, its political slant and motivation, and even more importantly, its financial backers? We have thought police. We have information police. Now we have picture police.

Clearly, our government and corporations don't trust us to police ourselves.

THINGS TO COME

In March of 2018, Dr. Robert Epstein appeared on an interview with Fox News host Tucker Carlson to discuss the power of SSE and SEME and their potential to influence elections. SSE stands for "search suggestion effect," meaning the power of autocomplete suggestions to influence a user's internet search, and SEME stands for "search engine manipulation effect," meaning the power of search engine results and manipulations to influence user behavior. Epstein, a research psychologist at the American Institute of Behavioral Research and Technology, talked about how the institute conducted a study of the power of Google and Facebook to influence elections over a five-year period.

Dr. Epstein told Carlson that we should all be paranoid because what the two tech giants could do was "really mind-boggling."

Dr. Epstein told Carlson that we should all be paranoid because what the two tech giants could do was "really mind-boggling." He used as a hypothetical example Facebook founder Mark Zuckerberg on election day choosing to send out a message early that morning to the supporters of a particular candidate that would send out an additional 450,000 voters to the poll with no one knowing he had even done anything. Google, he claimed, could do even more by taking a 50-50 split among undecided voters and changing it to a 90-10 split with no one noticing because there is no paper trail. When you type in search words related to undecided voters, you would see anything Google wanted you to see, including its fabricated and altered percentages.

In an article by Dr. Joseph Mercola titled "Google—A Dictator Unlike Anything the World Has Ever Known," Dr. Epstein was interviewed about the direct interference of Google on the 2016 election and how Google was no doubt planning more of the same in the next election. Epstein reported on Google blacklists and the difficulties scrubbed websites have in getting off the Google blacklist. With no customer service department, you can't just call and ask why Google decided to ban your site. Epstein learned that Google could block websites even via non-Google platforms.

He stated, "The thing that really caught my eye—because I've been a programmer my whole life—was I couldn't figure out how they were blocking access to my website, not just through their own products ... Google.com, the search engine, or through Chrome, which is their browser, but through Safari, which is an Apple product, through Firefox, which is a browser run by Mozilla, a nonprofit organization." Epstein found these tactics astonishing.

Biased search results, as Epstein discovered through his research beginning in 2013, can be used to influence public opinion and sway undecided voters. "What's more," he stated, "the strength of that influence was shocking.

With Americans already paranoid about foreign intervention in U.S. elections, an added blow is the possibility of homegrown tampering via giant tech companies with their own agendas and a powerful method for assuring that the votes go the way they prefer, regardless of what the public wants. Whatever news stories benefit their bottom line may be the news the public sees, and whatever results of polls best serve their chosen candidate may be the only polls the public is made aware of, while any polls that place the unwanted candidate at the top may be hidden away. This should terrify people on both sides of the political spectrum because what is one day done to one will the next day be done to the other.

SHADOW BANNING

Social media outlets like Twitter and Facebook have consistently been accused of "shadow banning" conservative, pro-Trump, alternative health, and antivaccine accounts, conspiracy-related posts (even those jokingly questioning if, for example, an alien invasion would be the next disaster to strike the United States), and accounts questioning the official COVID-19 narrative. Shadow banning involves manipulating algorithms to minimize exposure to viewpoints you don't want people to see and to make it more difficult to share those viewpoints. Facebook in particular has been accused of engaging in selective banning and censoring of this type, but Twitter has all but caught up to them with its trending hashtag lists, which are believed to minimize links involving, for example, certain political leanings, alternative and natural health sites, antivaccination groups, and people and

The popular social media site Twitter has been accused of "shadow banning," a technique of manipulating algorithms to show users only what you want them to see.

groups challenging the mainstream media's accounts of major news stories.

During the 2020 U.S. primary elections, shadow banning was suspected of being extended to cover many pro–Bernie Sanders accounts, which were removed, tagged, or blocked until Sanders dropped out of the race and backed presidential candidate Joe Biden. So shadow banning isn't always directed toward a political party. Sometimes it is used to manipulate beliefs and perceptions within a party to elevate a particular candidate or segment of that party. In the case of Sanders, he was attacked for his socialist beliefs, and accounts supporting his policies found themselves victims of shadow banning. What is ironic is that just a few months later, socialist accounts were freely allowed on social media and promoted widely, but conservative accounts were being shadow banned.

Evidently, then, the enemies change according to who is in power, who wants power, and whether or not it is an election year.

Despite both social media sites repeatedly claiming they do not shadow ban, Twitter and Facebook do so daily, and freely, without repercussions, acting again as publishers, not platforms. By the time this book is released, perhaps they will be forced to give up some of the liability protections that are meant for platforms and stop acting as free speech editors, banning or minimizing alternative points of view. Facebook has come under tremendous pressure to prohibit hate speech, and CEO Mark Zuckerberg announced a ban on advertisements that claim society is threatened by members of a particular race, ethnicity, gender, or other protected category.

This happened after big corporations pulled their advertising for the month of July 2020 unless Zuckerberg tagged politicians' posts that incited violence or suppressed voting, and after Attorney General William Barr stated the company was under investigation, along with other tech giants, on the grounds of antitrust laws. The Facebook CEO promised to follow through by taking down content that violated its rules "no matter who says it," but only time will tell whether that applies to both sides of the political spectrum or just the side the advertisers and propagandists agree with.

Demonization

Emotional Appeals

Patriotic Appeals   **Name Calling**
Humor or Caricature

Half-Truths or Lies   Catchy Slogans
Evocative Visual Stategies

Tools of the Propaganda Trade: The Techniques of Coercion, Persuasion, and Disinformation

"We'll know our disinformation program is complete when everything the American public believes is false."
—William J. Casey

"Propaganda is most effective when it's least noticeable."
—Nancy Snow

The tools and methods of the propagandist are varied, but all have one thing in common: they are about information—how we spread it, how we get it. Information is what shapes our individual and collective realities. We experience things with our five senses and create perceptions, beliefs, and subconscious programming based on those experiences. Then we do everything we can to validate our beliefs and perceptions and to share them with others so we can feel heard, understood, and acknowledged. Basically, we are intaking sensory input and putting it out into the world in the form of behavior, thoughts, actions, and beliefs.

The problems arise when not everyone agrees with the beliefs we do. Then it becomes a battle to sway one another to our way of seeing things, whether that perception is true for the other person or not.

SPEED AND ACCURACY

Our primitive ancestors didn't have the means of making their beliefs and perceptions travel around the world in five minutes on social media. They drew and carved on the sides of caves, on rocks, and later on crude items they made with their hands. Oral history came first, with stories and traditions passed down throughout generations via spoken word or song. Over time, as the information moved down the chain, it changed.

The written word allowed for more detail and accuracy, but it also allowed for more embellishment and fantasy. Still, writing something down could be a way to preserve a story more accurately than relying on human memory recall. On an individual and collective level, we may be influenced in our communications by peer pressure, cultural shaming, the push to conform, guilt by association, retribution, and a whole lot of other obstacles standing in the way of speaking our experiences and beliefs. Sometimes our own personal censor intervenes before we even attempt to communicate.

Today we use both oral and written vehicles for transporting information either to the world or just to our family and friends. We do the work of the media when we spread information that we haven't fully researched or vetted. We spread viruses of the mind just as we spread viruses of the body, infecting as many people as we come in contact with. And the mental viruses we spread the most involve fear and danger to survival.

MIND VIRUSES AND THE CONTAGION OF INFORMATION

A mind virus—a type of meme—is a masterful tool of the propagandist. If you infect enough members of the public with such a virus, they will distribute your version of the truth for you. In his book *Thought Contagion: How Belief Spreads through Society—The New Science of Memes*, author and former Fermilab physicist Aaron Lynch writes of the theoretical and mathematical models of how ideas are transmitted throughout a culture or society. To Lynch, an idea is something encoded in human neurons or other media that takes on a life of its own as it evolves and spreads, often creating a whole new belief set. This can breed everything from false and inaccurate news reporting to misinformation, with the potential for extreme hysteria, copycat crimes, and mob mentality.

Spread via thought contagion, there are seven key types of mind viruses or memes that Lynch describes:

1. Quantity of parenthood—Ideas influencing birth rates and how many children a person has
2. Efficiency of parenthood—Ideas embraced by children adopting them from their parents
3. Proselytic—Ideas spread to other people who are not family or children and have a tendency to spread horizontally across populations, rather than vertically as from a parent to a child
4. Preservational—Ideas that are held for longer periods of time, more traditional
5. Adversarial—Ideas that those who believe in them use to attack or sabotage others with competing or opposing ideas, often aggressive in nature
6. Cognitive—Ideas that are logical, reasonable, and convincing enough to be widely held within a population
7. Motivational—Ideas that are accepted by people because of a benefit to their own interests

According to Richard Brodie ... memes are spread "by influencing people's minds, and thus their behavior, so that eventually someone gets infected with the meme.

According to Richard Brodie, in his book *Virus of the Mind: The New Science of the Meme*, memes are spread "by influencing people's minds, and thus their behavior, so that eventually someone gets infected with the meme. If a meme is in your mind, it can greatly or subtly influence your behavior." Brodie offers his own categories for such memes:

1. Distinction memes help categorize and describe the universe around us by giving them distinctive labels.
2. Strategy memes tell us what to do when we find a solution applicable to a specific problem or goal we wish to achieve.

3. Association memes link two or more things to create a commonality, such as 4th of July fireworks and patriotism, or a Tahitian beach with retirement.

Mind viruses allow the flow of information to spread across mental networks in much the same way a silly video is emailed from one computer to another across a network. The diffusion of ideas and information is not random. It happens via networks of minds, computers, social media, you name it. The more central you are to any given network—say, of friends or family—the more connections you have to pass your ideas along and spread the information you think important, which may then be spread further by each individual in your network (if they share common beliefs and ideals, of course).

When mass media engages in this kind of diffusion an idea or belief, no matter if it's true or not, it can reach a tipping point where the idea then begins to take off on its own. This occurs when a large enough group accepts and promotes it as the real deal. Tipping points occur in the political arena as much as they do with cultural trends, and with the internet and social media, reaching a tipping point occurs a lot sooner than by old-fashioned word-of-mouth or the old-school media of newspaper headlines and radio or TV reports.

Memes can spread like viruses, starting with one person, who sends it to several others, and each of those sends the meme to several people, and so on. Certain qualities of the meme determine how rapidly and well it will spread.

Even tipping points operate by certain rules, according to Malcolm Gladwell, the famous British Canadian journalist who wrote the classic book *The Tipping Point: How Little Things Make a Big Difference*. Gladwell categorized tipping points as follows:

The 80/20 Principle—Special networkers called connectors, mavens, and salespeople who know a lot of people spread the most information, like a computer network hub.

Stickiness Factor—Ideas that are sticky, or memorable, have a higher ability to reach critical mass as they are more impactful.

Context—Mind viruses that succeed on a grand scale have context that a large number of people can relate to, use, or find relevant to their lives.

Gladwell states the reason certain concepts spread further and wider than others: "It's that ideas and behavior and messages and products sometimes behave just like outbreaks of infectious diseases. They are social epidemics."

We can see this effect in religious movements, cults, social and political movements, trends, celebrity worship, and the spread of urban legends and myths. When it comes to the mass media, knowing how to reach a tipping point or release a social epidemic is critical to a successful propaganda campaign. Often, these mind viruses work best when they utilize humor, fear, or instructional content. It works a lot like advertising, with the most successful commercials selling you products that make you feel good, scare you into thinking you need them, or offering something you want to learn how to do or master. If we find value in an idea, whether that value is a good laugh when we need one, a scary reminder we need to do something to protect ourselves or loved ones, or a piece of information that helps us improve the quality of our lives, we eat it up, then regurgitate it back out to whoever we have in our networks that will listen. Just get on social media and look at how recommendations for the best shows on streaming services get spread around, or how a great gardening tip, recipe for a Keto shake, or a funny or scary story—which could be entirely made up out of thin air—spreads like wildfire and is, by many, accepted as true.

Content is king, but only when it meets certain parameters by which it can be sent viral and spread to more people in less time. Because we tend to spread information and ideas that are important to us, others are more inclined to consider them, and

Web surfers today are easily influenced by trending hashtags, quickly spreading them to family, friends, and coworkers with barely a second thought. We would be wise to consider content more carefully, pause, read, and think before spreading whatever comes our way on the internet.

may even find them important enough to themselves to pass on. Less important or impactful information falls by the wayside, with our overwhelmed brains ignoring it or denying it. We operate on a need-to-know basis when it comes to the onslaught of information coming at us every moment of every day. If information is manipulated to give the impression that it's worth knowing, we will pay more attention to it. It's the difference between something being "buzzworthy" and something failing to push the buzz button at all.

Today trending hashtags and stories tell us what we should think is important and deserving of our attention. We are easily manipulated by what everyone else is doing, to the point where our government and mass media knows they can put out a story or piece of information and make it reach the tipping point, go viral, and reach critical mass in less than a day. Maybe even an hour. This should give everyone pause, because we are all guilty of glancing at headlines and passing them along to friends or family without even reading the stories. Our loved ones assume that because we found them of value, they should, too, and they pass them on to their friends, and before we know it, these stories have permeated the population and are accepted as true.

If it is buzz-worthy, we become like preachers or evangelicals spreading the gospel with such fervor and passion that we can easily infect others into buying what we have to say or sell. But it doesn't mean it was even accurate information to being with.

MISINFORMATION AND MALINFORMATION

People make mistakes. They spread bad information, sometimes intentionally but not usually. So, too, do the government and mainstream media. They misinform and malinform all the time.

Misinformation is the spread of bad, false, or inaccurate information, usually without any malicious intent. It's done out of ignorance, speed, and lack of attention on behalf of those spreading it. This includes mass media, which often gets things wrong and rarely redacts bad information or apologizes for shoddy reporting. If they do, the admission is often stuck somewhere few people will ever see it. Who wants to admit you put out a story without checking your sources? People's reputations are often destroyed that way, but that seems secondary in importance to putting out the flashy headline first.

Misinformation often comes in the form of rumor and gossip or accusations and allegations from "anonymous sources" who later prove to be totally false or nonexistent. This happens a lot with crime reporting, where we hear of suspects who are deemed guilty or innocent from the get-go, without any proof or evidence. It also comes in the form of posting the winners of elections long before the final vote counts are in. Misinformation is the easiest to spot if you do some cross-checking for accuracy. Sadly, most people don't, which is why it goes viral like wildfire before someone spots the inaccuracies and cuts off the oxygen to the flames.

Malinformation is similar, except in this case the information is real but is intended to harm or destroy, such as posting compromising sex videos or pictures, or spreading a less-than-virtuous news item that is factual. Malinformation is used all the time on the internet in social media and forums, especially among individuals out to hurt an ex or shut down a competitor. It is also found when someone posts a photo without context to ignite a negative reaction in a particular group or to turn people away from a particular world leader or politician. An example is a picture of a half-naked child in a cage. Without telling where the picture was taken, who the child is, and what the situation surrounding the picture is, you could ruin someone for life. Is it a refugee child at a detention center? A child being used in a child porn video? The abused child of an arrested couple? Or none of the above?

Malinformation is used all the time on the internet in social media and forums, especially among individuals out to hurt an ex or shut down a competitor.

DISINFORMATION CAMPAIGNS

Disinformation is deliberate manipulation, and in the hands of the government and mass media, it is used to keep the public from finding out a particular truth. Disinformation is a horse of a darker color. It is intentional and meant to manipulate, confuse, distract, discredit, destroy, derail, and deliberately harm a person, group, movement, ideology, or entity. When it's used by the powers that be, it's a lot harder to spot than simple misinformation or a hostile, reputation-destroying malinformation attack. Disinfo can be so clandestine, and so well planned and executed, that the majority of people have no clue they are being lied to.

Disinformation is used to undermine an opponent, create a consensus for a political or military action or coup, turn the public for or against something, mislead a populace about a scandal or crime, create a distraction from a troublesome situation, divert attention to or away from something, or sway opinion for or against a policy or law, among other things. It is a covert form of manipulative propaganda. The word comes from the Russian "dezinformatsiya," which was taken from the name of the KGB's own propaganda department.

During wartime, disinformation is critical to keep the enemy from knowing the moves of the allied troops, or to divert them away from a sensitive installation. It works much the same in business and the corporate world, with competitors lying and deceiving their rivals to stay one step ahead or to keep their rivals from knowing their plans and possibly stealing or sabotaging them. A pharmaceutical company might launch a disinformation campaign about a new drug they are touting that has unpleasant side effects but would bring them massive profits. A government might disinform their citizens about a terrorist threat to keep people afraid and subservient while they pass draconian laws taking away basic civil rights. A high school football team might put out a false playbook for their opponents to find to keep their rivals from winning a big game. A political party might lie about polls to make it look like they are on the winning side.

Stories about UFOs have been a cultural phenomenon going back to the 1950s. The internet age has brought disinformation and conspiracy stories about alien spaceships to an entirely new level.

People use disinformation to mislead family, friends, and lovers when it serves their purpose. Those who commit crimes might plant false evidence or do something deceptive to divert attention from themselves and toward another potential suspect. At the same time, the detective or investigators of said crimes might use disinformation to confuse a suspect in hopes they will become emboldened and make a careless mistake.

One of the most widely known disinformation campaigns involves whether UFOs exist and are the source of an alien presence on Earth. There has been so much false and misleading information released to the public courtesy of government, military, and intelligence entities that it's hard to distinguish fact from fiction. Despite millions of sightings, many from highly credible witnesses, the truth evades us because someone—or a group of someones—does not want us to know all the facts. The result is a host of sightings and reports that are faked or misleading, muddying the reports of citizens actually seeing objects in the sky they cannot identify. This isn't a book about UFOs, but the subject matter is rampant with attempts to lie, discredit, divert, and deceive.

During the coronavirus pandemic, there were accusations of disinformation from every camp and corner. The World Health Organization (WHO) and U.S. Centers for Disease Control and Prevention (CDC) were busy accusing individual doctors and researchers of lying to the public if their science didn't match the official narrative, even as hundreds of individual doctors and researchers accused the WHO and CDC of faking and inflating the numbers of COVID-19 cases to push mandatory vaccines (once some were developed), from which both organizations would financially profit. President Trump accused China of spreading disinformation about the origins of the virus, which it claimed came from bats near a market close to the Wuhan biolab, and other nations accused the United States of promoting a conspiracy theory to punish China. Meanwhile, a portion of the public accused philanthropists Bill and Melinda Gates of disinforming the entire world with bad and rushed science to bring about their desire to vaccinate the planet no matter what the dangers might be.

It was one big mess of misinformation, disinformation, propaganda, spin, and beneath it all, people trying to dog paddle and not drown in the chorus of chaos, waiting for facts that only time would reveal.

Social media outlets are filled with bots and trolls intent on disinforming and spreading fake news and propaganda for whatever their respective agendas are. Mainstream media disinforms day in and day out to maintain the narrative that they are beholden to politically and financially. Google promotes search results that may not always be accurate but follow the agendas of its masters. We are all seeing one big puppet show, and the puppet masters are hidden from view as they disinform us, manipulate us, and confuse us.

Censoring content and information is a form of disinformation, too, because it prevents any facts that go against a chosen narrative from being seen, thus creating a false reality that can harm the public. An example occurred in June of 2020 when Twitter began banning and blocking alternative and natural health accounts that discussed vitamins and minerals, exercise, positive thinking, and natural methods of fighting viruses such as the one that causes COVID-19. One of these accounts was Mercola.com, owned by Dr. Joseph Mercola, an osteopathic physician and marketer of alternative health supplements. The site was highly regarded by many—and criticized by at least as many—for its penetrating if controversial articles about the darker side of the pharmaceutical industry, mandatory vaccinations, GMOs, chemicals and toxins in food, and the growing epidemics of cancer, heart disease, obesity, and autoimmune diseases.

A platform that does not allow its audience and users to see alternative sources of information, even when fully sourced and backed up by science (albeit a different science from the one used by the chosen narrative), is not only engaging in censorship but possibly harming public health by cutting off potential sources of solid, health-related information. Obviously Twitter was, and is, catering to its financial backers, most likely associated with the pharmaceutical and agribusiness industries, cutting off many voices with opposing opinions to the giant corporate puppet masters. Facebook and Instagram weren't much better, each censoring and tagging as "fake news" any posts that didn't align with the narrative

chosen by the mass media and, in the case of COVID-19, the CDC and the WHO. Meanwhile, YouTube was accused of banning a documentary called *Plandemic*, which features a prominent cellular and molecular biologist, Dr. Judy Mikovits (called a "discredited former researcher" in Wikipedia), because it went against the official story. *Plandemic* asserted, among other claims, that the new coronavirus that causes COVID-19 did not arise naturally but was manufactured, that flu vaccines contain coronaviruses and increase the chance of contracting COVID-19, that the drug hydroxychloroquine is effective against COVID-19, and that wearing a mask does not protect the wearer but actually activates the virus.

Osteopathic physician Dr. Joseph Mercola has long been a proponent of alternative medicines and supplements. His website often criticizes modern-day medicines and nutrition, including vaccinations, GMOs, and Big Pharma.

Google went so far as to remove this documentary from people's private personal files after the *Washington Post* demanded it. The newspaper's correspondent Elizabeth Dwoskin complained about the documentary being accessible through Google Drive even after it had been banned, and Google responded by removing the private content, stating the company felt it was "misleading content related to civic and democratic processes" and was related to "harmful health practices." Suddenly the *Washington Post* had become Big Brother, and Google jumped when it said jump.

Google Drive also blocked users' personal access to a hydroxychloroquine study that showed that the simple and cheap drug worked to fight COVID-19. YouTube banned a video by an epidemiologist named Knut Wittkowski who challenged lockdown orders on a scientific basis. He was told his information violated community standards. Apparently, scientific inquiry was no longer permitted.

YouTube was engaged in a campaign to remove conservative and alternative health voices in 2020. Among other methods, it employed its "Up Next" viewing feature, which is an algorithm designed to show viewers chosen videos that might be of interest. The problem was that viewers had little choice in what they saw unless they went looking for different perspectives or alternative narratives to the ones that are "up next." YouTube deplatformed posts from Larry Cook, X22 Report, Charlie Ward, QAnon, Obiwan Qenobi, and other conservative, alternative, and anti-Big Pharma sites. YouTube would tag and flag videos, too. (Tagging an account means adding a line at the end of the post claiming it is not verified by official sources. Flagging an account means a warning the account will be taken down, or that it was taken down for violating the site rules.)

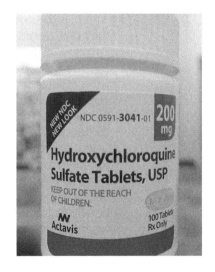

An untested and unproven treatment for COVID-19, hydroxychloroquine was promoted by various posters on social media as an effective treatment for the coronavirus. Even President Donald Trump was convinced by the unsubstantiated claims.

All social media outlets were flagging accounts that offered different perspectives surrounding the tragic death of a black man named George Floyd, who was killed on May 25, 2020, by a white police officer named Derek Chauvin, even when those perspectives came from the black community or those calling for an end to violence as a way of fighting violence. Only those celebrities, personalities, and people repeating the mainstream media's narrative were allowed to be heard. Even members of the Black Lives Matter movement were censored or banned if they dared bring up important questions or viewpoints about race, the media, and how politicians used both whites and Blacks for their own agendas that no one on mainstream media was talking about. If it didn't fit, it had to quit, to paraphrase a famous quote from the O. J. Simpson trial. Whatever viewpoint, opinion, or even fact that doesn't fit into a specific box doesn't make the cut. You won't even know what news you are missing. You don't know what you don't know, you know?

In *Mind Wars: A History of Mind Control, Surveillance, and Social Engineering by the Government, Media, and Secret Societies*, which I wrote with Larry Flaxman, we discuss how difficult it can be to discern real information from misinformation or disinformation. We quote Lenon Honor, author of *Media Mind Control: A Brief Introduction*, who summed it up perfectly: "While in the midst of the global mind control apparatus an individual will not realize that they are being subconsciously influenced nor will they realize the sometimes overt, but mainly covert, manes of subconscious manipulation presents." Because we are immersed in the apparatus, we don't always see it, in the same way a fish in the ocean doesn't necessarily see the water surrounding it. It's just a normal and natural part of its existence. Honor goes on to state that we are always distracted from whatever the media wants us to know. The same media keeping us in the dark of what they don't want us to know directs our attention to what is acceptable, even preferable, if it helps their agenda spread.

Blacking out information is as bad as lying about it. This applies to warfare, product advertising, politics, race riots, cures for cancer, and everything else. The media is complicit with their owners in choosing the news you get to see as your "new normal" reality. Freedom of speech and access to that free speech is what true democracy is based upon. You take that away, and you have totalitarianism made up of greedy, power-mad politicians and corporations putting a giant sticker over something you could possibly benefit from, something that might even save your life. Disinforming the public by cutting off their choice of who to listen to or what facts and research to consider is social engineering at its finest.

SOCIAL ENGINEERING, PREDICTIVE PROGRAMMING, AND FRAMING

In 2012, Facebook conducted a stealth experiment involving thousands of its users—700,000, to be exact. The social media site conducted a social experiment that manipulated news stories seen by users to gauge their emotional responses without telling the users what it was doing. This involved planting specifically positive or negative news stories in users' news feeds and also omitting positive or negative news stories with the help of an algorithm. The goal was to see how the guinea pig users would respond to the content over a one-week period. The social engineering experiment was published in the March issue of the *Proceedings of the National Academy of Sciences* the following year, and since then, similar "experiments" have been conducted on users across social media outlets to influence and gauge emotional responses.

Another social engineering experiment of sorts involved the hugely popular Google-owned Pokémon GO app that allows players to look for and capture virtual Pokémon creatures in real-world locations. Players had no idea they were being used as pawns in an experiment to manipulate their behavior in real-world settings as they sought out the rewards that often had them meeting up at local venues, where they would no doubt spend some money. Writer Addison Del Mastro reported on the phenomenon in "Pokémon GO: America's Social Credit System" in the July 5, 2019, *American Conservative*. Del Mastro speculated about the potential for an app like Pokémon GO but owned and operated by the government and designed to do something similar to the game—to track and influence social behaviors by giving rewards and credits. Del Mastro even suggested that the company that created the game, Niantic, knew of the more harmful potential aspects this technology, writing: "Pokémon GO, in a way, is social engineering. If a company can get you to take long walks or meet people to battle—even if you kind of want to—why couldn't a government app incentivize people towards pro-social behavior, by similarly gamifying real life?"

In the popular game app Pokémon GO, players search for monsters to capture in real locations using their phones. Unknown to users, the app was also designed to lead them to places where they might make purchases.

Del Mastro admitted the game is fun and that what you do on the app won't really harm your life, unless you get too addicted to it, but warned that a potential government app of a similar nature would most likely have much more intense consequences for your chosen behaviors and actions. "Perhaps Americans would rebel against government-sponsored social engineering in the guise of an app or video game.... But if America were to have its own social credit app ... it might not feel that different from Pokémon GO." Gotta catch 'em all!

Google has come under fire for censoring and manipulating, and at the time of the writing of this book, it was being considered for federal action to remove its liability protections under Section 230 of the Communications Decency Act for acting as a publisher and not a platform by engaging in editing and censoring public content. Demands to break up the monopoly Google holds—it controls over 90 percent of search engine activity—are on the rise as more accusations are leveled at the tech giant for controlling and restricting access to information its gatekeepers disagree with or find offensive, politically or otherwise.

Demands to break up the monopoly Google holds—it controls over 90 percent of search engine activity—are on the rise....

Social engineering, also known as social programming, is a tactic used in religion, advertising, politics, and corporate consumerism to mold the behaviors and beliefs of social groups. Just as the word "engineer" means to use scientific principles to build machines and structures, social engineering uses psychological principles to do the same to human beings. It may be gradual and subtle, but it is a form of mind control and manipulation because it involves coercive tactics, subconscious stimuli such as symbolism and subliminal messages, the use of tactics such as neuro-linguistic programming (NLP), and shaping public opinion for consent and approval, individually and collectively.

In August of 2020, a study was undertaken by Yale University to compare the effectiveness of various messages on participants' willingness to take a COVID-19 vaccine once one became available. The goal was to learn what forms of messaging could work to persuade the public at large to adopt such a vaccine— that is, what kind of pro-vaccine propaganda would work best.

Though the media was quick to jump on the Big Pharma bandwagon and guilt and shame anyone who might actually question a fast tracked vaccine without major testing (labeling anyone who dared ask questions an "anti-vaxxer" and conspiracy theorist), clinical trials were set up to investigate the use of guilt, shame, and anger techniques (you can view the trials at https://clinicaltrials.gov/ct2/show/NCT04460703). There were different subgroups including "trust in science," "guilt," and "anger," with each looking at ways to use coercive persuasion techniques to basically control and coerce people into taking an injected substance they might not have felt comfortable with and that may not have gone through enough studies to be deemed safe.

The 4,000 participants were randomly selected to get one of 12 different messages, which included 10 message variations about the COVID-19 vaccine, a control message about bird feeding, and a baseline message consisting only of a statement about the vaccine that was also included in all the other messages. Participants then reported their willingness to get the vaccine at three and at six months of it becoming available. Some of the messages were as follows:

- Personal freedom message—How COVID-19 is limiting personal freedoms and how society can preserve personal freedoms by getting everyone vaccinated.
- Self-interest message—How COVID-19 poses a danger to one's individual health and how getting vaccinated is the best way to prevent oneself from getting sick.
- Community interest message—How the dangers of COVID-19 could harm loved ones and how more vacci-

Many signs and billboards about COVID-19 take the community interest approach of asking people to wear masks because it will save lives.

nated people means less risk for disease; society must work together to all get vaccinated.

- Anger message—COVID-19 dangers are real and imagine how angry people will feel if participants don't get vaccinated and then spread the disease.
- Guilt message—Same as above but imagine the guilt participants will feel if they don't get vaccinated.
- Not brave message—Those who choose not to get vaccinated are not brave.

More information about the study can be found at the website of the U.S. National Library of Medicine: https://clinicaltrials .gov/ct2/show/NCT04460703.

Separate from the study comparing the effectiveness of the different kinds of messages, columnists and media outlets contributed to the propaganda push by publishing their own provaccine opinion pieces and articles. For example, three professors (of law, medicine, and bioethics, respectively), Michael Ledermanis, Maxwell J. Mehlman, and Stuart Youngner, together contributed an opinion piece to USA Today titled "Defeat COVID-19 by Requiring Vaccination for All: It's Not Un-American, It's Patriotic," published August 6, 2020, voicing similar messages to the ones offered in the study. So, the media jumped on the "get the vaccine bandwagon" even before a vaccine was developed, furthering the provaccine propaganda.

USING FAMOUS FACES

In May of 2020, a "soft power" propaganda campaign on behalf of the World Health Organization (WHO) was launched involving the use of celebrities and media influencers to try to persuade people to trust the WHO's recommendations on the use of masks to slow the spread of the coronavirus and on the development and eventual use of a COVID-19 vaccine. President Trump had recently suspended funding to the organization, an agency of the United Nations, unhappy with its response to the COVID-19 pandemic. The WHO paid a PR firm, Hill and Knowlton Strategies, $135,000 to seek out influencers willing to be a part of the campaign.

This was the same PR firm, by the way, that was hired to promote the war in Iraq and, back in 1950, hired by the tobacco industry to dupe the public into believing cigarettes were safe and did not cause cancer. Now here they were again, this time pushing an agenda that would benefit the WHO and their many associates. It started with a "One World Together" concert shown online to raise money for the WHO and promote the message we could get through this together. People like married actors Tom Hanks and Rita Wilson, who had both tested positive for COVID-19, served as spokespeople for the propaganda campaign. It successfully raised millions of dollars.

Meanwhile, the United Nations had its own narrative control campaign with an initiative called "Verified," using an army of 10,000 "digital volunteers" tasked with spreading UN-approved information about COVID-19 across social networking outlets.

Celebrity movie star Tom Hanks, who had COVID-19 but recovered, became a spokesperson for coronavirus awareness along with his wife, Rita Wilson.

These media and social media propaganda campaigns are called "soft power" or "soft sell" because they don't hammer the knowledge to the public via scientists and experts. Instead, recognizable and well-loved celebrities and social influencers softly and gently spread the messages. It's a perfect method of propaganda, especially for young people who are heavily influenced by social media and YouTube stars but also for those who believe famous faces wouldn't lie to them. PR firms like Hill and Knowlton know that people respond to those they admire. Whether those people are telling the truth is of little concern.

PUBLIC RELATIONS AND ADVERTISING TECHNIQUES

Selling a service or product requires a set of tools and methods that often parallel those in political propaganda. It's about shaping public opinion and manipulating behavior, especially when it comes to how we spend our money. Some of the methods of the advertising and PR world include:

- Snob Appeal and FOMO ("fear of missing out") — Ads work well that appeal to our desire not just to keep up with the Joneses but to pull ahead of them, as do those that show higher social classes and people enjoying a level of wealth we aspire to. FOMO can be a powerful motivator by appealing to our anxiety.
- Bandwagoning — The desire to fit in and belong is a strong one. Humans are creatures who seek connection and

community, so ads that play upon our need to go along and be one of the crowd hold particular appeal.

- Loaded Words—Words have power and emotion attached to them, and loaded words can be especially convincing. Highly negative words and phrases can be used in ads and messages that want to keep the public from doing something, perhaps out of fear or doubt. Positive words and phrases are used to persuade the public to do something, encouraging them with hope, fun, joy, happiness, and success.

- Music and Songs—The pharmaceutical industry, the insurance industry, the auto industry, and many others are known for the use of catchy songs with lyrical hooks to entice viewers to remember a company name or ask their doctors about this or that drug. Sometimes the music is so prominent that you don't even know what is being sold until the end of the commercial. The more the song can hook you, the more you'll remember it, and before you know it, you will be discussing the drug with your doctor to see if it's "right for you."

- Transferring—Propaganda often makes associations or transfers attention between two unassociated topics, concepts, or objects. This allows the propagandist to invoke images of positive or negative things that are then transferred onto the object being sold or promoted. Auto com-

An example of transferring is a car commercial that associates the product with the beauty of nature and fun of camping. It has nothing to do with the quality of the car and everything to do with image.

panies, for example, do this by showing images of people camping on a mountaintop or dressed up and exiting a fancy restaurant, so the viewer will associate those images with the car being advertised.

- Unreliable Sources and Testimonials—See those people telling you how great this drug is, or how much their lives have changed because of that yogurt brand? You know they are actors, but sometimes commercial producers use real people and real testimonials. You have to listen to the disclaimers or read the fine print at the bottom of the ad. Even when they use "experts" or "real testimonials," there is still the possibility the person isn't an expert in the field in question, or the testimonial is not normal in relationship to others who have tried the product. It is also possible the person was paid to hype a product whether they used it or not, as is often done with celebrity spokespersons.

- Card Stacking—Advertisers card stack when they only tell you all the good features and benefits of the product they are selling and omit the problems or faults. Pharmaceutical companies stack by telling you how wonderful your life will be on their drug before telling you all the negative side effects you might experience.

- Name Calling—We are not talking about calling your competitor a ninny or a jackass. The "name calling" form of propaganda calls out competitive products for their flaws and problems as a way to boost your own. This involves labeling and insinuating that another product on the market is unsafe, unhealthy, too expensive, not sturdy enough, and so on as a way to make your product automatically appear superior.

- Vagueness and Generalities—The more vague and general your claims are, the harder they are to dispute or refute. You can make statements like "Anything tastes great with ____ beer" or "Our cleaner works on all spots" and give the impression you have something that is tops all around, without having to get too specific or point out flaws or negatives. When an ad is too specific, the advertiser risks losing a portion of the prospective buyers. Generalizations rely more on the buyer's interpretation than on their critical judgment, as it is hard to judge something you don't know much about.

- Plain Folks Propaganda—This works well with politics and with advertising. Playing up the "we're just good ol' plain folks like you" angle creates a sense of belonging, comfort, and familiarity. It also attempts to breed trust in the buyer by saying the product is used by ordinary people, not superior snobs and elitists. The product is directed to regular folks and often shows them indulging in regular folk activ-

Jim Jones, the leader of the People's Temple cult, was able to convince hundreds of people to follow him to a camp in Guyana and commit mass suicide in 1978.

ities in the background. This type of propaganda appeals to those who don't want some rich celebrity telling them what face cream to use or wine to drink. They want to know what noncelebrity people like themselves think and buy.

Propagandists are usually masters at social engineering and programming the masses with persuasive, coercive phrases and visuals with the goal of regulating behavior and adjusting thought. Social engineering can be as subtle as manipulating what shows up on your social media walls or as forthright as a public service announcement telling you to keep yourself and others safe by wearing a mask and washing your hands. It doesn't have to be for a sinister or negative purpose, but it does have to connect with the populace on some level to work. Often social engineering campaigns will urge citizens to conform or to hold themselves to an acceptable standard in society, or risk some type of punishment or regulation. This works just as well on corporations and businesses to keep them in line with the government's desires or on the side of the "greater good."

Totalitarian governments use social engineering methods to condition their populations to be submissive and accepting or to shape public attitudes to benefit them. Engineering public favor can help support illegal wars, military coups, voting inconsistencies, fraud, and the crimes of powerful people. Just look at how easy it was for Hitler to engineer the people of Germany to support his heinous behaviors, or how cult leader Jim Jones was able to convince over 900 people to take their own lives at Jonestown in Guyana in November of 1978. A good social engineer is a good PR person, a good salesperson, and a good snake charmer all rolled into one. Now imagine that on a larger scale, as in politics, social movements, and global conflicts.

SEME: SEARCH ENGINE MANIPULATION EFFECT

During the 2016 presidential campaign between Republican candidate Donald Trump and Democratic candidate Hillary Clinton, the search engine giant Google was suspected of using its search engine methods to sway public opinion toward a particular political candidate. Google had the power to choose which news items came up in a search and keep certain news items at the top of that search list via SEME, which stands for "search engine manipulation effect." SEME can change and manipulate search engine results and create a discernible effect in the actions of consumers, including helping to shape their voting preferences.

Though Google avidly denied manipulating search results, or rankings of politicians, a handful of experiments involving more than 4,500 participants altogether showed how it might have been done. In one experiment, participants were shown two candidates and given brief descriptions of the two, and they were asked which one they liked or preferred. Then they were allowed 15 minutes to do some online research into both candidates. All participants had access to 30 search results that linked to actual website pages from a past election. For one group of participants, results were ranked to favor one candidate; for another group, results were ranked to favor the other candidate; and for the third group, results were not reordered at all. Only the ordering of the results differed among the groups; but people had free choice to click on whichever results they desired.

The result was a distinct shift in the opinions of the participants toward whichever candidate was favored by the rankings, with a large percentage of the participants not even aware that their results rankings were biased. Further studies confirmed that people do change their opinions based upon seeing and being exposed to top search results and higher rankings, whether for a political candidate, a cause, or some other matter.

During the 2016 election, Democratic presidential candidate Hillary Clinton hired Stephanie Hannon, a Google executive, as her chief technology officer. Google's holding company chair, Eric Schmid, had started a company in 2015 called Groundwork that was devoted to getting Clinton elected. Then, in 2016, an organization called SourceFed stated that Google search results in Clinton's favor were manipulated only because the recommended searches of her name were different from those of searches on Yahoo and Bing. Does this mean her opponent, Donald Trump, didn't have ways of

Stephanie Hannon was the director of product management for civic innovation and social impact for Google when she joined Hillary Clinton's campaign for the presidency in 2016. Hannon had also worked for Eventbrite and Facebook.

using Google search engine optimization and algorithms for Republican gains? Certainly both parties use every means necessary to manipulate the control of information, but what is key here is that the Clinton campaign had links to two Google executives. This suggests that the voters should always research and follow the source to the money, and the money to the source.

In Clinton's defense, it's clear that if more people search for her than for her opponents, results about her will rise to the top of the search rankings. It's not a conspiracy but simply how the algorithms work. Still, during the primary campaign, Vermont senator Bernie Sanders was highly popular and had a devoted following, yet his name was always ranked below Clinton's. It might seem reasonable that more searches would be conducted for Clinton, a former U.S. secretary of state, senator, and first lady, than for Sanders, a current senator, but how do we know? Perhaps we need to demand transparency into which political candidates are connected to Google before the next election is influenced by the manipulated flow of information to either political party.

Before the election, which Trump ended up winning based on electoral college votes despite Clinton winning the popular vote, *Politico* ran an article by Robert Epstein in August of 2015 called "How Google Could Rig the 2016 Election." Epstein laid out the various ways Google was associated with the Clinton campaign, and he described the potential of its SEME and search engine optimization (SEO) algorithms to influence the public, especially voters in search of reliable information. He also looked at SEME influence in the national elections in the U.K. and outlined ways to protect people in the future against this technological type of information manipulation.

Epstein warned, "Biased rankings are hard for individuals to detect, but what about regulators or election watchdogs? Unfortunately, SEME is easy to hide. The best way to wield this type of influence is to do what Google is becoming better at doing every day: send out customized search results. If search results favoring one candidate were sent only to vulnerable individuals, regulators and watchdogs would be especially hard pressed to

SEME and SEO are an indirect form of propaganda and censorship because they redirect inquiries to information sources that are deemed acceptable, are already popular, or are paid for.

find them." He ended the article stating that it is hard to imagine that Google would degrade its product or undermine its credibility by manipulating search results, but that the only way to protect free, fair elections might end up being government regulation.

An even better way would be for individual users to make use of other search engines as well as Google and expand the amount of information they have to choose from. In June of 2020, natural health groups accused Google of using the same SEME methods to manipulate search results on the coronavirus/COVID-19 to favor the websites of the WHO and the CDC. Results involving other sites, including studies by other scientists and researchers, were given lower rankings if not censored outright. People (including this author, who was researching another book at the time) flocked to DuckDuckGo, a search engine that offers a wider range of search results and much better privacy while searching, to find alternate viewpoints and information that did not align with what was being touted in the mainstream media. These included natural ways to improve immunity and health and research studies showing successful treatments that were not acceptable to the pharmaceutical industry.

SEME and SEO are an indirect form of propaganda and censorship because they redirect inquiries to information sources that are deemed acceptable, are already popular, or are paid for. It doesn't always mean they are truthful.

So you still have choices, but you have to, uh, "search" for them.

PREDICTIVE PROGRAMMING

In November of 1977, a science fiction movie titled *Close Encounters of the Third Kind*, directed by Steven Spielberg, was released to critical acclaim and huge ticket sales. The film told the story of a man and a woman who were thrown into extraordinary circumstances after they witnessed a UFO sighting. UFO buffs and conspiracy theorists alike claimed the film was predictive programming, or programming that predicts a future trend or event. They claimed the release of this film, along with many others, was part of a concerted and intentional effort on the part of the U.S. government, working with Hollywood, to gradually disclose to the public the presence of UFOs and aliens on Earth. Scientific consultant Dr. J. Allen Hynek, an astrophysicist, worked on the Spielberg classic, adding more fuel to the "are they trying to tell us something?" fire, but what really set this film up as classic predic-

In Steven Spielberg's 1977 movie, *Close Encounters of the Third Kind*, aliens set up a meeting with humanity at Devil's Tower (shown here) in South Dakota. Some conspiracy theorists felt that the movie was predicting the future.

tive programming were rumors of government agents involved with the filming itself, if only for accuracy.

Certainly if the U.S. government decided it needed to come clean on the UFO subject, it could either hold a huge press conference on the White House lawn and freak people out, causing chaos and upheaval the likes of which have never been seen, and probably be accused of creating the whole thing as some huge conspiracy ... or it could go with the trickle-down effect and slowly tell the truth via other means. It could whack the public over the head with it, or it could slowly acclimate the citizenry through a series of smaller and no doubt less painful taps on the head. UFO disclosure might best be doled out via television shows like *The X-Files*, movies like *Contact* and *CE3K*, and a host of novels and video games that gently nudge the public toward accepting the alien presence. What better way to tell the public something so utterly shocking than via entertainment and a popcorn-perfect blockbuster featuring adorable and friendly little gray aliens?

Then again, perhaps it was just the creative endeavor of a guy who loved the subject matter. This is where predictive programming gets a little tricky. Science fiction novels, films, and television shows touch on subjects long before they become realities, such as artificial intelligence, robotics, aliens, genetic manipulation, computer–brain interfacing, and so on. It is the realm of the imagination to look ahead and predict what might be coming, and writers and creatives of any sort are experts at doing so. Are filmmakers and writers putting certain subject matter out into the public for a larger, more mysterious purpose? Or are they just writing about and creating what they, themselves, are interested in? One can argue either way. There are numerous television shows, books, and movies that talk about pandemics, race riots, political assassinations, military coups, deadly pharmaceuticals, the dangers of microwave radiation, and more. Are they just good fun, or are they part of some government-initiated scheme to acclimate the public to some future event?

Writers pride themselves on trying to predict what is to come and then write about it. But now and then, strings of coincidences seem to point to something far more bizarre.

Sometimes, the programming gets way too specific to be coincidental, or merely the stuff of an active and forward-projecting imagination. The cartoon *The Simpsons* is the king of predictive programming. Tom Murray wrote in the February 3, 2020, edition of *Business Insider* of "18 Times *The Simpsons* Accurately Predicted the Future." The long-running cartoon is the masterpiece of creator Matt Groening, who has been accused of being a time traveler, a psychic, and a government agent! Some of the many predictions the cartoon nailed are:

- The discovery of a three-eyed fish near a power plant, on an episode that aired in 1990. Ten years later, a three-eyed fish was discovered in an Argentinian reservoir near a power plant.
- The advent of the dreaded "autocorrect" feature on the Newton phone in 1994, which mirrored the feature on the much later iPhone.
- The concept of the smart watch in a 1995 episode, 20 years before the Apple Watch was released.
- The mass of the Higgs boson particle in an equation in a 1998 episode, which was later discovered in 2013.

The long-running Fox network cartoon *The Simpsons* has had quite a few comedic bits about things that have come true in terms of everything from politics and culture to scientific discoveries.

- The Ebola outbreak episode in 1997 that predicted the outbreak of 2014.

Add to this the appearance of Lady Gaga flying over the Super Bowl halftime audience and, of course, the election of Donald Trump long before he even announced interest in running. The show writers have claimed they are simply trying to guess what might happen down the road based on observing what is happening in the present. The sheer number of episodes they must write means a certain percentage of what they predict might just nail it on the head. Some events are just coincidental, as in the claim the show predicted the 9/11 terrorist attacks in an episode where the Simpsons go to New York City and buy a city guidebook that says "$9" on the cover next to a picture of the Twin Towers, which look in the image like the number 11.

Imagination? Or an effort to show you glimpses of the shape of things to come? No doubt if the powerful elites and government leaders wanted to convey something they felt was too heavy for a normal press conference, they might just embed it in a story by working with the filmmakers or suggesting content to them and acting as consultants.

The darker side of predictive programming is a favorite among conspiracy theorists who believe the government and powers that be plant clues and hidden references to upcoming false flag operations in popular media to soften up the public and take away some of the shock and sting if the actual event occurs. From terrorist attacks to school shootings to mass murders, there are references throughout pop culture that, in hindsight, can give the impression of exposing something real via hidden or shrouded references. It could also be a way to subconsciously prep the public to accept something they might otherwise reject outright, such as pedophilia, child abuse, rape, sexual assault, and the torture of political prisoners.

This suggests the people involved in the making of the film, television show, or cartoon in question know about the atrocity to come and thus become complicit with its perpetrators. One example is the commonly heard allegation that the movie *The Dark Knight Rises*, which was released in theaters in July 2012 and contained a scene showing a map with "Sandy Hook" marked on it, was predictive programming of the Sandy Hook school shooting. The event took place in December 2012 in Newtown, Connecticut, and took the lives of 26 people, 20 of them children. If indeed the film reference was meant to foretell the shooting, wouldn't any of those involved with the film have confessed or felt some semblance of guilt and removed the scene? Surely it was pure coincidence, given meaning only in hindsight after the shootings occurred. Put the name of any town in a film and you might be able to later reference it to some larger event that took place there. It's a numbers game.

Since humans rarely learn the lessons history tries to teach them, history tends to repeat itself over and over, thus making it pretty easy for someone to predict the future.

BAIT AND SWITCH

Bait and switch is a popular sales and advertising tactic, especially with online "clickbait" that lures you in with the promise of a cheap product that either doesn't exist or is no longer in stock, only to persuade you to buy the more expensive one. In the political arena, a bait and switch occurs when someone offers a promise in return for support but then delivers something less desirable or below expectations in return. A candidate running for Senate might promise favorable legislation to a lobby group representing tech companies or environmental concerns in return for the group's support only to help pass antitech or antienvironmental legislation once elected.

Bait and switch is similar to the "low-ball technique" in sales…. It is manipulative and deceptive because it is premeditated.

Bait and switch is similar to the "low-ball technique" in sales, where the goal is to get somebody to buy something that is either inferior to or more expensive than the object the person intended to buy. It is manipulative and deceptive because it is premeditated. A store advertising an incredible deal on a new 60-inch television set may not even have the set in stock, but it uses the ads to draw in customers. The store can then try to sell the customers a similar television set for a higher price or an alternate one of inferior quality.

In such a scenario, the advertised item is the "bait," and the alternate item is the "switch." Often a store will have a limited supply of the bait product, as on Black Friday or during a huge holiday sale, and they just run out, and in that case the bait and switch is acceptable or at least understandable. But as a regular practice, although it is legal, it's pretty unethical. Even in the world of real estate some agencies entice buyers by listing homes and buildings that are already sold or never were for sale in the first place.

One type of political bait and switch involves "caption bills" that put forth minor changes to an existing law (bait) that are drastically rewritten later, after they are introduced into the legislature (switch). The goal is to get the legislature to pass major laws or law changes without time for community feedback and review that, if they were introduced another way, might be too controversial to receive approval.

FRAMING

One way to shape public perception is to frame a news story or event. Think of a plain photograph of a cow. You can dress it up or down with a frame depending on whether you wanted to draw more attention to it, or less. A fancy, ornate frame would catch the eye much more so than a simple wood or plastic one. You can also use the frame to show just part of the cow, or even just part of the background without showing the cow at all.

Framing takes basic information (true or not) and either surrounds it with exaggeration, embellishment, spin, rumor, innuendo, misinformation, and disinformation, or it removes some of the information to leave only partial truth. It's a manipulative effort to present information in a way that it is acceptable or appealing to a given audience or to sway an audience to perceive a piece of information in a certain way. An example would be a breaking news story about a toxic substance found in an orange juice supply. Health and environmental groups would frame this with warnings about pesticides and toxins and possibly call for sanctions or a boycott of the company behind the product. The company might frame it as a mistake made by another, unrelated party as a way to deflect blame and offer to stop selling the product or refund money to anyone who purchased it. Politicians might frame it as an example of inadequate oversight or a reason for more governmental regulations of orange juice factories.

Everyone has their own angle of the same news story, and everyone wants to put their own style of frame around it. Framing is most often used to dress up a negative news story, but it can also help promote a positive one. It's up to the public to see beyond the frame to the picture of the truth it is distracting from.

Everyone has their own angle of the same news story, and everyone wants to put their own style of frame around it.

Language is an especially powerful form of framing. Words have the ability to influence human emotions and responses to things just as visual images do. Incendiary language is the most potent, as we have seen in the past with racial and gender conflicts, in wartime, and during political elections, where it's par for the course for candidates to frame themselves as the good guys while framing their opponents as the bad guys. It goes hand-in-hand with the "us versus them" mentality that seeks to portray people or circumstances in a way that benefits the framer.

Accreditation, whether false or true, is a form of framing that gives credence to news stories and scientific studies by claiming that the news is coming from experts on the subject matter. By framing a new pharmaceutical or vitamin supplement as a wonder product based on expert research studies, which may or may not exist, a company can encourage people to take the product without hesitation. A piece of information deemed worthy because it came from an "accredited source," even if the source is not named, will be accepted as fact by many people who won't bother to ask who the source is.

Governments, corporations, and anyone who wants to sell us something bank on the general hesitancy of the public to do their own research and find out things for themselves. Many people tend to trust what the leaders of the world tell them, including what they see on the nightly news, not because they necessarily trust the government or the mass media, but because they are too uncertain and overwhelmed as to how to go about finding out the truth on their own.

It's much easier to let someone else tell you the truth, even when it's hiding in plain sight.

CANCEL CULTURE AND HISTORICAL REVISION

"Cancel culture" refers to the withdrawing of public support for a person or organization in protest of some action or statement by that person or group. In mid-2020, protests against racism and police brutality filled the streets of many American cities, and many people called for statues, flags, and other symbols of the Confederacy to be removed from public spaces. Some argued that monuments to the proslavery Confederacy should have no place in modern society, while others lamented the loss of such historical symbols. Some statues of Confederate heroes were defaced by protestors, and others were removed by the cities or counties where they stood. Hollywood responded to concerns about racism and police violence by withdrawing or reframing movies depicting racial stereotypes (HBO Max, for example, added introductory material about racial characterizations and slavery to its showing of the classic *Gone with the Wind*, and Disney added warnings about racial stereotypes to some of its classic animated movies, including *Peter Pan* and *Dumbo*) and canceling long-running television shows like *Cops*, which was said to glorify violence on the part of both police and criminals. Some attributed the changes merely to a fear of offending someone, while others cited respect for more enlightened and inclusive social norms.

Racist and blatantly offensive names of products and sports teams were questioned and even changed. Companies such as Mars, Quaker Oats, and Land O'Lakes changed product names or imagery to reflect compassion and remove any semblances of stereotyped racism. Mars, the makers of Uncle Ben's Rice, had named its product after a rice farmer of that name and since 1946 had used the image of a beloved Chicago chef and

waiter named Frank Brown. In 2020 Mars changed the product name to Ben's Original, dropping the "Uncle" for its potential for racial stereotyping. Similarly, Quaker Oats announced that it would change the imagery and name of its Aunt Jemima products, which were inspired by a minstrel song called "Old Aunt Jemima." The Native American woman pictured on Land O'Lakes butter and other products was named Mia and had been on the products for about 100 years, and in 2020 the company decided to remove the image of the woman and leave just the background showing the lake and trees.

A Confederate monument is removed in Raleigh, North Carolina, in 2020 on order from the state's governor. Public opinion against such statues has, in turn, caused television and movie studios to censor or reframe movies that might be considered pro-Confederacy or proracism.

Sports teams named after Native Americans or Indigenous peoples like the Atlanta Braves, the San Diego State Aztecs, and the Kansas City Chiefs have long been pressured as well to use less offensive names, logos, and chants, and in 2020 the Washington Redskins agreed to change its name. The movement toward less offensive names became prominent but was not new in 2020, as Brian Welk pointed out in an article for the *Wrap* on July 13, 2020, citing Eastern Washington University's name change in 1973 from the Savages to the Eagles, Dartmouth College's abandonment of its Indian mascot in 1974, and Miami University of Ohio's name change in 1997 from the Redskins to the Redhawks, among many others.

Protestors against the Washington Redskins mascot argued that the image and name were offensive to Native Americans.

Some commentators considered such changes to be a form of historical revisionism and feared the possibility of removing valid historical data and evidence from the record just to appease people who wish history hadn't turned out the way it had. Others pointed out that as new facts and knowledge arise, interpretations of history need to be revised, and that changing an offensive name or practice, while it represents a change in the present, doesn't change anything from the past.

Historical negationism or denialism is the denial of an event or situation, such as the moon landing or the Holocaust. Negationism is more extreme than revisionism and often involves a distortion of the public record rather than an honest, fact-based revision of it. It includes mistranslating texts in foreign languages and forging documents. Granted, freedom of speech is important, but when it comes to documenting history, it's more important to ensure accuracy and the removal of bias to present as objective a record as possible of what happened, when, and to whom.

While revisionism is concerned with accuracy, negationism is about using historical events to serve a particular political or social agenda. Sometimes it's hard to tell who is on the side of truth and fact, as conspiracy theorists and truth seekers both claim a special knowledge of the truth and accuse governments, leaders, or certain experts of lying to the public. On some occasions, the traditional historic record gets the full consent of the government, which promotes the record as a form of propaganda, and on others it's the revisionism that receives official support, as in the use of negationism to advance a nation's political agenda or importance in world history or to hide it from blame, guilt, or shame, as with the Holocaust. Elements of revisionism and negationism can make their way not just to media messages but into textbooks.

WHO PUTS THE TEXT IN TEXTBOOKS?

Medical students often learn from books that were paid for by pharmaceutical companies. Does that sound right to you? The students believe they are getting a well-rounded education, when in fact, depending on the books they study, they might be being indoctrinated by Big Pharma and pushed in the direction of prescribing pills rather than seeking other treatments. Somebody pays for the books our kids learn from in school, and often the funding sources are skewed politically. Which means since grade school, kids might be exposed to a version of history that is dependent upon the funding sources of the books they are reading from.

In "Textbooks Are the Education Ground Zero of America's Culture Wars," written by Joseph Williams for the November 29, 2016, *Politico*, Williams looks at some of the challenges to textbook content over the years. A Texas high school desired to teach its students about Latin American culture, only the textbook the school chose, *Mexican American Heritage*, was filled with racism, stereotypes, and incorrect information. The books were shelved and replaced.

In Tennessee, a parents' group fought to have a social studies textbook removed because they felt it had a distinct "pro-Islamic" angle.

In Tennessee, a parents' group fought to have a social studies textbook removed because they felt it had a distinct "pro-Islamic" angle. The Portland, Oregon, school board voted to remove textbooks that questioned climate change. Colorado voters replaced their school board during a fiery debate over whether to teach kids about the uglier sides of history, such as slavery.

Some controversies boiled down to a battle of ideologies between the right and the left. In addition, scholarly examinations into U.S. textbooks found many to be sorely lacking in accuracy, deeply flawed in choices of information presented, and incomplete in reports of the events covered. Students don't have a chance to learn the true course of historical events at school if the books they are reading from are as spun and skewed as the nightly news, whether because of incompetence or intention.

University of Vermont sociologist and historian James W. Loewen authored a book in 1995 titled *Lies My Teacher Told Me* that documents his analysis of a dozen high school textbooks. He found that these books framed history by promoting inaccurate perceptions, racist attitudes, and repeated misinterpretations, coming to the conclusion that the history education of U.S. students was fundamentally broken. He concluded that America's schools bred adults who would go on to conflate empirical fact and opinion, and who would lack the media literacy needed to navigate conflicting information. Welcome to 2020, when mainstream media adds to the fray with its own reinterpretation of historical events, depending of course on the political bent of the network.

In an interview with Alia Wong for the August 2, 2018, issue of the *Atlantic*, Loewen is quoted as saying, "History and social studies, as taught in school, make us less good at thinking critically about our past." He believes history is the worst-taught subject in modern schools, in part because textbooks are outdated but not identified as such to the students. There also seems to be a drop-off point in teaching about the recent past. Most history teaching concerns the distant past, but students need to know what is going on now, in the present, objectively and factually. In the time this book was written, racism was the topic on everyone's lips. Loewen points out that history books teach that slavery and racism went hand in hand, but once the discussion of slavery is finished, the discourse on racism does not continue in those textbooks, and we all know racism did not end along with slavery. One reason for the omission may be because current history is more controversial, so it gets left alone in favor of the past.

Sometimes textbooks are removed from classrooms because they are old and outdated. Other times they get removed because a group of people doesn't agree with something they teach, even if it is true. Sometimes the books get revised because their content is skewed toward one group or another, not based on the historical record presented but on its interpretation.

School books—especially in the subjects of history and social studies—have often been censored or redacted by school boards in America to remove material about such topics as racism and other injustices perpetrated by the establishment.

One thing is clear: parents should read their kids' textbooks to see exactly what is being taught and maybe even find out who funds those textbooks.

An old African proverb states that until the lion learns to write history, the story of the jungle will always be written to glorify the hunter. As an adult, you can choose what to read, but our children are being taught history, science, and social studies from textbooks that may or may not be inaccurate or have a hidden agenda. Either way, they grow up believing history is just the way they read it was and risk spreading that belief to the next generation.

SCIENCE AND MEDICAL PROPAGANDA

Science is never settled, in that there is always more to learn, and sometimes it's purposely tampered with to benefit an organization, research group, or political agenda. The same applies to medicine and health care, where powerful insurance companies and pharmaceutical corporations call the shots. Because so many of the advances in science and medicine come to the public only after clinical studies and publication in prestigious journals, the use of propaganda happens during the process as well as afterward, where money and influence dictate the science and health policies of the government as well as what passes for good science and good medicine in the public square.

Who pays for the scientific studies and medical research papers that determine public policy issues, and who publishes them? Predatory journal publishers made the news in March of 2017 as part of a sting operation. As reported by Ivan Oransky in a blog post for *Scientific American* titled "Science Sting Exposes Corrupt Journal Publishers," the sting involved a group of researchers from the University of Warsaw, Poland, who tried to get a fake scholar a seat on the editorial boards of 350 academic publications. With fake scientific degrees and a fake profile on Academia.edu, the fake scholar was offered acceptance by 48 journals that were labeled "predatory" because they accepted manuscripts without review and printed without editing, and some even required payment to be published.

None of the legitimate journals approached fell for the ruse, which was good news, but the indiscriminate publication and paid-for research of the predatory journals could muddy the waters of true scientific inquiry and results.

The phenomenon of "those who sell the panic, sell the pill" is rife in the medical industry, with pharmaceutical companies paying for research studies or placing articles in magazines without being transparent about their involvement. You would have to do some digging to find out where all the articles in, for example, the weekly health newsletters from major university research centers really come from—that is, who funds them and which industry players are involved. Most people don't bother to ask, instead believing that the scientific and medical communities would never lie, cheat, or use propaganda. What a big mistake. Who can we trust to give us the facts about science and medicine?

 *The vast majority of the public gets its scientific and medical advice in an indirect way from these research studies, and if the journals are corrupt, the information isn't trustworthy.*

Gaia online asked the question in its July 28, 2017, article "6 Corporations Control Most Scientific Publications." The article stated that in the past, money for scientific research came from universities, government grants, and other legitimate sources and were peer reviewed for accuracy and objectivity. But today, only a handful of huge corporations own the journals, and they not only control the flow of information and what gets studied, but they control the results, too.

The article reported on a paradigm shift that occurred when a scientific journal called *Cell*, which originated in 1974 at MIT Press, began placing more importance on showing the implications of its research, which gave bigger, broader discoveries greater value and prestige. The more mundane research was not so exciting and took a back seat, creating a newly competitive playing field where the biggest, glossiest research got the attention. Eventually, the publishers of journals under control of the big six media outlets allowed shoddy research methods and inaccurate results. It became more about quantity than quality. The journals began to charge more for access and increased their profits tremendously.

In addition, the big media corporations are buying up more and more scientific journals and bundling in some lesser journals with the more prestigious ones. They then have control over what research is published in those journals and can charge whatever they want to the scientists and researchers who want their work published. It's a great scam. Yet this is just a small part of a systemic problem in the scientific world, and without antitrust laws to stop the monopolization of information, it's hard to fight. Some countries are enacting policies to fight this extortion by the big publishers and promoting use of the Public Library of Science (PLOS), an online, open-access forum for scientific research and literature to avoid the pay-to-play scheming.

The vast majority of the public gets its scientific and medical advice in an indirect way from these research studies, and if the journals are corrupt, the information isn't trustworthy. Whether a university health newsletter publishes a research study secretly paid for by a drug company that comes out with results in favor of that drug and fails to mention deadly side effects, or a medical facility changes its policies or procedures based on faulty scientific studies, it all comes down to one thing: danger for the consumer.

Conflicts of interest are widespread in science and medicine, with organizations like the CDC owning vaccine patents they then push on the public, or the makers of a certain drug revealed to be on the board of directors of a medical journal. Then there is junk science, which is often passed as real science. In "The Rise of Junk Science" by Alex Gillis for the March 27, 2020, issue of

The chemical company Monsanto was found to be covering up negative research studies about the dangers of its herbicide Roundup. The news spurred a number of public protests.

the *Walrus*, the author writes, "The dark ages may already be here. Increasingly journalists, politicians, and the general public are— sometimes inadvertently, sometimes not—relying on fraudulent and flawed research to guide major decisions." He points to the "scientifically indefensible" studies that, by downplaying the possible causes for concern, contributed to the 2015 drinking water crisis in Flint, Michigan, where some 9,000 children were exposed to lead in their drinking water.

Another example occurred in 2018 when the agrochemical company Monsanto, now owned by Bayer, was caught funding junk studies that discredited legitimate research about its herbicide product Roundup, which can cause cancer. "Fake and flawed studies are so pervasive," Gillis writes, "that the presumed authority of an expert or researcher in a scholarly journal is no longer what it used to be." With more universities focusing on output and funding, and companies preying on academics with money, the traditional knowledge-sharing process is now corrupt. It's a crisis of legitimacy, and the scientists and academics are partly to blame for it.

If we cannot trust the research to always be accurate, and if we cannot trust the researchers and the journal publishers to put forth the highest-quality research, then how on earth can anyone say the science is settled about a given topic, and how can we trust what the scientists, doctors, and medical experts tell us? This is a good question to ask as Johnson & Johnson was ordered in 2020 to pay over $2 billion to ovarian cancer victims who used the company's talc-based baby powder, which the company has removed from the market. The very same company began in 2020 to develop and test a potential vaccine for COVID-19, asking the public to trust its product.

WAG THAT DOG

The best way to get the public to stop focusing on a critical issue, especially one that might be embarrassing or damaging to oneself or one's interests, is to provide them with another thing to focus on. There's an old saying that if something big is happening in the news, look behind it for the story you should really care about. Has a senator been caught with his pants down with an underage girl? Wag that dog and put out a distracting story about a massive drug bust off the coast of New Jersey! Does the massive drug bust off the coast of New Jersey involve the local mayor? Wag the dog and direct the public's attention to a bigger story about a sex scandal. Human beings by their very nature have short attention spans and are always seeking novelty. The public is easily manipulated and distracted from one topic to the next, especially if the next topic is steeped in fear or sensationalism.

The point of wagging the dog is to intentionally divert attention away from a really important thing to a much less important (but perhaps more sensational) thing. The phrase comes from an article written in 1871 about the Democratic National Convention, referencing a play called *Our American Cousin*, which happened to be the play Abraham Lincoln was watching at Ford's Theatre when he was assassinated by John Wilkes Booth. In the play, the lead character is one Lord Dundreary, who is always using confusing catch phrases, which were then known as Dundrearyisms. The line in the article read, "The Baltimore American thinks that for the Cincinnati Convention to control the Democratic Party would be the tail wagging the dog."

The tail is the smaller event that ends up controlling or distracting from the dog, the larger event. It was the title of a 1993 novel by Larry Beinhart and then a 1997 film based on the book, in which the actual plot about a president up for reelection who tries to use a military action to save his failing campaign appeared prescient one year later, in President Bill Clinton's second term. Clinton was facing impeachment for his scandalous affair with Monica Lewinsky when he ordered missile strikes against Afghanistan and Sudan, followed by bombings in Iraq and Yugoslavia. Some said the strikes were meant to distract attention from his impeachment scandal.

President Bill Clinton and then-intern Monica Lewinski are shown in this c. 1996 photo. Clinton was accused of having an illicit affair with Lewinski, and some say he ordered missile strikes on Sudan and Afghanistan in order to distract from the affair that led to impeachment proceedings.

President Donald Trump was accused of wagging the dog during an investigation into possible Russian interference in the 2016 presidential elections by ordering airstrikes against Syria, and again in January of 2020 during impeachment proceedings against him by ordering the assassination of Iran's General Qasem Soleimani. During the 2020 coronavirus pandemic and after the murder of George Floyd by a police officer, which gave rise to protests all over the country, many people accused the government of promoting stories of both the virus and the protests to cover up what they claimed were bigger stories. These "bigger" stories involved everything from billionaire Bill Gates pushing for a global mandatory chipped vaccine that would depopulate the planet, to declassed Foreign Intelligence Service Act (FISA) documents from the Obama administration reportedly exposing illegal spying on the Trump administration; the ushering in of the New World Order courtesy of George Soros, nemesis of the extreme right, and other extreme leftists who were planning on stealing the 2020 elections; and claims that Trump and the Republican Party were also planning on stealing the 2020 elections.

No doubt wagging the dog happens all the time, keeping the public off the scent of a bigger story every time another bone is thrown its way as a diversion.

HEGELIAN DIALECTICS

For those who do question if, and why, the government or elite powers might engage in predictive programming, one possible explanation takes us into Hegelian dialectics, in which the perpetrator, says the government, creates a problem or crisis that is meant to elicit a desired reaction from the public. The government then offers a preplanned solution to save the day and further its agenda. Create a problem—get the reaction—offer a solution. It's controlled manipulation.

"Hegel's dialectics" refers to the dialectical method of argument used by a nineteenth-century German philosopher, Georg Wilhelm Friedrich Hegel. His method "relies on a contradictory process between opposing sides," according to the online *Stanford Encyclopedia of Philosophy*. It is also described as an interpretive method in which the contradiction between a proposition or thesis and its antithesis is resolved at a higher level of truth, or synthesis. Hegel's intention was to reduce reality to a synthetic unity within the system of absolute idealism. The three dialectical stages of development that Hegel proposed are the thesis (giving rise to its action), the antithesis (which contradicts or negates the thesis), and the tension between them that gives rise to a solution.

For example, you have a government with an agenda or problem whose solution requires centralizing power. The "thesis" would be a manufactured or false flag terrorist event. The "antithesis" would be a police state and martial law to quell the public protests. The "synthesis" or solution would be the removal of civil rights and freedoms and a transfer of power from the many to the

The use of false flags by a government in order to create a climate ripe for taking power is an example of how the philosophy of Georg Wilhelm Friedrich Hegel (pictured) has been misappropriated by corrupt politicians.

select few (who started the agenda in the first place).

Hegel may have never imagined his work would be used to justify terrorist attacks or false flag shootings, or envisioned how the governments of the world would manipulate the masses by creating newsworthy events to get a reaction, then offer the perfect solution to fix it all up.

During the 2020 coronavirus pandemic, many conspiracy theorists suggested this was an example of Hegelian dialectics at work. They alleged the government created or unleashed the pandemic to elicit a response of fear and worry so they could then save the day with mandated vaccines that would include a chip for tracking people, among other diabolical actions. Some believe the virus was unleashed on purpose to vaccinate the masses with a deadly toxin to cull the human population.

The anti–police violence protests that followed the pandemic were also said to be Hegelian dialectics. Create an incendiary event such as a white cop killing a Black man—elicit a response of anger, protest, and riots in the streets—crack down on civil rights, and stop the free speech of those with opposing agendas in its tracks.

The terrorist attacks of September 11, 2001, are also believed by many in the so-called truth movement to have been government false flags to create hatred for the countries U.S. politicians needed citizens to fear enough to allow the country to go to war with. If they were, they worked like a charm, with invasions of Afghanistan and Iraq. Interestingly, the one country that funded the attackers, Saudi Arabia, was not invaded or attacked. The terrorist attacks served the purpose of scaring U.S. citizens and enraging them enough to also allow basic rights to be taken away courtesy of the Patriot Act, which many identified as right out of George Orwell's *1984*.

There is a famous quote of unknown origin that says, "Those who sell the panic, sell the pill." When it comes to controlling the masses, what better form of propaganda than for the controllers to provide the solution to the very problem they created, making them look like the good guys?

False Flags, PsyOps, and Conspiracy Theories

*"No matter how paranoid or conspiracy-minded you are,
what the government is actually doing is far worse
than you imagine."*
—*William Blum*

MISDIRECTION CAMPAIGNS

Deception can come from anywhere, including the world of stage magic, where sleight of hand and distraction work to fool an audience into looking toward one place when the real story is happening somewhere else. While attention is drawn to something over here, the magic occurs over there. The magician helps the misdirection by chattering away, telling jokes, using props, or utilizing music and optics to keep the audience's focus exactly where the magician wants it.

The same sort of deception and distraction works off the stage, too. In the 1930s and 1940s, British stage magician Jasper Maskelyne, who came from a family of magicians, joined the Royal

Engineers during World War II and trained at the Camouflage Development and Training Centre at Farnham Castle. He believed his skills on stage could be used to help teach the British military a thing or two about the art of deception and camouflage.

Maskelyne was recruited to work in Cairo, Egypt, creating ways to assist soldiers in escape methods and techniques, and he made devices that could help them, such as little blades hidden in combs and maps embedded on playing cards. Eventually it was determined these ruses were not great successes in wartime, and Maskelyne ended up entertaining the troops with his good old stage magic. His 1949 autobiography *Magic: Top Secret* is said to have embellished his critical role as a master deceiver in wartime, positioning the magician as a myth and legend, and future books about him were varied in their opinions on how instrumental he was.

Still, the idea of using misdirection was a valid one. During World War II, Operation Bodyguard was the code name for a deception program that began in 1943 to mislead the German High Command as to the time and location of the invasion of northwest Europe in 1944. The Allies often used misdirection to keep one step ahead of the enemy forces, and the planning for Operation Fortitude, under the general Operation Bodyguard campaign, involved leading the Germans to believe the invasion would take place much later than it was planned, and that it would happen in a different location. The operation succeeded on all fronts when the landings at Normandy took the Germans by surprise.

These diversionary tactics proved successful in wartime situations and became a part of advertising and news media. The tobacco industry often used misdirection in their public information campaigns in the 1970s and 1980s by using paid experts and celebrities to advocate for social responsibility in smoking ads. This kind of advocating gave the impression it was okay to promote smoking as long as you took responsibility for your own smoking habit, but it totally ignored the many campaigns targeted to youth or the health effects of tobacco products. The industry saw huge profits by directing the attention away from health issues related to smoking and onto smoking as a personal rights campaign.

The U.S. Army used some cleverly deceptive tactics during World War II's Operation Bodyguard. For example, this photo shows a blown-up Sherman tank that was deployed to mislead the Germans on where American forces were deployed before the Normandy invasion.

This same shift was seen in the 1970s with gun ownership and gun control. The National Rifle Association (NRA) had been promoting gun rights as a sportsman's right to own firearms, portraying itself as a sportsmen's association, and showing some understanding and tolerance for those seeking gun control, labeling them misguided but not the enemy. In the 1980s, things changed, and the NRA began politicizing guns and diverting attention away from debate by labeling anyone against gun rights as "unpatriotic" and "un-American," even if all the gun control advocates sought were better background checks.

Misdirection campaigns are used as a method of discrediting whistleblowers and researchers who may be on the verge of exposing government, corporate, or military secrets. A journalist or researcher might be approached by some mysterious individual or sent a package or thumb drive containing alleged top-secret documents, which they then publish through the media, believing them to be authentic. However, the documents could be fake and meant to divert attention from the truth, or the documents could be real and meant to redirect attention on someone or something other than what was originally being investigated.

The documents might look authentic and may indeed contain factual information the journalist can corroborate, but they could still be fabrications and distortions meant to keep eyes off the prize. One area where misdirection seems to be popular is the field of ufology, where UFO researchers are often given "inside information" to release to the public, only to find out they've been set up. This happened to UFO researcher Paul Bennewitz in the early 1980s when he believed he was tracking alien signals on his computer sent from an underground base where aliens were held outside of Albuquerque, New Mexico. He spread his information about the Dulce Base and alleged alien occupants to other researchers and research organizations and eventually caught the attention of the intelligence community's Air Force Office of Special Investigations (AFOSI), which began a complex disinformation campaign to misdirect and discredit Bennewitz.

Another ufologist, William Moore, later admitted to being approached by AFOSI to assist in the misdirection campaign and said that it drove Bennewitz into a state of paranoia and mental

One area where misdirection seems to be popular is the field of ufology, where UFO researchers are often given "inside information" to release to the public, only to find out they've been set up.

distress, landing him in a mental hospital. A former special agent for AFOSI, Richard Doty, also admitted to being a part of the campaign, claiming he was responsible for giving Bennewitz and other UFO researchers false documents and information.

Clearly, giving someone bad directions is a great way to keep them from arriving at the place where they hoped they were heading. When that place is the truth, and the ones giving the bad directions are the government, military, mass media, and advertisers, it becomes a frightening form of propaganda.

PSYOPS

Psychological operations were once thought to be the stuff of spy novels and conspiracy theory documentaries, but psyops are used all the time by the government, military, mass media, and corporations. Anytime there is a need to convey specific and selected information or news to the public with the intention of influencing their emotions, thoughts, and actions, you can be sure there is a psyop going on. PsyOps use manipulative and coercive tactics to reinforce a particular behavior or to diminish an undesirable one. The methods of psyops used in warfare and geopolitical maneuvers are the same as the ones used on the public to coerce them into accepting a certain ideology, movement, situation, circumstance, or mode of behavior in alignment with a goal, usually war or some type of public compliance. The psyops motto of the U.S. Army is "Persuade, Change, Influence." The U.S. Air Force uses "Never Seen, Always Heard."

The mass media might adopt as its psyop motto "We report what we want you to believe." The government and politicians could always use a few good mottos of their own. Any ideas? "Trust no one, and especially not us"?

PsyOps are divided into three categories:

1. Strategic psyops include information activities conducted by the U.S. government usually, but not always, separate from the military.
2. Operational psyops are military operations conducted even during peacetime to promote the effectiveness of a military campaign or strategy.
3. Tactical psyops are campaigns assigned to a tactical commander in a military operation to support the tactical missions against an opposing force.

Pysops, whether in a military sense or used on the public as a form of disinformation or misdirection, can involve combining persuasion with a credible threat, downplaying the enemy's ability, disrupting and confusing decision-making capabilities, undermining command and control, reducing the enemy's will to fight, planting or arranging false flag scenarios to gain complicity or to create anger toward the enemy, or destabilization, among others. Psyops can be anything from a coordinated campaign to invoke protests or riots to divert attention from a bigger story or to make a certain political party look bad, to disrupting an election with a false threat, to using fear tactics to get the public to accept a mandatory medical procedure.

It's all about carefully and strategically disseminating the right message at the right time to create a desired result.

It's all about carefully and strategically disseminating the right message at the right time to create a desired result. These messages are broken up into white, black, and gray. White products are used in overt psyop operations, and gray and black are used covertly. The colors are not indicative of whether the operation is good, bad, or in between, but rather the methods used.

White psyops use a known or trusted source, often an official government source or one strongly associated with the government, and the information used is true and based on fact.

Gray psyops use a source that is ambiguous or impossible to track, and the source is not revealed to the public. The content of the psyop will benefit the position of the government and any of its allies by presenting viewpoints that are acceptable to the intended audience and more palatable than an official U.S. government statement. This works well for those less trusting of the government.

Black psyops are covert and originate with an alleged hostile source. Black psyops conceal the position of the U.S. government, and often the government denies any responsibility or association with the psyop program. All three use various forms of media to get the message out, such as radio, television, leaflets, publications, air drops, and so on.

No matter the method, for a psyop to work it must be grounded in reality. It must, in other words, be something that could easily happen and is not so far-fetched as to draw too many questions once it is executed. A successful psyop also clearly defines the mission to align with national objectives, and it is based on a preanalysis of the potential targets that would be most beneficial to that mission. Such an analysis might include determining the strengths and weaknesses of the targeted audience and how best to undermine their weaknesses in order to shift their attitudes and perceptions in the direction chosen by the psyop. It involves all aspects of informational warfare to demoralize, disempower, and destabilize the intended target by focusing on psychological manipulations that create confusion and fear, disaffection within the ranks, defection or desertion, the destruction of morale and will, and the breaking of the human spirit. In a previous chapter, we looked at propaganda techniques that demoralize the enemy by dropping leaflets into their territory urging them to surrender or by broadcasting radio messages suggesting the enemy is losing a battle they are actually winning.

In more modern times, tactics could include publishing inaccurate political polls showing that one candidate is ahead by a landslide as a way to discourage voters for the opposing candidate from turning out on voting day, or funding and instigating violent acts against a certain part of the populace to destabilize the local government or provoke a desired response.

The branches of the military use psyops regularly, with the army as the most active branch to pursue these tactics. The Pentagon and intelligence agencies employ psyops regularly to

The Pentagon uses psyops all the time to collect and distribute information. Psychological warfare can be just as effective in attacking an enemy as direct military action in some cases.

gather and disseminate information. World governments use them to shore up or destabilize enemy nations or disempower threats. Corporations use them to squash competition and increase their own profit margin and influence. Media outlets use them to spread fake news that benefits their financial interests or political agendas. Politicians use them to harm their opponents and win elections. Cults use them to gain and keep members. A thousand books can be written about the various psyops employed throughout history. But in the world of propaganda, they can be used by governments, corporations, political entities, or social movements, and they are almost always directed at one target group—the public.

We might say that anyone who engages in the use of propaganda is engaging in a psyop. As Sun Tzu wrote in the ancient Chinese classic *The Art of War*, "All warfare is based on deception. Therefore, when capable of attacking, feign incapacity; when active in moving troops, feign inactivity." These fake-out tactics work because they are simple, tried, and true. Remember the Trojan Horse? During an ancient war between Greece and Troy, the Greeks left the gift of a giant wooden horse at the gates of Troy as an offering to the goddess Athena. Then they high-tailed it out of there. The Trojans were delighted and took the wooden horse into their city's gates, thinking it a victory trophy. Out from the horse that night jumped Greek soldiers, who opened up the gates for the rest of their army, thereby taking the city of Troy and putting an end to a 10-year battle. It was classic psyops, and it worked.

Fooling your enemy is pretty easy. Genghis Khan (1162–1227) did it by having his troops each light three torches at night to give the enemy the impression that his army was bigger than it was. He also attached instruments to the tails of the Mongolian army's horses to kick up dust clouds and give the impression of a massive horde to opposing armies. Obviously, modern warfare now has the advantage of a host of high-tech methods and weapons, but the strategies are the same. Deceive by any means necessary.

But how do you deceive millions of people in the twentieth or twenty-first century to do what you want, especially when they have access to the internet and social media? Is it even possible? Welcome to the world of false flags.

FALSE FLAGS AND STAGED EVENTS

False flags and staged events, also referred to as false indication and warning events, combine psyops with physical situations meant to provoke a response, usually fear or rage. A false flag operation is intended to trigger a desired situation while keeping those behind it from the public eye, all the while pointing the finger of responsibility toward a chosen "enemy." The phrase comes from the sixteenth century and signifies a "deliberate misrepresentation of someone's affiliation or motives," according to the *Oxford English Dictionary*. These tactics have been used throughout history to promote a certain political, social, or geopolitical goal, but the term originated in naval warfare where it was common to fly the flag of an enemy or a neutral country to fool the enemy.

The frightening thing about false flags? Often it's the government itself that perpetrates an attack on its own people or territory. The 9/11 terrorist attacks are believed by some conspiracy theorists to have been a false flag both to secure support for the draconian Patriot Act, which whittled away freedoms and civil liberties, and to justify invading Afghanistan and later Iraq. Was the U.S. government complicit in the attacks? Did the government coordinate the attacks? Some continue to ask these questions, even citing a report released in 2020 by a group of engineers stating that World Trade Center Building 7, which was not hit by a plane but caught fire after the attacks, did not fall from fire but from an explosion.

Naturally people wonder if their own government would do such a horrific thing—to kill its own people as a means to an end. The answer, sadly, is that it would, and it wouldn't be the first time. While there is still no proof that 9/11 was a false flag–styled psyop meant to plunge the nation into fear, rage, and submission, that is exactly what resulted. The Patriot Act was renewed in mid-2020 with bipartisan support, amidst a virus and political protests that certain observers believe were false flags to push for more restrictions of freedoms, mandated vaccines, and the defunding of police, among other goals. Most false flag accusations, including the ones just mentioned, get thrown aside as "conspiracy theories," but they have their foundation in history.

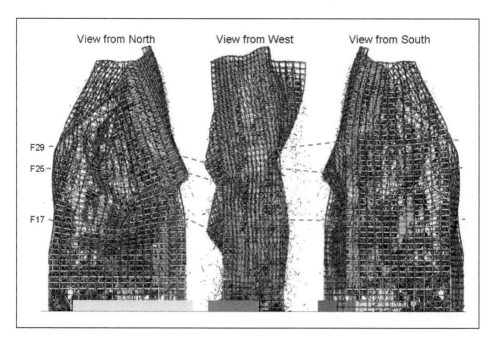

A simulation depicting the collapse of World Trade Center Building 7, which conspiracy theorists say could only have happened if the structure had been demolished by explosives.

The main reason for false flags is to offer a pretext for war or the invasion of another country. War is a costly and scary commitment, and it can be a hard sell to the public. What better way to do it than to create a physical event that terrifies the public into complicity and acceptance? And how better to achieve that goal than by showcasing the horrors of the evil enemy "other"? One of the biggest strategic components of a successful false flag is to make it so big and so shocking that the public will refuse to believe it was an inside job—something their own government would do to them. It worked for Hitler, who wrote in *Mein Kampf* about the "big lie":

> All this was inspired by the principle—which is quite true in itself—that in the big lie there is always a certain force of credibility; because the broad masses of a nation are always more easily corrupted in the deeper strata of their emotional nature than consciously or voluntarily; and thus in the primitive simplicity of their minds they more readily fall victims to the big lie than the small lie, since they themselves often tell small lies in little matters but would be ashamed to resort to large-scale falsehoods.

Thus, the majority of people will not ever consider that a shocking event, especially a global one, could be based on such lies. It couldn't possibly have been planned, staged, or faked. It can't happen here!

Nonetheless, there have been dozens of known false flag events throughout history:

- In 1933 Nazi leader Hermann Goering was accused of setting fire to the German Parliament building and blaming it on the Communists.
- In 1939 Operation Himmler was a plan by Nazi Germany to stage false attacks using innocent people, including concentration camp prisoners, to pin the blame on Polish aggressors.
- In 1954 Israel admitted to planting bombs in several buildings in Egypt, including various U.S. diplomatic facilities, and then blaming it on the Arabs.

Today it is well known that in 1933 the Nazis deliberately set the Reichstag building (the German Parliament) on fire, blaming the arson on the Communists to get the German public on their side.

- In 1954 Operation Washtub occurred, in which the CIA planted phony Soviet Union arms caches in Nicaragua to portray Jacobo Arbenz, then president of Nicaragua, as working with the Soviet Union.
- From the 1950s to the 1970s, according to a U.S. congressional committee, an FBI counterintelligence campaign used provocateurs to cause violence, which was then blamed on political activists.
- In 1999 the KGB blew up apartment buildings in Russia and blamed it on the Chechens to justify an invasion of Chechnya.
- In 2001, during the G8 Summit of Nations, police officials in Genoa, Italy, planted Molotov cocktails and faked the stabbing of a police official to justify a crackdown on protestors.
- In 2001 anthrax attacks on American citizens and politicians were falsely blamed on Iraq to justify the coming invasion and push for a regime change.
- In 2007 violent protestors on the streets of Quebec carrying rocks were discovered to be undercover police officers.

The list goes on and on. Notice that many false flags involve squashing protests and dissent by introducing violent elements that are later blamed on the protesters or on one political party or another, but are in fact plants and "crisis actors" hired to turn a peaceful assembly into a riot. Sound familiar? At the time of the writing of this book, protests against police brutality in the African American communities were large and usually peaceful, but a small and vocal violent element began disrupting the protests with violence, looting, and beating of protestors and police who tried to stop them. Pallets of bricks were found strategically placed throughout the cities where most of the protests were taking place, as if inviting violence. (Most, if not all, however, were determined to be related to ongoing construction projects.) Some protesters in Seattle set up their own community, which became known as the Capitol Hill Autonomous Zone (CHAZ) and lasted through June 2020, consisting of a six-block area of "autonomy and freedom" from police presence. Depending on who was reporting, the community was described as largely peaceful or largely violent. Meanwhile, right-wing white nationalists showed up in some cities to counter the protests with their own violent attacks and actions. The peaceful and effective protests in some places spiraled out of control because of these small but vocal groups, and soon the point of the protests became lost in the destruction. America was divided—a perfect storm for the powers in Washington to manipulate the masses and take control.

One main factor influencing all of this was division. The nation was filled with fear and anxiety, ready to give up its security and police forces altogether instead of demanding reform, and racial divisiveness and anger on the streets and across social and mainstream media were destroying families and friendships. During this incendiary time period, some freedoms and rights were curtailed with, for example, temporary curfews, and people monitored each other's speech by guilting and shaming each other when they expressed themselves. The media was so complicit in promoting the violence with sensationalistic headlines and video coverage that those who noticed and asked questions were called "ridiculous conspiracy theorists." More on that later.

Conspiracy theories claiming the COVID-19 pandemic was a false flag to usher in mandated vaccines or a result of newly constructed 5G cell towers permeated social media in early 2020.

Conspiracy theories claiming the COVID-19 pandemic was a false flag to usher in mandated vaccines or a result of newly constructed 5G cell towers permeated social media in early 2020. People put forth all kinds of theories about the pandemic being a lead-in to total lockdowns, martial law, and the ushering in of the New World Order of one global government and one global currency. As outlandish as these claims might seem, there were 5G towers being erected in cities worldwide; their purpose was to increase cell phone connection speeds, but some people claimed they caused cancer, spread COVID-19, or otherwise endangered people. Others suggested the pandemic was a drill or a trial run to see how people would react and how quickly they would obey various orders, from staying home to wearing a mask. Others believed it was engineered in part by billionaire Bill Gates as part of the ID2020 program, with the goal being to insert a computer chip into everyone via a vaccine to control and track the population.

Many pointed to Event 201, a global pandemic exercise that took place in New York City on October 18, 2019, that simulated a coronavirus pandemic and how it could spread, and even included fun stuffed coronavirus toys handed out to the attendees. The event occurred before the novel coronavirus outbreak occurred in Wuhan, China, and was not meant to predict the pandemic that occurred soon afterward. The 3.5-hour tabletop exercise was sponsored by the Johns Hopkins Center for Health Security in partnership with the World Economic Forum, and the

The Gates Connection to EVERYTHING

Many people have wondered how a tech billionaire like Bill Gates came to exercise so much influence and managed to appear on so many media outlets during the COVID-19 pandemic. Despite having no medical background whatsoever, Gates became extremely prominent in discussions about the crisis and in leading the charge for developing COVID-19 vaccines. A little bit of research uncovers his connections to many of the companies that could benefit from vaccine sales, but why was the media fawning over him so? One word: money.

Billionaire Bill Gates is both a respected and feared figure, with many people concerned about how much power and influence he has in today's media.

A shocking article by Tim Schwab in the *Columbia Journalism Review* dated August 21, 2020, titled "Journalism's Gates Keepers," looked at the disturbing influence Gates wields over a large number of media outlets via gifts and grants from the Bill and Melinda Gates Foundation directed at training journalists and encouraging coverage (almost invariably positive) of his global goals for health and in the food industry. The article exposed Gates funding recipients, including the BBC, NBC, NPR, the *National Journal*, the *Guardian*, Univision, the *Atlantic*, *Washington Monthly*, a *New York Times* charity, and Al Jazeera, among many others.

The Gates Foundation gave financial donations to media outlets totaling over $250 million just from January to June of 2020. Why? Perhaps because as a leading donor to these news outlets, Gates was able to procure favorable reporting and next to no criticism, including journalists looking to him for advice more than any other individual during the pandemic. Again, he has no medical background. "In the same

way the news media has given Gates an outsize voice in the pandemic," wrote Schwab, "the foundation has long used its charitable giving to shape public discourse on everything from global health to education to agriculture—a level of influence that has landed Bill Gates on *Forbes*'s list of the most powerful people in the world." What is more, the Gates Foundation does not disclose all of the money it awards through charitable grants, so it's impossible to know the true extent of the influence Gates has over global everything. According to Schwab, in part quoting Gates, money is spent on "producing sponsored content, and occasionally funding 'non-media nonprofit entities to support efforts such as journalist trainings, media convenings, and attendance at events.'"

Schwab speculates in his article about the ethics of one person, or just a few, having so much power over media outlets. He cites a handful of billionaires who, through their philanthropy and their media ties, wield enormous influence, including Charles Koch, who donates to the Poynter Institute and the Daily Caller News Foundation, among others; Mark Zuckerberg, owner of Facebook and cofounder of the Chan Zuckerberg Initiative; and Jeff Bezos, owner of Amazon and the *Washington Post* and founder of the Bezos Family Foundation. Consolidating such power is asking for trouble and eliminates other voices of truth and information that don't benefit the bottom line or the often-messianic, power-hungry goals of the Big Boys Club. And it is worth keeping in mind that there are tax advantages for such philanthropy. In fact, Gates and his peers constitute what are known as "philanthrocapitalists"—those who donate large amounts of money but end up making more than ever. "He has 'donated' tens of billions of dollars over the years, yet his net worth hasn't dropped—it has doubled, and this is largely because his donations are treated as tax deductible investments," writes Joseph Mercola in his article "Bill Gates Secretly Dictates Global Food Policy, Too."

There is nothing wrong with making a lot of money, but using that to buy influence and literally dictate the rules of society in terms of health care, education, and mass media is dangerous to a free and open society.

Bill and Melinda Gates Foundation, and it resulted in the sponsors' recommendations should such a pandemic really happen—which it did just a few months later. Information about this event is available for viewing on the Center for Health Security's website at www.centerforhealthsecurity.org/event201/.

Coincidence, or conspiracy?

OPERATIONS NORTHWOODS, MONGOOSE, AND BINGO

Although the 9/11 terrorist attacks in the United States remain the biggest and most widely known potential false flag operations, there are three others that stand out, all of which took place on American soil, proving that our government and military leaders should never gain the total trust of their citizens. They sure haven't earned it.

The goal was to blame Cuba as a pretext for invasion and war by making Cuba out to be the enemy and garnering support from both American citizens and nations abroad.

In 1962, a set of proposals under the code name Operation Northwoods was put together by the Joint Chiefs of Staff and presented to President John F. Kennedy. The operation called for false flag terrorist attacks by the Pentagon against the country's own U.S. ships and aircraft, as well as the possible assassination of Cuban refugees. It also suggested terror attacks in American cities. The goal was to blame Cuba as a pretext for invasion and war by making Cuba out to be the enemy and garnering support from both American citizens and nations abroad.

There were sub-proposals that included hijacking planes and bombing buildings followed by planting phony evidence to point the finger at Cuba. (In a similar way, those who believe 9/11 was a false flag suggest that the untouched passports of the bombers had been planted in the rubble to point fingers away from the true perpetrators.)

Some people suggest the Operation Northwoods documents, later declassified and released in 1997, were faked, and the whole thing never happened. The released documents do

Signs of a False Flag

- The event occurs on a large scale.
- There is immediate national news coverage.
- The event inspires intense emotions such as fear, hatred, rage, and anger.
- There are mass casualties.
- There may be drills of a similar type of event going on beforehand.
- There is a political motivation or agenda.
- Initial media reports later conflict with the official story or narrative.
- No dead bodies are ever seen, but IDs such as passports or driver's licenses may be found intact near the scene of the event.
- There are curfews, lockdowns, and martial law or the threat of such.
- Propaganda fills the airwaves and social media.
- Facts don't add up, or they contradict other facts.
- Whistleblowers begin to emerge with a different story or narrative.
- One political party or social movement benefits more than another, as during election cycles.
- War is declared on a country already targeted ahead of time or used as a scapegoat.
- The stock market reacts before the event.
- Certain world leaders or government officials leave the country or go missing beforehand.
- A scapegoat person or group is immediately blamed, or immediately takes credit for the event even when no evidence supports the claims.
- The person or persons blamed end up dead or "commit suicide" to avoid trial and interrogation.
- Anyone questioning the official story is marginalized or labeled a conspiracy theorist.

General Lyman L. Lemnitzer, chair of the Joint Chiefs of Staff and Supreme Allied Commander, Europe, led the charge on Operation Northwoods, a plan to have the CIA and other agencies stage or commit actual acts of terrorism against Americans and blame the attacks on Cuba.

show that they were drafted by the Joint Chiefs of Staff, signed by Chairman Lyman Lemnitzer, and sent on to the secretary of defense, who authorized the proposals. President Kennedy did not sign on, and he removed Lemnitzer from his position.

Similar to Northwoods was Operation Mongoose, which also suggested the use of false flag attacks to gather support for war with Cuba and the Castro regime. Twelve selected proposals were part of a larger 1962 memorandum, "Possible Actions to Provoke, Harass or Disrupt Cuba." Operation Bingo was yet another proposal to use false flag attacks on U.S. facilities in Cuba to blame on the current Cuban government. The goal was to get the necessary support from the military, government, and public for a full-scale war.

For an idea of what the proposed Operation Northwoods false flag suggested, and what President Kennedy refused to implement, here are a few of the U.S.-initiated ideas taken from the declassified documents put forth in Northwoods:

- "A series of well-coordinated incidents will be planned to take place in and around Guantanamo to give genuine appearance of being done by hostile Cuban forces."
- "A 'Remember the *Maine*' incident could be arranged in several forms: ... We could blow up a US ship in Guantanamo Bay and blame Cuba...."
- "We could develop a Communist Cuban terror campaign in the Miami area, in other Florida cities, and even in Washington."
- "The terror campaign could be pointed at refugees seeking haven in the United States. We could sink a boatload of Cubans en route to Florida (real or simulated)."
- "Use of MIG type aircraft by US pilots could provide additional provocation. Harassment of civil air, attacks on surface shipping and destruction of US military drone aircraft by MIG type planes would be useful as complimentary actions."

To read this is like reading a playbook of many events that have occurred since, and it gives one pause as to whether they were false flags that had been approved by the presidents in office at the time.

GULF OF TONKIN

The Gulf of Tonkin incident, also known as the USS *Maddox* incident, was a unique false flag in that it involved two incidents, one real and one false flag, relating to confrontations between an American ship and North Vietnamese ships in the waters of the Gulf of Tonkin. Declassified documents in 2005 showed that the *Maddox* had engaged in two separate incidents two days apart, but that the second one was false.

On August 2, 1964, the first incident occurred when the destroyer USS *Maddox* was performing signals intelligence patrols in the Gulf of Tonkin. Three North Vietnamese P-4 torpedo boats tracked the *Maddox* and were communicating with each other, and their communications were intercepted to reveal they were

The Gulf of Tonkin incident involved the USS *Maddox* off the coast of Vietnam in 1964. False claims were made about the ship being attacked by the Vietnamese, which led to greater U.S. involvement in the war.

planning an attack on the *Maddox*. The *Maddox* fired three warn-ing shots when the torpedo boats got too close. The North Viet-namese boats returned with torpedoes and machine gun fire, and a battle at sea began, resulting in the deaths of four North Viet-namese sailors.

Two days later, on August 4, the second Gulf of Tonkin in-cident resulted in another battle at sea (some claim it might have been triggered by false radar images called "Tonkin Ghost"), but it was later discovered that there were no North Vietnamese ships present. The National Security Agency (NSA) claimed that the event took place, but decades later an internal NSA study re-vealed the second incident never happened. Former U.S. secre-tary of state Robert S. McNamara confirmed this in a 2003 documentary called *Fog of War*. And whistleblower Daniel Ells-berg, who was on duty in the Pentagon on the night of August 4th and fielded messages from the *Maddox*, later leaked the Pentagon Papers, aka the "Report of the Office of the Secretary of Defense Vietnam Task Force," to 17 newspapers. These papers revealed the history of operations regarding the Vietnam War, and most of them were not known to the public, including the truth about the second Gulf of Tonkin incident, which was used to pass the Gulf of Tonkin Resolution and escalate U.S. involvement in the war.

We know the world's leaders engage in false flag opera-tions, as history has proven. We know that the U.S. government is not above faking attacks and bombings to coerce public sup-port for war and regime change. But what might the ultimate false flag attack look like—the one that would cause global chaos, up-heaval, and bring about a united front that could lead to this mys-terious New World Order so many speak of?

How about an alien invasion? Not a real one, but a faked one, using technology that already exists, at least according to many who have researched the government's deep black pro-grams. The goal of a psyops operation such as a false flag is to create the illusion of an enemy threat by conducting an attack on your own people, blaming the enemy of your choice depending on your goals. If your goals are the full domination of world economies and governments, you might want to trigger widespread panic with the appearance of alien ships over major cities, like something out of a science fiction movie. You could play upon people's fears, panic, false nationalism, and survival instincts and create a "boog-eyman" for them to take out their anger and hatred upon.

The bigger the threat, the bigger the panic. Thus, the easier it becomes to lock down nations and allow a small, elite group of people to take over and protect everyone from the evil alien invaders. It's perfect. It's classic. It's been slowly introduced to the public via books and movies and television shows. The public has been set up for just such an event to the point where the vast majority would surely fall in line out of sheer fear for their survival, not questioning a thing. The mainstream media would be in heaven, with enough shock and awe stories to satisfy their "if it bleeds, it leads" thirst, and they would no doubt ignore the many truly important stories going on in the background, including emergency laws being passed to remove basic human rights and negate the Constitution.

But who would care, because the big, bad aliens were going to kill us all! People would get in line to give up their liberties for some security in such a scenario. Those who did speak out would be silenced, banned, blocked, or worse. Thankfully, the persistent tinfoil-hat conspiracy theorists would be the first ones to attempt to poke holes in such an event, with so many moving parts for the key players to control and keep track of, and they would find their own creative ways to spread dissent and evidence they found to prove this was a false flag event. Many would be "suicided" or mysteriously die of natural causes.

Only when those behind the false flag event locked in what they wanted, be it a one-world government, a global currency system, the culling of the population, or control over world leaders, would the event come to an end. The aliens would suddenly depart. We won! It's our new Independence Day! (Cue Will Smith whooping and hollering.) We would all go on to a "new normal," just happy to have survived such an ordeal.

No scenario would make more people submit to their leaders and give up their rights and freedoms than the threat of little green, or gray, men.

OCTOBER SURPRISES

Right before a major November election in the United States, it has become the norm to expect some big, shocking event that serves to shift or manipulate the voting sentiment. An "October surprise" is an event engineered to do just that, especially during presidential election years. The hope of a late October surprise event is to sway the election one way or another, and the closer it can happen to voting day, the better. Of course, it has to happen with enough leeway for mainstream media to play it up, so timing is everything.

This is a photo of 52 of the American hostages at a Wiesbaden, Germany, hospital several days after being released by the Iranians. Some people wondered about the timing of the release, which happened right after Ronald Reagan won the 1980 presidential election over incumbent Jimmy Carter.

The phrase "October surprise" comes from an alleged plot during the 1980 presidential election involving Republican challenger Ronald Reagan and Democratic incumbent Jimmy Carter. At the time, the news was filled with stories of 66 Americans held hostage in Iran since November of 1979. According to a conspiracy theory, prior negotiations for their release had not worked, but lo and behold, the release of the hostages was announced the day of Reagan's inauguration, prompting accusations that he had worked to withhold the release of the hostages until after the election to make Jimmy Carter look bad before the election and himself like the hero after it.

Several important people who were involved stand by their allegations, including Reagan's former White House analyst and Reagan-Bush campaign staffer Barbara Honegger, who wrote a book called *October Surprise* in 1989 documenting what she witnessed and knew. She claimed to have discovered collusion between George H. W. Bush and William Casey to assure Iran would not release the hostages until Carter had been defeated (which gives one pause to ask how they were so sure Carter would be defeated). Another high-profile witness who claimed it happened was Gary Sick, a former naval intelligence officer and National Security Council member. A banker named Ernest Backes claimed to have been involved in the transfer of $7 million from Chase Manhattan Bank and Citibank in January of 1980 to pay for the freeing of the hostages. He provided copies of the transactions to the National French Assembly.

Several congressional inquiries found the allegations false, but one must ask: How many of them were involved themselves in the ruse? Would people withhold bringing home hostages from a hostile nation just to win over the public?

It happened before and many times since:

The election between Hillary Clinton for the Democrats and Donald Trump for the Republicans was filled with October surprises....

- 1972—Twelve days before the election between Republican incumbent Richard Nixon and Democratic challenger George McGovern, in the fourth year of the Vietnam War, National Security Advisor Henry Kissinger appeared before the media to announce, "We believe peace is at hand." Nixon, who had not done much to end the war during his first four years, won the election, but military involvement in Vietnam continued another three years.

- 1992—In June of 1992, Independent Counsel Lawrence E. Walsh was accused by Republicans of timing the indictment of Reagan's defense secretary, Caspar Weinberger, for involvement in the Iran-Contra affair. This was blamed for incumbent Republican George H. W. Bush's loss to Democrat Bill Clinton.

- 2004—In late October, Democratic challenger John Kerry was running against George W. Bush, the Republican incumbent. Several events transpired that are suggested to have influenced Bush's win. The *New York Times* released a story about a cache of looted explosives in an Iraq warehouse. The Kerry campaign blamed the Bush administration, but the Bush administration claimed the *Times* had reported the story wrong, as the cache had been cleared out of the warehouse before the alleged attack. There were claims that Saudi prince Bandar bin Sultan Al Saud, a friend to the Bush family, purposely cut the price of oil to reduce gas prices in America and help Bush grab the win.

- 2008—On October 31, just four days before the election between Democratic candidate Barack Obama and Republican John McCain, the Associated Press broke a story that Obama's aunt had been deported from the United States in 2004 after living here illegally. Obama went on to win anyway, despite that accusation working against him.

- 2016—The election between Hillary Clinton for the Democrats and Donald Trump for the Republicans was filled with October surprises, including the revelation that Trump had openly admitted he could grope women and get away with it because of his celebrity, as well as other allegations of sexual harassment, which led to him apologizing after losing much support from women and from his own party. Clinton, meanwhile, was suffering from the email releases from Wikileaks known as the Podesta Leaks, supposedly linking her to everything from child sex trafficking to corruption within the Clinton Foundation, as well as her six-figure pro-Wall Street speeches and associations with alleged pedophiles.

The biggest of all may have been the October 28 announcement from FBI director James Comey that he would take steps to investigate additional emails found on Clinton's private server, as well as the discovery of emails found by the FBI on somebody else's laptop—that of congressman Anthony Weiner, which was also used by his wife, Huma Abedin, Hillary Clinton's aide, some containing sexually suggestive emails to a minor. Most of the emails have yet to be investigated.

With two candidates facing a plethora of accusations, many voters felt they were choosing between the "lesser of two evils" or were reduced to going along with their preselected party line. It didn't matter if the accusations being leveled were real or not. Facts rarely matter. Once accusations are made, the damage if done, and any clean-up that might occur later is downplayed or ignored.

The public has now come to expect one or more October surprises every two years during the election cycle, with the biggest coming right before the four-year presidential elections. An intelligent, aware person might ask how these politicians continue to get away with it, not to mention those behind other false flags that lead the country into war or allow leaders to take

Hillary Clinton was the target of an investigation by the FBI after she was accused of using a private email account to send official emails.

away basic human rights. They might ask how the public can so easily forget the previous times it happened and become blind to the patterns when they are so obvious. These tactics continue for one reason, and one reason alone.

Because they work.

QUESTION AUTHORITY

If these events prove anything, it is that governments, military leaders, and media outlets lie all the time. When the act of questioning authority, the media's narratives, and inconsistencies becomes something to be ridiculed, we have reached the point of no return. Propaganda has won. It controls us. But how can we not ask questions when so few things add up? For example, after the two tallest World Trade Center towers fell during the 9/11 terrorist attacks in New York City, there were rumors of an explosion in nearby Building 7 and speculation that the building fell from the explosion, not a fire as officially reported. Years later, the National Institute of Standards and Technology (NIST) released its long-awaited report on Building 7 and claimed, "Our take home message today is that the reason for the collapse of World Trade Center 7 is no longer a mystery." Lead investigator Shyam Sunder told the press that "WTC 7 collapsed because of fires fueled by office furnishings. It did not collapse from explosives or from diesel fuel fires."

Yet in May of 2020, another report was released, this time by a group called Architects and Engineers for 9/11 Truth (AE911T) claiming the collapse of Building 7 was a "near-simultaneous failure of every column in the building." The group dismissed the earlier findings of the NIST and asked for a retraction of that report. These engineers and architects stated that from their perspective, the NIST study was fundamentally flawed and that science and engineering knowledge showed the building fell to a controlled demolition.

Could the conspiracy theorists have been right about 9/11? Was it really a false flag attack? Who was telling the truth about how Building 7 fell? Will we, the people, ever know what goes on behind closed doors? And why, when we bring up these inconsistencies, are we told to go put on our tinfoil hats?

CONSPIRACY THEORIES OR CONSPIRACY FACTS?

It all comes down to trust. The loss of trust in authority figures to tell the truth comes from decades, if not centuries, of betrayals. We know they lie. We know they manipulate and act in the shadows of secrecy.

They conspire.

Why, then, do we treat conspiracy theories like the mumblings of madmen and women and the stuff of tinfoil-hat-wearing rabbits down a rabbit hole? Conspiracy theories are both a form of propaganda and a response to it. Most people who believe in conspiracy theories do so because they know that we have not been told the entire truth about events and situations throughout history. There is also a mistaken belief that if you buy into one conspiracy theory, you will buy into them all. This is far from the truth. It's possible to question the official story on 9/11, for example, but reject the notion that the earth is flat.

Conspiracy theories are both a form of propaganda and a response to it.

When you challenge an official story, narrative, or explanation, whether on a personal level or as a citizen concerned about an event in the news, you are engaging in critical thinking and inquiry. But too often, you are labeled a tinfoil-hat-wearing nutjob for doing so and told to stay in your corner. You're called paranoid, crazy, disillusioned, mentally incompetent, and lacking in intelligence. Yet to you, the questioner, you are anything but, and it's those who do not question what they see and are told who lack intelligence and insight.

By focusing on a person's competence and intelligence, it's all too easy to dismiss their questions as baseless when they might be valid. The labels we give to those who believe in conspiracies cut off any debate or discourse that might point us to a new truth or a whole new set of facts we had not considered before. Conspiracy theorists, like the theories they study and research, come in all sizes and shapes, and they range from mild to moderate to extreme. The pejorative labels might better fit the extremists who see everything that happens as a grand conspiracy and deny any attempts to view something as not a conspiracy. This contrasts with the more moderate believers, who suggest that some things do happen in the shadows of secrecy, and the public does not always have a need-to-know golden ticket.

The Watergate scandal was a conspiracy before it broke out into the light of public and media perusal. Military operations are conspiracies because they are covert and must be guessed at, not occurring in the light of day for all to see. Most of what government leaders do behind closed doors won't be made public and can therefore be called conspiracies. Until something that is being conspired between people out of the view of others is made public, it is, by definition, a conspiracy. This applies even to mundane events, such as a married person cheating with a neighbor unbeknownst to their respective spouses.

Conspiracy theories arise when the official narrative is flawed, inconsistent, or full of holes that those who are inclined to be observant can see while the rest are distracted and their attention diverted. Noticing that there are two possible explanations for something, seeing photos that don't jibe with official descriptions, witnessing an event differently from how it is portrayed on the nightly news—these glitches in the Matrix grab the attention of the observant, the paranoid, the untrusting, and the wary who have been betrayed by powerful authority figures before.

One of the key questions that conspiracy theorists ask when looking at an event is: Who benefits from keeping this secret? Pursuing the answer can lead to the discovery of new facts and information that redefine the official story, as with a presidential assassination as witnesses come forward and evidence is revealed. By their nature, conspiracy theorists tend to be knowledgeable about propaganda, brainwashing techniques, mind control, media manipulation, false flags, and psyops already, and they may be more adept at spotting these things than the average person.

Some who are attracted to and even obsessed by conspiracy theories are often as much in denial about reality as they claim realists are in denial about the presence of a conspiracy.

Or they may just see things that aren't there. Perception is everything. Some who are attracted to and even obsessed by conspiracy theories are often as much in denial about reality as they claim realists are in denial about the presence of a conspiracy. They might also dismiss out of hand any evidence that counters their beliefs or exhibit confirmation bias toward the conspiracy they have invested in (or away from any proof that their chosen narrative might be wrong). Sometimes, they want to be the ones to uncover a deep truth or show a surprise twist in a story everyone thought they knew about. Being a conspiracy theorist means being in a club where you are supported and accepted for thinking outside the box—sometimes way outside.

There are those who claim conspiracy theorists are dangerous because they spread misinformation and disinformation for a particular agenda. That's ironic because the reason a person believes in a conspiracy is because they feel they've witnessed the use of misinformation or disinformation and propaganda for a particular agenda. We know those things happen and that propaganda is everywhere. And if propaganda is manipulating us to look over here, not there, and to believe this, not that, why would we dismiss those who cry "conspiracy" just as we might cry "foul" when someone does something nasty to us? Perhaps we just need to hold both sides of the coin accountable to greater levels of proof and evidence. Extraordinary claims require an awful lot of proof to back them up, but that should go for both sides of the narrative, and just as a person shouldn't believe everything they hear without question, they also shouldn't discount everything they hear.

Balance and discernment may be the conspiracy theorist's two best weapons. They would serve everyone else well, too.

Not too surprisingly, those who attack conspiracy theories are often those with the most to lose if people get too close to a potential truth. Conspiracy theorists are not always completely paranoid. They just may be more observant. According to a study in 2018 published in the *European Journal of Social Psychology*, psychologists from the University of Mainz in Germany looked at conspiracy theorists and paranoia and found that, "while paranoid people believe that almost everybody is out to get them, conspiracists believe that a few powerful people are out to get everybody." As true as this may be, the problem is going to the extreme of believing everything is a conspiracy by an elite group of sinister individuals. The psychologists also pointed to a negative portrayal of conspiracists, often thought to be crazy by those who encounter them, and indicated that conspiracy beliefs are generally associated with a decreased trust of government and that belief in conspiracies is more of a political attitude than a symptom of a psychopathological one.

Often, "big tent" thinking makes it hard for many people to take conspiracy theories and those who believe in them seriously. The big tent refers to a tolerance, within a particular party or group, for diverse ideas and theories over the quality of reason and evidence behind them. A big tent that includes all kinds of conspiracy theories, running the gamut from UFOs to chemtrails to who shot JFK, might be one categorized as the truth movement. The truth movement and others like it embrace a broad spectrum of theories and ideas in the singular quest to find truth. Big tent thinking may find links and connections between various conspiracies that may or may not be real, such as UFOs and Bigfoot, or racial protests and the fascist left, or mandatory vaccines and federal emergency detention centers. Conspiracy theorists put together the pieces of a giant jigsaw puzzle that they make fit even if the pieces have to be adjusted.

"Big tent" thinking combines a variety of concepts and theories involving conspiracies or the paranormal. For example, some people believe in connections between UFO aliens and Bigfoot.

Big tent thinking also tends to divide believers and skeptics into two groups, leaving little wiggle room for someone who is a bit of both. It also plays into the idea of the echo chamber or "preaching to the choir," referring to surrounding oneself with like-minded, agreeable individuals. Inside the echo chamber, you basically hear your own opinions bounce back to you via those who think just like you do. Don't believe in alien bases beneath New Mexico? You're out! Wrong tent, pal. Don't think 9/11 was a false flag planned by George W. Bush and company? Hey, you belong in tent number 3.

Everyone loves a good conspiracy, and often where there is smoke, either there was a fire, there is an ongoing fire, or there is about to be a fire. According to "5 Theories about Conspiracy Theories" by Max Read for the February 6, 2020, *Intelligencer*:

1. Conspiracy theories are a long-established method of organizing and understanding the modern world.
2. Conspiracy theories are a way for people to exert control over or within unstable, complex systems.
3. Conspiracy theories are a symptom of a crisis of legitimacy among representative institutions.
4. Conspiracy theories are a function of information overload.
5. The world is rife with conspiracy.

In the article "The Value of Conspiracy Theory," author Ed White writes, "If we define conspiracies more loosely, as programs of strategic action fashioned at a remove from public notice and

Even in mainstream media and on talking-head news shows, we hear extremist opinions and watch people go to extremes to defend their position....

either not acknowledged publicly or acknowledged only under coercion (or by defection); ... then it becomes impossible to dismiss the ubiquity and significance of conspiracies." Max Read writes that if you are a good student of history and politics, you probably are a conspiracy theorist yourself. It's hard not to be when the government, the media, and the authority figures we look up to betray our trust time and time again.

Even in mainstream media and on talking-head news shows, we hear extremist opinions and watch people go to extremes to defend their position and deny any evidence or data that counters it. Yet if one of those talking heads dares cross the invisible political identity barrier to ask a question about some inconsistency or evidence of hypocrisy, they are slammed with the "conspiracy theory" label. Perhaps we should be careful not to censor them too much, lest we become brainwashed puppets of the puppet masters who do not want us to question anything, no matter how blatant or obvious.

There are reasons why people are drawn to conspiracy theories. David Ludden writes in "Why Do People Believe in Conspiracy Theories?" for the January 2016 issue of *Psychology Today* that people desire to understand the world and find some certainty in it. They also seek order out of chaos and disorder, seek a positive self-image, and want a sense of control and security. Believing in something like a conspiracy theory gives a sense of control and order, along with a sense of importance and acceptance with others of like mind. Conspiracy theorists ultimately seek to understand the world they live in and to be in some way socially relevant.

The validation that comes with studying and researching a theory and possessing knowledge of it above and beyond others gives a strong sense of accomplishment or a feeling of mattering in the world. If your chosen conspiracy theory is proven real, it can be a huge boost to your self-esteem, especially if, after years of being dismissed, you finally get to utter those magical words, "I told you so."

Our Favorite Conspiracies

There are hundreds of conspiracy theories to choose from, but some stand out as fixed parts of our past and present, and many stand out because they remain unsolved crimes or mysteries that have yet to be proven true one way or another. Here are some perennial favorites.

- Aliens on Earth and UFOs are real
- The JFK assassination
- Sirhan Sirhan was under MKUltra mind control
- 9/11—Inside job or not?
- The Illuminati and the coming New World Order
- The Deep State is in power
- Jesus married Mary Magdalene and had children
- Secret societies run the world
- Reptilians are running our highest political offices
- AIDS was man-made
- COVID-19 was man-made in the Wuhan, China, lab
- Bill Gates and George Soros are eugenicists
- The moon landings were faked
- The Holocaust never happened
- All school shootings are false flags
- FEMA has death camps for vaccine deniers
- Chemtrails are poisoning us
- Fluoride is poisoning us
- Hollywood is full of pedophiles
- Bigfoot roams the woodlands
- The Clinton Death Count
- JFK Jr. is still alive
- George Floyd is still alive
- Russiagate
- Barack Obama was born in Kenya
- Donald Trump is a time traveler

Mind Games: Manipulating Thought, Behavior, and Action

"This is the secret of propaganda. To totally saturate the person, whom the propaganda wants to lay hold of, with the ideas of the propaganda, without him even noticing that he is being saturated."
—*Paul Watzlawick*

The human mind is the most powerful weapon on earth. It has the ability to create and to destroy. Manipulating the human mind is behind all propaganda. Anyone can coerce, convince, or control another mind if they know the tools and techniques and if they know the weak spots to attack—the Achilles' heel.

It works in politics, religion, media, advertising, and our personal lives. Knowing the tools and techniques doesn't mean you won't fall prey to them from time to time, but it helps to see the methods being used to usurp control of your mind. Once you see it, you cannot "unsee" it, and the knowledge gives you tremendous power to begin deflecting these attempts to make you a puppet to someone else's agendas and motives.

It begins within.

IDENTITY AND IDEOLOGY

Identity is how we see ourselves and how we imagine others see us. It is what we think makes us individual. It is the collection of ideals, beliefs, and programming we carry into the world that represents who we are. We may identify ourselves with politics, religion, gender, race, worldview, or mentality as a way to describe ourselves to others. "I identify as ..." or "I am a ..." and you fill in the blanks accordingly. We associate identity with our personality and mistakenly believe this is what gives us worth.

Identities may define us, but they are not us. They are descriptions and categorizations, and they can help us identify those we align with and those we consider our enemies. We find friends and lovers who match our identities, or come close, and we do our best to avoid those who contradict the way we see ourselves and the world around us. Identity, like personality, is nothing more than an adopted set of beliefs we have about ourselves, many of which were imposed upon us by society, parents, peers, and the education system. We carry this into adulthood, rarely questioning it. "I've always been this way," we say to ourselves and others, without stopping to question not only why it is so but whether those beliefs serve us in the present, even though they worked for us in the past.

Identity, like personality, is nothing more than an adopted set of beliefs we have about ourselves, many of which were imposed upon us by society, parents, peers, and the education system.

When it comes to propaganda, the way we identify ourselves opens us up to untold methods of manipulation, coercion, and control. Identity politics is at the heart of division in modern society as we end up warring with those who identify differently, rather than focus our attention and our fight against the elite powers manipulating the various sides. There's an old saying that the left wing and the right wing are part of the same bird, yet in today's political arena and the mass media, the two sides seem like different animals altogether.

Right/conservative versus left/liberal is a powerful divisionary tactic that is easy to fall into, even for some who belong to a third political party or have no party preference. Propagandists play to our desire to take sides and to attack the other side as the "evil" one, even as we become blind, deaf, and dumb to the sins of our own side. Differences in worldviews that make us liberal, conservative, or anything in between are ignored in favor of stoking the fires of hatred and intolerance. The need to be right and the desire to show one's own side as more virtuous and righteous than the other has led to violence, wars, death, and destruction, with no end in sight.

Propagandists play to our desire to take sides and to attack the other side as the "evil" one, even as we become blind, deaf, and dumb to the sins of our own side.

DIVIDE AND CONQUER

Our fixed identities are at the heart of the "us vs. them" mentality that divides us. Instead of celebrating differences while understanding our common humanity, we too often allow our political and religious beliefs, bolstered by media manipulation, to force us to take sides. This way, we are so busy fighting each other that we can easily allow those with a larger agenda to control us. "Divide and conquer" works so well that propagandists use the tactic over and over again, especially during election cycles or to increase support for a war abroad. Think how many ways there are to divide a population:

- Republican vs. Democrat
- Liberal vs. Conservative
- Fox vs. CNN
- Free speech vs. Censorship
- Red vs. Blue
- Religious vs. Atheist
- War vs. Peace
- Sheep vs. Woke
- Conformist vs. Nonconformist
- Black vs. White
- Male vs. Female
- Traditional vs. Modern
- Old vs. New
- Millennial vs. Boomer
- Pro vs. Con

That we are so easily divided against our fellow humans means that we can be manipulated easily when someone plays upon those divisions, especially when they can dredge up our deepest fears and insecurities toward the opposing party or belief system. Putting ourselves and others into neat little boxes may help us create order out of chaos in our world, but does it really serve humanity? Polarization occurs when we are pushed into seeing only two sides to every story (and picking which one is right for us), when there might be three—our side, their side, and the truth. Once polarization occurs, we are hard pressed to stay in our chosen corners, and rarely do we switch sides or agree to meet in the middle.

Both conservatives and liberals believe that their side is the side of love, and the other side is the side of hate. But how can they both be right? That kind of polarization leads to ongoing gridlock in which ideology overshadows any possibility of learning from one another or finding common ground.

Our egos protect our identities and hold on for dear life, even when doing so prevents us from seeing what is really going on around us. Propaganda is best served with a heaping helping of division and a side of self-righteousness. And the politicians that we elect and the mass media who give us our news and information sit back and watch us turn on each other as they go about their business of deceiving us all.

In a country that claims to promote harmony, equality, and unity, if an alien were to drop down in a UFO and take a look around the United States, it would no doubt see a whole different story playing out. We find every possible reason to divide ourselves into categories and then stay there come hell or high water.

Human beings easily form "us vs. them" mentalities, then quickly make judgments about people who don't live their lives or make choices that align with their own personal identities.

What better way to control people than by feeding them with news and information that backs up their beliefs and shores up their identities, while portraying the opposing people as monsters, terrorists, and enemies to be vanquished? Here's an experiment. Get on social media and claim to be a Trump supporter, or a Hillary supporter, or a Bernie supporter, and watch your comments burst into flames with supportive comments, shaming, outright hatred, and possibly a few death threats. Say you are a feminist, or a supporter of male rights, and lose friends by the dozen. Make a stand as provaccine or antivaccine and run for cover from the flying verbal bullets.

Why are we so threatened by other people's identities, perspectives, perceptions, beliefs, or ideals? Maybe it's because we sense the fragile and insecure nature of our own.

You've heard of "playing the race card" or "playing the gender card." Now it's all about playing the identity card. Propaganda pushes an agenda geared toward one ideology over another that promotes one description of identity as superior to another, and that pushes an acceptance of one identity and ideology across the board even when half the country disagrees with it.

The mental gymnastics they employ are stunning.

IDEOLOGY

We are what we believe. Ideology is a set of beliefs or opinions held by a group or an individual. Because we are political creatures by nature, political ideology is a huge part of the belief system we choose to latch onto. There are four basic ideologies in American politics: liberalism, libertarianism, populism, and conservatism, but we might also include economic categorizations such as capitalism, Marxism, socialism, and communism. When we take on one or more of those identifiers, we become so attached to them that we are defined by them, which makes it very difficult to move outside of them should we be presented with information to the contrary of our chosen ideology.

If we identify as liberal, we tend to always support liberal causes, vote liberal, and act liberal. In doing so, we often turn blind, deaf, and dumb to anything that suggests something negative about liberalism or liberals. We are all in. That goes for identifying as a conservative, too. Or a socialist. Because our life experiences have led to the opinions, beliefs, and worldviews that cause us to align with a particular ideology, we believe it to be the only one that is right. How can anyone think differently? How can they not see that we are right and they are wrong?

The problem is, each person has their own life experiences that lead them to embrace a particular ideology and identity, political or otherwise. And to them, their worldview is right. To them, their life experiences aren't bad or evil, they just are, and why should they be judged wrong for believing what they believe?

This applies to groups in society, too. The inability of humans to accept that their singular life experience is not the only one is at the heart of racism, gender bias, violence, terrorism, inequality, and injustice—not to mention a whole lot of family division, with liberals at one table and conservatives at another.

Politics and mainstream media play upon our inherent need to be proven right and come out ahead by amplifying and antagonizing political identity. Liberal news media will do all it can to trigger hatred and division toward the right. Conservative media will do the same toward the left. Same for our politicians who run their campaigns on division and intolerance of other people's experiences and ideals, instead of trying to find some common ground and a respectful tolerance of those differences.

There will never be an end to racism, sexism, homophobia, injustice, and inequality when we are pushed to keep the walls of division strong between us. Only when we rise above the manipulations of mass media and the puppet masters who want to keep

A group of Trump supporters mock the news channel CNN for its left-leaning spin on the news. National news channels tend to favor one side or the other of the political spectrum to cater to certain audiences and gain ratings.

us hating on each other will we realize that every single person's life experiences lead that person to a set of beliefs and opinions by which they identify themselves in life and in society. And no one is wrong or right.

In *How Propaganda Works*, author Jason Stanley writes that ideology is often resistant to adjustment. "The distinctive and controversial property of ideological belief is its resistance to rational revision. Skeptics about the theory of ideology tend to hold that those motivated to theorize about belief-like mental states that are rationally resistant to revision just have a hard time accepting that beliefs they reject have large independent plausibility." He goes on to say that beliefs that are connected to one's identity, which one shares with others, are the hardest to revise and must be undertaken one by one, because it is "hard simply to abandon one's identity." Aha! So we will do anything we can to avoid abandoning our chosen and fixed identity and all it entails unless we absolutely have to, and then we will only do it one idea or belief at a time. Because it is just too painful to admit you were wrong about yourself, and just too difficult to admit you belong to a group that no longer aligns with your inner beliefs and opinions. Most people would rather die than change or revise their vision of who they are and how they fit into the world.

Most people would rather die than change or revise their vision of who they are and how they fit into the world.

So why is it so hard to see this? And why is it even harder for people to see beyond the confines of their staunchly defended identities and ideologies to the possible truths that lay outside the walls of division? Why won't the liberal sit down with the conservative and talk about life and how they each arrived at their belief system? Can you imagine what we might learn about each other? Why are we so against acknowledging anything that goes against our identity, our ideologies, even when we are presented with knowledge backed up by fact? Why are we not encouraged to think outside the boxes we have given to ourselves and to others? When our opinions are challenged, we feel like it's a personal attack and go into fight or flight mode, which means we are reacting from a place of fear and distrust of the other.

It's almost as though the powerful elite don't want us to ever do such a thing.

DENIAL

The mind is a terrible thing to challenge. We are so easily manipulated when we are not forced to challenge any preconceived notions about who we are and how the world works. It's easy to make us go along to get along, just by playing to our beliefs and biases. We experience friction when those beliefs and biases are challenged, often slamming up against the wall of abject denial. We refuse to look at facts and evidence to the contrary of what we've already buckled down to accept as reality, usually dependent upon our political, religious, and cultural leanings. If a new narrative doesn't fit our chosen one, we find many creative ways to reject it even if it is truer and more accurate than what we are choosing to believe.

Try to tell a Democrat their political candidate or leader is flawed, and they will probably reject your accusation without bothering to check for themselves. Try to tell a Republican their political candidate or leader is flawed, and—well, you get the picture. Propaganda slanted toward what we already believe will always work and knowing this allows those who use propaganda to manipulate us fairly easily. They may pander to us, pretend to agree with us, or shore up our existing beliefs to fool us into thinking they are the good guys, on our side, even as they are using and abusing us. They also manipulate our views about the bad guys to the point where we will then deny the bad guys are capable of any good and refuse to acknowledge evidence that shows the bad guys and the good guys might be working for the same goals.

Denial is powerful. It blocks us off completely to another perspective, not to mention to facts and evidence to the contrary of what we believe. Instead of having the courage and self-confidence to open our eyes to the other side of the coin, we deny that the coin even has two sides to begin with. There is only *our* side.

We see this every day in politics and social issues. "The liberals are evil." "The conservatives are evil." Is that true? No, both statements are categorically false. There may be some evil members of both parties, but it doesn't follow that they are all evil. Projecting all blame for the evils of the world onto the side opposite the one you belong to is not operating from facts and truth. It's operating from inherent biases and beliefs that are the accumulation of your life experiences and how you've chosen to perceive them. "Hollywood is all a bunch of pedophiles." "Rich people are all selfish." "Poor people don't work hard enough." These are not absolute truths. They may have some truth to them, but they are not the complete truth. Yet people level these kinds of accusations as if they were gospel. We deny anything that might change our minds. Sometimes, however—slowly, hopefully—we might begin to wonder, ask questions, look deeper into things. Maybe if we are brave enough, we look at what the other side is saying and do some research, with open minds and hearts. It is possible.

Denial is the most difficult to escape when we are presented with information that challenges and potentially shatters our most entrenched ideals. Such a catastrophic and fundamental shake-up of our foundation, our core, with new information might cause us to change our minds, and worse, admit we were wrong. About some

Once people have made up their minds about their worldview and self-identity, it is extremely hard to change their views, and even presenting them with indisputable facts will rarely sway them.

things, we would rather be dead than wrong. When presented with such potentially identity-altering material, we shut down or deny it. Sometimes we don't quite know how to process it.

Imagine supporting a political movement or candidate only to find out that movement or candidate is corrupt. Most people would rather not know the sins of their own party and instead point the finger at the other guy as full of sin. The blame game works best when you are not the one being blamed. Rare is the soul who can stop and demand to know the corruption of their own political party before judging the other. Rare is the soul who can engage in meaningful and respectful conversation and dialog with those who are on the other side of the fence to see what good might be growing there. Denial prevents that. So does cognitive dissonance.

COGNITIVE DISSONANCE

According to *Simply Psychology*, "Cognitive dissonance refers to a situation involving conflicting attitudes, beliefs, or behaviors. This produces a feeling of mental discomfort leading to an alteration in one of the attitudes, beliefs, or behaviors to reduce the discomfort and restore balance."

A common example is a smoker who continues to smoke even when they know it might kill them. The term comes from the research of Leon Festinger, who observed participants in a study who were members of a cult. The cult believed that Earth was going to be destroyed by a flood, and researchers looked at how the members responded when the prediction did not come true. The committed ones had given up their homes and jobs. When the flood didn't happen, they were far more likely to reinterpret the evidence to show they were still right than to admit they had made a mistake. In the study, they came up with excuses such as "the Earth was saved because of the faith of cult members." Instead of admitting they'd screwed up and bought into something that proved untrue or baseless, they found a way to make it true to avoid experiencing the resulting anguish and discomfort.

Beliefs or values that are not consistent with the behavior being forced can lead to cognitive dissonance.

In his studies, Festinger proposed the cognitive dissonance theory, which posited that people have a powerful inner drive to hold their attitudes and behaviors in harmony and to avoid disharmony or dissonance. We seek cognitive consistency. He also found that there are three things that create the most cognitive dissonance:

- Forced or compliant behavior—in particular, being forced to do something we know is wrong. The dissonance is between cognition ("I know this is wrong") and behavior ("I did it anyway"). Beliefs or values that are not consistent with the behavior being forced can lead to cognitive dissonance. An example would be: "I know this drug will harm me, but my doctor demands I take it, so I take it."

- Decision making—in particular, having to choose between alternate choices that have good and bad aspects, such that when you choose one you cut off all other alternatives, and you may choose wrongly. Making the choice creates such dissonance around the possibility of making the wrong choice that you increase the positive associations with the choice you make, and decrease the positive associations with the choices you leave behind.

- Effort—We hit high levels of dissonance when we put a lot of effort into something that ends up being a total bust, be it a product, spouse, or job. We then must get rid of the pain of dissonance by reframing how we feel either about the amount of effort we put into the cause, or about what we ended up with (even despite evidence to the contrary).

When there is any inconsistency between someone's attitude and their behavior, this creates dissonance. Either the attitude or the behavior must change to eliminate the feelings associated with dissonance. The person could stay in total denial or completely reframe the situation, as long as they are willing to continue to live with the discomfort of things not quite lining up.

The achievement of a goal can also cause dissonance. If we expend a lot of effort to get something only to find out it isn't what we really wanted, we are more likely to convince ourselves that we either didn't put out too much effort or that the result wasn't so bad after all. We persuade ourselves to find a way to live with the result that doesn't cause us pain, and we resort to mental gymnastics to do so.

This is why propaganda is often aimed at creating a sense of cognitive dissonance in a person, group, or population. An example would be a politician who was apparently pure and saintly committing a horrible crime against a child. Many of that politician's followers would be in a state of cognitive dissonance, trying to put together the pieces of two alternating viewpoints: this is the politician I thought was a saint, and this politician is a criminal. It becomes much easier to deny or reframe the politician's behavior than to face the dissonance and admit that we had misjudged the person's character or were duped.

To reduce our emotional and mental discomfort, we will excuse our politicians, our political parties, our countries, our media, our corporations, our medical system, and so on of any crimes and injustices. We reframe what they've done. We look only for positive scraps and ignore the heap of negative scraps. We decide the effort to support this person, cause, or party was worth it no matter what the information we are presented with tells us. We find a way to make our minds okay with what we have chosen, even if we chose something that results in some very negative consequences for ourselves and others. If we are really brave, we realize we screwed up big-time and try to course correct by changing our actions, behaviors, or thought patterns.

The propagandists know this, and this is how they continue to get away with what they do.

A woman holds a sign complaining about the dangers of climate change deniers. While 97% of scientists agree that climate change is real and human-caused, deniers will assert that it is a plot to force people to change their behavior and threaten their liberties.

The bottom line is, cognitive dissonance will occur when our behaviors go against our core values and beliefs. It can produce a division within us that is so painful and disabling that we will justify our behaviors rather than face the mistake. But when our outer actions and inner beliefs don't align, we live our lives out of balance. We lose our integrity.

And all to hang onto being right.

CONFIRMATION BIAS AND CHERRY-PICKING

When we only seek or acknowledge information that confirms our existing beliefs, we experience confirmation bias. It's a type of cognitive bias that influences both how we find information in the first place and how we interpret it. When we exercise cognitive bias, we seek out only those facts that align with our beliefs while ignoring objective facts that don't. We interpret information only one way, ignoring that there might be other ways to interpret the same information. We remember only things that align with our beliefs, and we dismiss anything that challenges us on all these fronts.

Media outlets are filled with confirmation bias, depending on whether they lean left or right. News is cherry-picked to line up directly behind the bias, and expressed opinions confirm it. Now and then an opposing point of view might be permitted, perhaps to present some semblance of balance, but in a biased outlet this is tokenism, and most of the time a media outlet panders to one political ideology over another.

Viewers flock to the media that confirms their biases because it reinforces their need to be right and justified in their beliefs. Rarely will someone cross over to the other side and watch a news outlet with an opposing bias. Viewers beholden to one ideology over another will even avoid nonpartisan, objective media because it will still challenge half of their entrenched ideals by possibly presenting facts to the contrary, resulting in cognitive dissonance.

In the article "How Confirmation Bias Works" at the website *Verywell Mind*, writer Kendra Cherry outlines the following example.

Sally supports gun control and seeks only those news stories and opinion pieces that support gun control. When presented with a news report related to guns in the media, she spins her interpretation of it in favor of gun control, even if a story suggests owning a gun saved someone's life.

Henry is against gun control and seeks only news and opinions that are against gun control. He will always interpret news in favor of his own viewpoint against gun control, even if a story suggests a lack of gun control led to a mass shooting.

We are talking here about the same subject—guns—but two different ideologies, two different personal beliefs, and two different biases. We want to reinforce what we believe because it makes us feel right, just, and intelligent. Sadly, when challenged to look objectively outside of our biases, we too often refuse. We miss out on important facts and information by pretending on some level that it isn't there.

Cognitive bias ... arises from limited thinking, our own individual motivations, social pressure and stereotypes, our emotions, and how we process information.

Cognitive bias has common causes. It arises from limited thinking, our own individual motivations, social pressure and stereotypes, our emotions, and how we process information. It also is formed by mental shortcuts called heuristics that influence how we make decisions and our ability to remember things accurately. Other types of bias include:

- False consensus bias—Believing more people agree with us than is true.
- Attentional bias—Paying attention to certain things while ignoring others.
- Actor-observer bias—Attributing our actions to external causes while attributing other people's actions to internal causes. A good example is attributing your own weight to genetics while blaming another person's weight on their lifestyle or eating habits.
- Anchoring bias—Relying heavily on the first news or information you access to the detriment of additional information that follows.
- Self-serving bias—Blaming external causes for the bad things that happen and giving yourself credit for the good things that happen.

Some researchers suggest that our cognitive biases become more entrenched as we get older and lose cognitive flexibility. Memory has a lot to do with it, too, because as we get older, our memories become far less accurate, so we often fill in the blanks as it suits us.

Not seeing the other side of the story serves no one. Again, the media perpetuates this tendency, and political parties and social movements bank on it. It's a form of mental division and a way to perpetuate the "us versus them" and "I'm right and you're wrong" thinking that is behind so much of what is wrong with our world.

CONDITIONING, DESENSITIZATION, AND THE POWER OF REPETITION

In a 1958 interview with journalist Bill Wallace, author and visionary Aldous Huxley made chilling predictions of a time when the minds of the masses would be easily controlled and manipulated. It was an idea he had depicted in his 1932 novel *Brave New World*. "If you want to preserve your power indefinitely, you have to get the consent of the ruled, and this they will do partly by drugs," he stated. He went on to tell Wallace that the powerful would use new techniques of propaganda to bypass the rational mind of man and appeal to the subconscious and deeper emotions, and this would result in man loving his enslavement. This new form of propaganda focused on hacking the minds of the masses to enslave them.

Some of the techniques involved are conditioning, desensitizing, and repetition. The programming that drives our actions, thoughts, and behaviors comes from the subconscious, so by conditioning the subconscious via words, images, and events, it would be easy to bypass the analytical rational mind and fool someone into thinking they still have control of their mental processes.

There are two ways propaganda and disinformation become a part of our reality. One is with big, shocking events that completely destabilize us mentally, emotionally, and physically. Think 9/11 or the COVID-19 pandemic.

Aldous Huxley, the author of the dystopian novel *Brave New World,* said that propaganda would be used to control the masses by appealing to their subconscious emotions.

The second way is slower and more insidious. It's the "boiling frog" phenomenon. The premise behind this is that if you put a frog into a pan of boiling water, it will jump out immediately. But if you put a frog into a pan of lukewarm water, then slowly heat it to a boil, it will acclimate to the rising temperatures and passively boil to death. This is probably not true, as even frogs know when to jump out of a pan of increasingly hot water, but the idea is valid and works wonders to gradually influence and control a person or a group of people without them even knowing they're in the pot in the first place.

Conditioning

In human psychology and physiology, conditioning is a process whereby a behavioral response becomes more frequent or predictable in a given environment when it is reinforced either by the stimulus of reward or the threat of punishment. Much of the research we have on conditioning comes from studies done in the early twentieth century establishing the procedures and definitions of conditioning, with later research adding to our understanding of the techniques and methods.

Conditioning can be achieved with repetition, exposure, deprivation, and stimulus to train a response from someone based on a specific set of actions. Those actions can be the sound of a bell, as in the famous Pavlov's dog experiment, a trigger image, or repeated trained behavior, such as teaching a child to go to the potty when she has to urinate and not to, say, the trash compactor.

Conditioning can be achieved with repetition, exposure, deprivation, and stimulus to train a response from someone based on a specific set of actions.

We are all being conditioned by the news media, entertainment, our peers and families, and social pressures. Our actions and behaviors are either rewarded for conforming or punished for not conforming. We receive reinforcement training that keeps us behaving in a particular way and in a predictable fashion. This is how false flags and other methods of propaganda work: we are conditioned to believing the media and our leadership, and we are conditioned to do what we are told, especially in an emergency. Those who show variations in the conditioned responses are shamed, guilted, arrested, fired, or banished from a community (such as a school, a church, a social media platform, and so on).

Classical conditioning or Pavlovian conditioning involving an external stimulus is effective. Turning on the news and reacting with fear or anger to inflammatory headlines is a conditioned response. Instrumental conditioning, or operant conditioning, is focused on the reward or punishment that comes from performing certain actions and displaying certain behaviors.

Even our entertainment conditions used to be more accepting of everything from violence and gun use to crime and brutality, sex and romance, fear and paranoia, and assorted other bad behaviors, as well as positive things like tolerance, love, compassion, and empathy. It depends on what you're watching. There have been accusations galore that video games condition children to accept violence and sex, and that heavy metal music conditions kids to worship the devil. Adults can be just as conditioned by what they watch, read, and listen to. It's easy to become conditioned because most people are distracted and overwhelmed and have no idea their subconscious minds are being programmed by everything around them.

Rarely do we put our own thoughts and behaviors under the microscope.

Desensitization

In the same way that we can be conditioned to think, feel, and behave certain ways, we may also be numbed to things like violence, child abuse, sexual abuse, and crime. Seeing something over and over diminishes its effect, positive or negative, and we tend to become more passive and neutral toward things we might never have tolerated before—especially things like war, drone bombings, or deaths that don't affect us or anyone we love.

Mass media desensitizes audiences to violence with the "if it bleeds, it leads" mindset. The viewer is overwhelmed with images and stories of people being killed, accidentally or otherwise. Suffering gets the headlines, and soon we feel less and less outraged and affected by it. We lose our will to stop it or fight it. Some scholars suggest seeing violence all over the big and small screen helps us cope vicariously with it, whereas others feel it makes us immune to violence and more likely to accept it as a means to an end. Exposure does not always lead to acting out or changes in personality, but sometimes it does trigger real-life violence in those who see it as a form of inspiration or motivation.

Familiarity breeds contempt, but it also breeds boredom and numbness, especially when the subject matter is highly emotional and painful. We cannot mentally and physically keep processing intense emotions, so we shut down or put up a wall against them. We reduce our sensitivity to them. We almost treat such emotions like a food allergy and avoid the emotions altogether. It's a survival instinct, but it also threatens to do us harm when we go numb to the horrors of abuse all around us and stop collectively fighting them.

Desensitization can be used for good, as in the case of overcoming phobias. By gradually increasing exposure to the subject of the phobia—for example, for a phobia about flying, visiting an airport, standing near an airplane, stepping into an airplane, sitting in an airplane, then finally flying in one—you can stop reacting to it irrationally and fearfully. You get used to it, and the familiarity of repeated exposure leads to acceptance of the situation. That exposure happens in small doses, enough to build up a conditioned response that is more positive and beneficial than sheer horror and panic, without overwhelming the person and making their phobia even more extreme.

Did you ever wonder why there is so much violence in the news? One theory is that by showing viewers an endless stream of wars, disasters, riots, and other violence, we will become desensitized to it to the point where we become apathetic.

Repetition

Repetition is a favorite tool of the propagandist because it attracts attention and stays in the memory banks longer than random words or phrases. It works for advertisers and real estate agents. "Location, location, location." It's a hypnotic form of language that works well to embed itself in the subconscious, making ideas easy to remember and share.

Repetition is all about emphasis, impact, clarification, confirmation, continuity, musicality, and coercion. There are two kinds of repetition politicians and others use frequently in their rhetoric.

One is anaphora. In speech or writing, this is the deliberate repetition of the first part of a phrase or sentence to achieve an artistic effect and reinforce the meaning of the chosen words.

Examples of anaphoric repetition: "He was the wrong man for the wrong job at the wrong time." "I gave my heart, I gave my money, I gave my time."

The other is polysyndeton. This stylistic literary and speaking device uses several coordinating conjunctions in succession to achieve an artistic effect or emphasize flow and continuity.

Examples of polysyndeton repetition: "And I will walk a hundred miles and I will walk a hundred times and I will buy a hundred donkeys." "I try or I die or I keep trying or I keep dying."

Repetition breeds familiarity. It acts like a mind virus by infecting our subconscious with what we hear and see, and by our exposure to a certain opinion or point of view over and over again until we adopt it as our own.

If we are exposed to information that we feel is crucial for others to hear, we then repeat it to anyone who will listen. We evangelize, as if we are on some crusade. If we do a good job, we convince the next person to repeat the process and spread the mind virus further.

Repetition breeds familiarity. It acts like a mind virus by infecting our subconscious with what we hear and see....

RHETORIC

Language has hypnotic power. It can be used to control another person or to set them free. Rhetoric is a tool of politicians and leaders who use argument and discourse to persuade others to adopt their point of view. In ancient Greece, it was considered a positive and cooperative form of communication that involved three levels of appeal to change another person's mind:

- *Logos* — using logical argument and induction or deduction
- *Pathos* — creating an emotional reaction in the listener
- *Ethos* — Projecting trustworthiness, authority, power, or charm

Rhetoric is a huge part of any political candidate's speeches and interactions with the public and opponents.

DOGMA

Dogma is the foundation of beliefs and principles that are to be accepted as truths, whether or not there is a factual basis for doing so or adequate grounds for authority. Dogma is at the heart of any ideology or paradigm and is often used negatively to suggest control or brainwashing. Dogma is associated with cults and religions that force their members to believe and act as the leadership wants.

We also see dogmatic ideals and beliefs in political parties and leaders who strongly persuade their members to stay within the party lines and behave as good citizens, even if the party itself or its leaders break the rules.

Behavior modification using specific propaganda tools works best on the subconscious mind that does not analyze, criticize, judge, or question the dogma. Coercive persuasion is a more destructive type of control that involves the systematic manipulation of someone's behaviors, thoughts, information, and emotions. This is done by using fear, intimidation, and punishment; controlling the information given to the subject (or not giving them any information at all); and coercing the victim with promise of reward. In the torture of prisoners of war, this is done by threatening to withhold food, water, sunlight, and sleep. The controllers can persuade the prisoners to do whatever they want by promising to give or withhold the most fundamental basics of survival.

These are brainwashing techniques that work in any situation. The person or group you wish to control and manipulate may be exposed to a host of psychological tactics, which may include:

- Intimidation—Threaten the victim with certain punishments if they don't act and behave as the controlling party desires.
- Isolation—Keep victims isolated so they don't have human comfort and feel powerless and alone.
- Cut off the flow of information—Keep the victim off balance and in fear of not knowing what is happening in the outside world.
- Increase suggestibility—Use everything from subliminal suggestions to hypnosis, music, sleep deprivation, and food restriction to make someone more compliant.
- Create a sense of powerlessness— Subject the victim to frequent, often

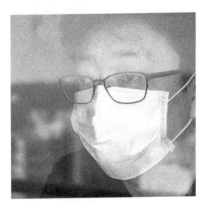

Forced isolation is one technique used in brainwashing. Interestingly enough, isolation policies have also been used during the COVID-19 pandemic, as well as cutting off or restricting the flow of information, intimidation, and creating a sense of powerlessness.

surprise actions that undermine their confidence and sense of security.

- Destabilize a sense of self—Work to destroy someone's ego and sense of self with the intent to recreate them as the controller wishes.

If you look at the above list, you think of a cult, but according to some commentators, many of these tools were used during the recent COVID-19 pandemic to create a public that was compliant to the orders of the government. Isolation resulting from stay-at-home orders created depression, anxiety, and an uptick in calls to suicide hotlines. Censored or cherry-picked information kept many in the dark as to the true extent of the virus's spread and virulence. Many people felt powerless throughout the ordeal. The techniques that work to brainwash prisoners of war also work to keep cult members from leaving the fold and to keep the public in the dark and submissive to government actions or external events.

NLP: NEURO-LINGUISTIC PROGRAMMING

Neuro-linguistic programming, or NLP, is not itself propaganda but is one of the tools of it. NLP teaches the structure of language and behavior and how to model or mirror structures to reproduce them in yourself and others. Critics consider it a pseudoscience, but those who have studied it prefer to call it a self-empowerment program that can help you amplify the successful structures and disempower the ones that don't work for you. It's a type of programming and reprogramming of the subconscious mind that involves teaching someone to observe desirable behaviors, mirror or imitate them, or even undergo hypnosis.

NLP posits that we each have an internalized map of our beliefs, perceptions, and viewpoints about the world that dictates our feelings and behaviors. That personal map can free us or enslave us until we acknowledge and modify the patterns and adopt more empowering ones. Modeling, or mirroring, is the process of adopting similar behaviors, actions, and thought patterns to someone you admire or aspire to be like as a way of duplicating the structure of their success map.

NLP was created in the 1970s at the University of Santa Cruz by linguist John Grinder and psychologist Richard Bandler. It was marketed early on as a success program and is used today in business, medicine, therapy, law, sports, the military, and the education system. It has successfully been used to remove phobias and cure addictions. Propagandists use NLP techniques such as anchoring, a form of classical conditioning that establishes what are called anchors between a person's senses and their emotional state. While a person is in a certain emotional state, if they are exposed to a stimulus of sight, sound, or sensation, that stimulus becomes an anchor that will put them in that emotional state whenever they experience it. Advertisers use anchors to create a link between their product and a certain emotion via the music and visuals in their commercials and ads.

NLP posits that we each have an internalized map of our beliefs, perceptions, and viewpoints about the world that dictates our feelings and behaviors.

Other techniques include:

Future pacing—Takes the person's thoughts into the future and uses language to show acceptance of a desired change or state of mind. In the case of advertising, it would be a desired product.

Association and dissociation—The strategies serve to create a strong association with a new and desired mental map or framework, and a dissociation with the present map or framework that no longer serves you.

Swish—This is a process meant to interrupt an existing pattern of thought from the unwanted behaviors to the desired behaviors. You visualize a cue or image and then "swish" it away, replacing it with an image of the desired outcome.

Reframing—This technique changes the way you perceive something and its meaning by putting a new frame of reference around it or by changing its negative aspects into positives.

State management—This teaches you to actively control your emotional and mental state by using other tools such as anchoring.

Covert hypnosis—This uses language patterns to hypnotize someone to persuade them to change.

NLP tools are said to work wonders to change the self and reprogram new patterns to replace old, stale ones. As a self-help method, it employs language to teach the individual or group to recreate the maps of their lives so they end up at their goals. It shows the user how to achieve success by learning how another successful person, or model, created their own map for success, and by copying and following that same map. It can be used for great good, but when used against you, with or without your consent, it can make you think and do things without even understanding why. NLP has been under fire for its use in cults, and it has also been praised as a powerful self-help strategy by influential names in personal power, including Tony Robbins.

STOCKHOLM SYNDROME

Sometimes victims, hostages, and prisoners of war become strangely attached to their abusers and controllers. Capture bonding and Stockholm syndrome describe the effects of a certain kind of mind control technique involving positive and negative reinforcement and the creation of confusion, cognitive dissonance, and a destabilized sense of identity to bond a victim with the abuser. Often, the mix of positive reward with negative punishment creates a situation where the victim has no sense of security or stability and waits for the positive, focuses on it, and sees it as an act of kindness and goodness when it does arrive. Intermittent reinforcement is more powerful at breaking someone's spirit than negative reinforcement because of the human desire and need for kindness, so even when the positive reinforcement is peppered with torture and abuse, it is more comforting than to have none at all.

Capture bonding may also be a survival mechanism in that we are forced to adapt to an extreme by coping with it or becoming accepting of it. We know if we fight back, we might die, so we become compliant and surrender to our captors. Often, we get to know our abusers and captors and find some common ground or empathy for their cause.

"Stockholm Syndrome" is a term that comes from a 1973 bank robbery at this building in Sweden. The robbers took a hostage, who after some time began to form an emotional bond with the criminals.

It is a powerful form of abuse and one that is seen in personal relationships, cults, and war. The term "Stockholm syndrome" comes from a bank robbery in 1973 in Stockholm, Sweden, involving bank employees held hostage in a vault for six days. As the criminals were negotiating with law enforcement, the employees were said to have bonded emotionally with the criminals.

CULT MENTALITY AND GROUP THINK

Why do you think it's called "deprogramming" when someone leaves or escapes a cult and undergoes specialized treatment to regain control of their minds? To a degree, we are all members of cults, whether we want to admit it or not. Once we become aware of this and begin to disengage, the deprogramming starts, and it can be so painful and isolating that the temptation to return to the cult is powerful.

Cult Mentality

Political parties are cults. Religions are cults. Sports team fans are cults. The definition of a cult is simple. It's a system of worship with followers who adhere to a certain ideal, person, object, or thing. Cults flock around a sacred person chosen as their leader, an ideology, or a thing like a golden calf, and they create rituals, ceremonies, and sets of behaviors for followers of the cult to follow. That describes a whole lot of groups and ideologies other than the religious groups people usually think of.

Cults share common characteristics, such as a charismatic leader or an object of devotion. Cults can be personal, focused on a person as leader or messiah, like the Branch Davidians under David Koresh. They can be ideological, focused on a set of beliefs or a particular worldview, like the Ku Klux Klan. Many cults are a combination of the two. Political parties fit the bill, combining charismatic candidates with a set of beliefs that align with the party.

Religions can be seen as devoted to an ideology or a leader, but there are distinctions between religions and cults. Cults usually:

- Isolate members and penalize anyone who leaves the fold
- Push a special doctrine outside of normal scripture

Branch Davidian leader David Koresh was considered a charismatic leader of this cult, which he led to disaster in 1993 when ATF agents raided their Waco, Texas, compound, killing Koresh and 76 of his followers.

- Dishonor the family unit
- Demand obedience and submission
- State they are the chosen ones
- Cross boundaries of purity with bad behavior (sex with minors, rape, drugs)
- Oppose individuality and critical thinking

Cults can be happy homes for those who are inclined to isolate from friends and family and abide by set rules and behaviors. But cults have a tendency to turn negative when members begin asking questions and suddenly wake up to the abuses of the leaders. Yet in everyday life, we deal with cult mentality any time we interact with more than one person at a time. It could be called groupthink. The same characteristics that cult members exhibit can be seen in political parties, sports fan groups, social movements, even entertainment, if viewers of popular shows like *Game of Thrones* become devoted enough. Individuality is not a part of a cult. It's all about the group, and that's where the members become the most vulnerable.

In the March 15, 1982, *New York Times* article "The Psychology of the Cult Experience," Glenn Collins writes that there are at any given time between 2,500 and 3,000 cults operating in the United States alone, with up to three million collective members. Many of these cults are not destructive. Collins interviewed Dr. Stanley H. Cath, a psychoanalyst at Tufts University, who stated that cults develop common conversion techniques. Cults, Cath states, are "groups of people who are joined together by a common ideological system fostered by the expectation that they can transcend the imperfections and finitude of life." They do this by setting up a "we–they" philosophy that states, "We have the truth, they do not." It's the cult version of the divisive "us versus them."

Freedom of expression or thought goes against the purpose of most cults, which is to allow the leaders to control others for their own agendas and motives.

Some cults take in homeless teens or former criminals recently out of prison and give them a home where they feel accepted. The cult might be a safer place than the home or the street. But inevitably the structure of the cult benefits the leadership. Freedom of expression or thought goes against the purpose of most cults, which is to allow the leaders to control others for their own agendas and motives. Even within a political party or social movement, there is only so much room for individuality. The goal is to blend in as part of the collective.

An unsafe cult leader or group shows these warning signs:

- Group leader always has to be right.
- Authoritarian attitudes toward members.
- Abuse of any kind.
- Unreasonable fear of the outside world.
- Obsessiveness of the leader about the group's goal.
- Doomsday talk and beliefs.
- No record of how group is financed.
- Justification for bad behaviors of leadership.
- Extreme forms of isolation and punishment.

Any group that displays any of these behaviors is suspect. Cult mentality follows blindly, rarely asks questions, and puts way too much power and authority in one person or leader. If you try to leave, you are threatened, shamed, guilted, isolated, and shunned. Same thing happens when you switch favorite football teams or political parties, eh?

Groupthink
"Birds of a feather flock together."

Groupthink can be a good thing. An office working toward a big sale. A community group working toward positive change or the passage of a law. Hanging out with those of a like mind, whether it be about a sports team, food, a vacation spot, a social or political mindset, a trivia team, or a love of corgis. Group dynamics are a necessity to work together in a variety of situations for the common good of all. The dark side of groupthink is what drives cults, what can turn social and political groups into intolerant extremists, and what makes propaganda so effective on a grand scale. Manipulate one person, and you have a personal slave. Manipulate a group, and you have an army.

Manipulate one person, and you have a personal slave. Manipulate a group, and you have an army.

Group dynamics lead to groupthink, which has some key characteristics:

1. *Illusion of vulnerability*—The group is all-powerful and indestructible
2. *Righteousness*—The group believes it is inherently moral and just.
3. *Thought police*—The group polices the thoughts and actions of members
4. *Self-censored*—The group never deviates from the narrative and consensus.
5. *Negativity toward other groups*—The group sees others as the enemy.
6. *Rationalization*—The group never questions its own viewpoints and assumptions.

When groupthink meets extremism, you have mob mentality, as evident in protests that turn into riots and violence courtesy of particular groups on the far left or the far right. Terrorist groups engage in this same groupthink.

Fear and intimidation play a large role in keeping the group glued together. There is a constant pressure to live up to the expectations of the group and to accept ideas that benefit the group mind. This is similar to someone who joins a political party and gets involved in the campaign activities before an election. But what happens when the person meets with some contradictory information about the group or its beliefs?

Those in the group will resort to fear and threats to either bring the person back around or punish them for the betrayal. The groupthink has been challenged by the one member's decision to walk away, potentially resulting in others in the group suddenly questioning their own devotion and commitment.

FEAR POWER

Fear works wonders not only to reinforce cults and groupthink but in the world of advertising, too. FOMO, or fear of missing out, means we want to keep the love of the group, so to be like the rest we buy the cool car or the expensive phone we can't really afford. Like politicians and the media, advertisers and corporations with something to sell play upon our fears. Pharmaceutical companies tell us we might have something wrong with our health and encourage us to ask our doctor if we need a certain drug. They scare us with threats of dying if we don't ask our doctor about the drug. We may not have any need for such a drug, but hey, shouldn't we ask our doctor about it just in case?

Advertising often works best when it makes us feel happy and good, yet we may be more inclined to buy the product advertised if we are afraid of something bad happening if we don't. A beer company can appeal to us by showing a group of people on a beach having a blast drinking their beer and dancing by the light of a bonfire. Or they can appeal to our fear of not being cool by showing a glitzy party with the hottest people and throw a few celebrities in for good measure, telling us we need to drink this beer or we will never be allowed to party with them. Fear sells because it appeals to our need to be accepted, loved, acknowledged, and special. In the case of medications, it appeals to our need to be alive.

Propagandists search for any reason they can find to keep us in a panic about something. They know we are not as easily manipulated when we are happy and healthy and everyone is getting along. A deadly new virus. Riots in the streets. A terrorist at-

Politicians often use fear to manipulate their followers, accusing certain groups of people of causing violence and crime. They then declare that they need public support to stop the scapegoats.

tack. School shootings. An electromagnetic pulse shutting down the power grid. Godzilla! Our presidents and congresspersons spew fear-based rhetoric about illegal immigrants, terrorists, weapons of mass destruction, foreign sleeper cells, super predators, rapists, sex traffickers, food shortages, water shortages, gas shortages. If it makes us afraid, it works for their purpose of keeping us collectively disempowered.

Even better, if it makes us afraid of each other, those in power can get away with almost anything while we are distracted, divided into groups that see others as the enemy while remaining ignorant to the groupthink spell we are under.

British philosopher Bertrand Russell once said, "Neither a man nor a crowd nor a nation can be trusted to act humanely or to think sanely under the influence of a great fear."

Group fear pushes us into the fight-or-flight response together, and we all know a lot more damage can be done by a mob than by just one person. Under the power of blind fear, we can become like a horde of zombies, with no capacity to stop and analyze our actions. People take on an all-or-nothing mindset, unwilling to look beyond extremes and limited thinking. Media outlets can reinforce this by publishing stories that make only one side of the equation look good, rarely if ever pointing out the positives of the other side. At the same time, they may refuse to acknowledge mistakes and scandals that reflect poorly on their favored side but constantly point out those of the other party.

Projection of guilt is a powerful tool when the projector you are using has a rabid audience of "believers" willing to accept it without ever holding a mirror up to their own guilt. "It's ok when my side does it, but not when the other side does it." If the other side is thinking the same, no wonder there is so much hatred, intolerance, and division in this country. We all think we are perfect and the other guy is a hot mess. That sentiment is amplified in group dynamics.

TAKING CRITICISM

Those who judge, attack, and condemn others for their opinions, beliefs, and points of view know that people generally don't take criticism well. It hurts to be judged and called names, especially in a public forum. Humiliation, degradation, and projection are the tools of the trade for some who seek to change others' beliefs and behaviors.

When facing personal attacks, it helps to realize other people are acting from anger or hostility that really isn't about you. You may have triggered it, but it's coming from their own perceptions and life experiences, even though it's being directed at you. Social media and talking-head cable news outlets are notorious for attacking others and projecting their own sins onto their opponents while rarely shining any light on their own. It's sad and divisive, but it's human nature to lash out when you feel your ideals and beliefs are being challenged, threatened, or ignored.

The best way to deal with the growing hostility is to avoid it altogether, but for most of us, being on social media and watching the news now and then is a part of our lives. We don't want to have to give it up completely. It's critical then to let it flow off you like water off the back of a duck. There is no need to take anything personally or let it get to you. The media and the powerful forces behind it thrive on people hating each other and taking sides so they can play those sides against each other. Don't fall for it.

The media and the powerful forces behind it thrive on people hating each other and taking sides so they can play those sides against each other.

Never argue with someone over opinions or beliefs. They are personal and everyone is different, so you will never change the other person's beliefs, and they will never change yours. At least, it won't happen with negativity and nastiness. Has anyone ever made you change your opinions on something by calling you names or yelling at you? Have you ever changed someone's mind by telling them they are an idiot for thinking the way they do? This kind of behavior only makes people dig their heels in even deeper, refusing to even consider that they should change something. The human ego prevents us from embracing the possibility of change when the person suggesting it is angry, rude, condescending, or inconsiderate.

In conversations online, watch out for hijacking, which is when someone comments on your post with irrelevant information on another topic, sends the conversation off on a tangent, or takes over the post and gets into debates and arguments with your friends, even insulting and offending them. Keep control of your social media and manage your posts accordingly. Don't hijack other people's posts either. You have your own page to express your opinions on. Respect others as you'd want them to respect you.

Twitter wars, Insta wars, and Facebook battles are the order of the day, but it's up to you whether you want to jump into the fray or to stay detached, keeping your peace and your sanity intact.

SHOW-AND-TELL AND ICE CREAM CONES

Quotes are frequently taken out of context in news stories. Sometimes they're fabricated completely and passed off as truth to readers, who have no reason to suspect they're being duped. Reporters and journalists sometimes use quotes to persuade the viewer or reader that if so-and-so said something, it must be true. Often the reporters add their own opinions to the news story, editorializing just enough to keep it looking like factual news. This serves to frame the story just enough to keep it from looking like fake or manipulated news.

Happy stories make people feel good. Everyone loves an ice cream cone, and everyone loves a feel-good story, which is often used as a diversion from a negative story to follow. It's best to make someone smile before you make them sad. Feel-good stories that are true build trust in the reporter and the news outlet so the viewers become more inclined to believe the stories that contain propaganda, spin, and disinformation.

Winning over the viewer means they will return to your network or outlet for all of their news and information. The more goodwill you can foster in viewers, the better, as viewer loyalty is critical considering the plethora of choices both online and off.

ECHO CHAMBERS, SHILLS, AND GATEKEEPERS

Echo chambers result from only joining groups or hanging out with people who are exactly the same as you are. Every message reinforces the accepted belief system, bouncing off the chamber walls like an echo, and no argument or opposing information is allowed in. Many modern media outlets have become echo chambers of the right or left, with very little time spent examining anything outside the chamber. Social networking allows us to follow and friend only those who share our beliefs and ideals, so we never have to challenge ourselves to look at anything that might contradict what we are so sure we are right about.

Having our own opinions mirrored back to us doesn't challenge us or allow us to grow in our understanding of others.

We tend to prefer an echo chamber because it's safe, comfortable, and easy, even if it is the lazy way out. Having our own opinions mirrored back to us doesn't challenge us or allow us to grow in our understanding of others. There's a great meme on social media that says, "You don't want to hear their opinions. You want to hear your opinions coming out of their mouths."

A shill is a spokesperson for a group, organization, or viewpoint. Shills are often experts or people with lofty titles. A news outlet might interview a shill to support its own agenda, point of view, or political or economic affiliation. Shills are somewhat like talking heads or pundits, but they tend not to have their own hosted show. Rather, they may appear as an interviewed expert to comment on an event or news story.

They may be part of a special interest group or the sponsor of the news outlet that has a common agenda to spin the news right or left or to satisfy a particular corporate agenda, such as supporting pharmaceutical products or pushing for bigger defense spending bills. A shill's tactics may include "fogging up an issue" by injecting confusing or obscure references into a news story that might otherwise be too big to distract attention from.

Gatekeepers are similar, but with a twist. Gatekeepers are paid experts and shills who control access to the real story by pretending to be on the side of the public or the consumer. They are two-faced, promoting a pro-public front while behind the curtain they are working for an organization. An example would be a climate expert claiming to care about climate change objectives at a public forum who works for the oil and gas industry and is against those very objectives.

Gatekeepers can also be personalities or celebrities working with a news outlet to come across as trustworthy and honest

Media mogul Rupert Murdoch, who owns such companies and publications as Fox News, *The Wall Street Journal*, *The New York Post*, and HarperCollins publishing, acknowledged that these outlets of news and opinion reflect his personal values.

while engaging in propaganda and toeing the outlet's party line. Biased news outlets only employ those who are on their "team" and have the same opinions and ideologies as their superiors. The public attaches to these personalities and believes anything they say even if they've been proven wrong about something in the past. The talking heads of cable news outlets, for example, have become extremely popular, with social network followings in the millions. People trust them, and that's how they get away with propaganda.

Rupert Murdoch, the Australian-born American media mogul and owner of News Corp (Fox News, Sky Group, 21st Century Fox) has been quoted as saying, "For better or worse, my company is a reflection of my character, my thinking, my values." This means the people he hires to give the news will slant that way, too, perhaps with a token talking head on the other side of the political divide to offer the appearance of "fair and balanced news." This isn't just a character-istic of right-leaning news. It happens on the left, too. The gatekeepers and shills will be a reflection or mirror of the person or corporation behind the curtain, pulling the strings.

Media personnel, too, are expected to hold that opinion no matter the news story, and if they dare express a different point of view, they may be fired and replaced.

The best shills and gatekeepers know how to embed a news story with editorial views, either their own or those held by the network or outlet. You as the viewer may not even know you're hearing opinion and editorialization, because it's coming from a "news" reporter on a "news" channel. Yet look close enough, and you'll see that in today's market, most news outlets engage in edi-torializing and stating opinions as facts, something you the viewer can easily research if so inclined.

FLIPPING REALITY

"War is peace," as George Orwell once wrote, and if you re-peat this enough, or if famous people and alleged experts say it over and over with great passion, no doubt the public will begin to accept war as the ultimate form of peace. Most people abhor violence, but encourage them to believe it is an acceptable form of social justice and perfectly okay when it's against the enemy, and suddenly you have a society that believes violence is acceptable or even normal.

This is called "leveraging the correct mainstream opinion" by portraying only the points of view you wish to promote as good, positive, strong, empowering, and right, and anything against them as dangerous and evil. This is good; that is bad. Push that enough and with all the tools of propaganda, and you can make people think up is down and down is up. You flip their reality.

Repeating lies as the truth is the same concept. This can be done with expert quotes, crooked polls (more on polls later), or disinformation that encourages the audience to accept as truth something they would not otherwise do under any other circumstances. If U.S. citizens are told enough times that another world leader is evil and must be replaced with regime change, even if that leader is well-loved in their country, and the only reason the United States wants him removed is to take that country's oil reserves by force, the citizens will soon be pushing for regime change to get rid of the evil dictator across the globe.

Author of the classic novel *Nineteen Eighty-Four,* George Orwell asserted that continuous war (which we have today) would become the accepted norm as the cost of peace at home.

If you speak out against regime change in that circumstance, pointing to news stories from that country showing the people love their leader and are treated wonderfully, you may be called a "terrorist lover" and cast as an extremist who hates the United States. Any alternative points of view or hard facts that go against the narrative will be attacked and maligned.

LABELING AND PIGEONHOLING

We love to smack labels on people or put them into neat little compartments, refusing to see them as more than their opinion on a single issue. Anyone who questions the official story is a "crazy conspiracy theorist" or a "truther" and thrown into the big box of generalizations and stereotypes. "Left-wingers" and "right-

A liberal protestor puts a spin on being labeled a "snowflake," a term used disparagingly by right-wingers to imply that those on the left are overly sensitive and weak.

wingers" might not take into account all those who lean one way or another but also embrace some attitudes and points of view from the opposite side of the spectrum.

Before propagandists can employ divide-and-conquer techniques on a populace, they first seek to label and pigeonhole people into groups they can then focus on dividing. Prolife or pro-choice? Believe it or not, it's possible to be both. "Climate change is real" or "climate change is a fraud" has a compromise in the center where people are willing to accept the truth about aspects of both claims. "War or diplomacy? Which do we choose?" Is it possible to believe in diplomacy first, then war as a last resort? Democrat or Republican? As if you must choose one and never even consider that the other party might have something to offer. Yet so many times we are labeled as just one thing or the other. Humans are more nuanced than that.

THE "MAY HAVE" TECHNIQUE

Most Americans accepted the war in Iraq in 2003 fairly quickly based upon stories that there "might be" weapons of mass destruction there. Watch the news on any given day and one or more news stories will feature speculation about somebody who "may have" committed this or that, or a country that "may have" bombs or terrorist cells. It's a common method to incite fear, concern, and doubt by insinuating something that "may have" no basis at all in reality or fact.

"Iran may boost their nuclear weapons arsenal."

"Russia may have tampered with the U.S. elections."

"China may have unleashed the COVID-19 virus from a bio-warfare lab."

By the time these statements have gone viral through the public, they are accepted by many as truth. Even when they turn out to be false, as with the weapons of mass destruction (WMDs) in Iraq, it's rare for the retraction or correction to receive as much attention as the original story. In the minds of most Americans, Iraq did have WMDs even if none were ever found and despite even President George W. Bush going on record as saying they did not exist.

This technique goes hand-in-hand with "cooked" or false headlines meant to embed propaganda. Most people never read beyond the headline, so planting ideas in them is a highly impactful method for conveying a certain message before having to clarify it. Another way to accomplish this effect is to overplay one headline and underplay another. An example might be a big, bold headline in a newspaper or online news outlet about how the COVID-19 virus saw an increase in cases after largely Democratic (or "blue") states opened their beaches and parks, followed by a back-page story with a smaller headline stating that COVID-19 cases spiked after openings in largely Republican ("red") states too, or vice versa.

This works wonders on the bottom tickers of news pro-grams, airport TV channels, and Times Square billboards, which feature bold headlines without the complete stories. When you only see the headline across the bottom of the screen, how often do you go seek out the story to corroborate it for yourself? Chances are, not too often.

ASTROTURFING AND PANDERING

Astroturf looks and feels like real grass, but it's fake grass. In politics and propaganda, astroturfing is the illusion of support for a particular person, movement, cause, or position. Political parties, candidates, and corporations all use astroturfing to give the impression they support something they don't. But as long as they can make the public believe they support it, that's all that matters.

Take a social movement like #MeToo. The goal was to give a voice and give support to women who were sexually assaulted and raped. If a candidate for the Senate wanted to astroturf, he might claim to support the movement and even agree to speak at a rally or event to help a women's group raise money and get bigger visibility. He will be interviewed in the media speaking praise for the movement and its leaders. In truth, he might not support the movement at all, but he needs women's votes to win his election. It's a grand deception with the goal of trying to gain public appreciation, sympathy, trust, or votes.

Another word for this might be pandering. Politicians pander all the time to get elected. Corporations use astroturfing to try to get regulations lifted or laws passed in their favor by first pretending to be sympathetic to the opposition. They may also try to get the opposition on their side by lying and deceiving them with promises of support and compromise.

During political debates, just about every candidate uses astroturfing to some degree, making promises and concessions to anyone and everyone they think will help them build their base and get them elected. Antigun Democrats might astroturf by agreeing to compromise on a concealed-carry bill. Prochoice Republicans might astroturf by feigning compromise on an abortion bill that only allows abortion in cases of rape or incest. Once elected, the true colors or true stance of said politicians is made clear.

Groups that pretend to be public servants but are supported by corporations or political parties can raise money for environmental protections their backers would never agree to. Pharmaceutical companies can support or sponsor patient advocate and support groups to make it look like they care, all the while using the patient groups to push their products into the marketplace. Often a group seeking to astroturf will use multiple online identities or fake focus groups to mislead the public into thinking there is widespread support for their position.

Often a group seeking to astroturf will use multiple online identities or fake focus groups to mislead the public into thinking there is widespread support for their position.

SCAPEGOATING

Blame the victim. That's become the motto of criminals and bad guys everywhere. Victim bashing and scapegoating—focusing blame on a particular person or group that may not be guilty—is a great way to distract attention from your own guilt. Ask any politician or celebrity accused of sexual harassment or rape. In this rape culture we live in, it's become the norm to blame the victim of sexual abuse, even if it's a child.

Scapegoating can involve an individual, group, or movement, casting unwarranted blame upon them for just about any sin, targeted for their race, gender, creed, or political affiliation. The scapegoat becomes the dumping ground for the projected sins of the real sinners, the one who is punished instead of the real perpetrator.

Scapegoating can be directed toward one of two groups even when both groups might be equally oppressed, or it can target a different group altogether. It might target a social class as a way of lashing out for social inequity and injustice. By placing blame and guilt upon another group or person, we remove the focus and attention from ourselves and our role in the crime at hand. It can also be a sneaky method of instigating violence and retaliation against an enemy by blaming them for something they didn't do.

Projection is widespread in politics, with one group or candidate projecting their own sins upon the opposition. Religious leaders often do the same, pointing the finger of blame toward their enemies even as they engage in the same criminal activities.

The public is left to focus on the scapegoat, letting the real perpetrators of the crime off the hook. Instead of holding a celebrity or politician accountable for rape accusations, for example, we instead attack the victims, calling them sluts or whores who asked for it. This discourages other rape victims from speaking out, thus protecting many more guilty celebrities and politicians.

The word "scapegoat" comes from the Bible. It references the goat that Aaron cast the sins of Israel upon and then banished into the wilderness. The poor innocent goat was punished for all the sins of the Israeli people and thereby became the first scapegoat.

MARGINALIZING

One of the best ways to cripple someone's personal power is to push them to the edges of society—to shun them or cast them

During the 2016 campaign, Democratic nominee Hillary Clinton called Trump supporters "deplorables," thus marginalizing nearly half the country with a single word.

out. Marginalizing people or groups of people labels them as undesirable or untouchable. During the 2016 presidential campaign, Hillary Clinton used the term "deplorables" to describe a segment of those who supported Donald Trump, and many liberals adopted the term to marginalize all Trump supporters. Many Trump supporters, meanwhile, referred to liberals as having "Trump derangement syndrome" when they expressed their loathing of the president. Both sides engaged in marginalizing their opposition as a way to relegate them to the fringes or the edge of society.

We marginalize people of a different race, creed, religion, class system, and gender to render them and their communities powerless or voiceless in society. It isn't just about race and belief systems, though, because people marginalize others in all kinds of situations. There may be a couple in the neighborhood that seems a bit odd and is never invited to block parties. Maybe there's one employee at the company whom the manager dislikes and gets everyone else to snub. Children can be marginalized at school for a disability, their appearance, the clothes they wear, the neighborhood they live in, their weight, or the color of their skin. People can be marginalized literally based on immigration status, even physically placed into detention camps or arrested and deported.

Some of the ways we marginalize others include:

- Isolating someone from a group or meeting.

- Using derogatory language and bullying tactics against someone.
- Denying someone a professional opportunity or advancement because of their color, creed, or gender.
- Perpetuating stereotypes.
- Making fun of someone.
- Guilting or shaming someone as punishment.
- Singling people out for being different.
- Disallowing the construction of a mosque or other non-Christian house of worship in a given neighborhood.

The marginalized person or group is disempowered and often feels invisible. This can lead to mental health issues or even, in extreme cases, violence and retaliation. It has damaging effects on an individual's mental, emotional, and physical health, and if it's a group, those effects are amplified within the group. Isolated individuals may resort to acting out or suicide. Making someone the "other" is a potent method of cutting off their ability to express themselves and voice their needs. This can lead to substance abuse, self-harm, or, if projected outward, violent uprisings. As Martin Luther King Jr. once said, "Riots are the language of the unheard."

Propaganda often attacks and marginalizes an "other" while persuading people to join in and cast out certain groups.

Propaganda often attacks and marginalizes an "other" while persuading people to join in and cast out certain groups. This may be done with ridicule, which is one of the most effective tools for destroying someone's sense of self. Those in power can ridicule a person or a group and know that they won't likely be challenged in the media because of the complicit relationship they have with news outlets. Ridicule also works well to disempower groups challenging the official narrative of a news story or event, such as the 9/11 truth movement. All you need to do is personally attack the members of such a movement as conspiracy theorists, ridicule them and their claims openly and regularly, or distract researchers and the public away from any information that could back up the movement's claim, and you keep the narrative rolling.

Shame, guilt, ridicule, fear, personal attacks, and of course, good, old-fashioned intimidation can go a long way to shut down opposing voices and place them out in the margins of existence, on the outside looking in. Social exclusion, especially in the age of social media, blocks and cuts people off to opportunities to be seen and heard, and it punishes them for exercising critical thinking and being different.

The alienation and exclusion can lead to disenfranchisement in many forms, including loss of jobs and opportunities, discrimination, loss of rights, inability to vote, and economic and material deprivation. Social exclusion and marginalization take away a person's right to freely engage in a society that claims to honor freedom and equality for all.

POLLS AND PROPAGANDA

The year is 1948. It's November 3, and Harry S. Truman has just been elected president of the United States over the Republican challenger and governor of New York, Thomas E. Dewey. At a press conference at Union Station in St. Louis, Missouri, one of the most iconic photographs in history was taken showing Truman holding up a copy of the *Chicago Tribune* with the headline "Dewey Defeats Truman." The newspaper had printed an incorrect banner stating Dewey won, having gone to press before the final results were known. The *Tribune* wasn't the only news outlet that had predicted Dewey would win. The *New York Times* had suggested likewise, only it hadn't printed an actual banner yet. No doubt polls were showing Dewey in the lead enough to prompt the *Tribune* to print the issue, even if only as a "just in case."

Jump to the day after the presidential election of 2016, where a shocked nation wondered how political newcomer Donald Trump could have beaten former senator and secretary of state Hillary Clinton when, just days before, she was leading in many polls by double digits. Did the Russians interfere? Did the Republicans rig the election? What happened? She had won the popular vote, to add insult to injury—and by quite a lot. But ... those polls?

Polling has been used as a political guide and weapon for as long as there have been elections—and other things, for that matter, to be polled about, such as products, services, favorite singers, favorite baseball teams, and more. But polls are ripe for manipulation and misinterpretation, and as the two examples above show, are not entirely accurate portrayals of how people will vote come election day, what their true buying habits are, or what their honest opinions are. In political polls, this would help explain the huge discrepancies between exit polls and actual vote returns. Some of a more conspiratorial bent suggest polls are mini–false flags setting the public up to accept the coming results of a rigged election. If a poll shows that someone has a high lead in a dozen polls, and then they lose, they can claim it was a rigged election. If they win, they have all they need to prove the vote was *not* rigged if the opponent questions the results.

Donald Trump won the 2016 presidential race, even though Hillary Clinton had about three million more votes. People wondered about the legitimacy of the polls and the election afterwards.

Polls and polling techniques have been faulted for everything from deceptive questions to leading the person being polled, having sample groups that are too small or too targeted, only contacting people of a certain age group, using landlines to skew to older subjects, using the internet and cell phones to skew younger, focusing only on echo chamber groups, and using confusing language to cause subjects to affirm something they disagree with. (Ballot measures can be similarly confusing, such that you end up voting con if you're pro or pro if you're con.)

The largest polling company is Gallup, which conducts over 350,000 polls every year. Gallup claims it can accurately represent the views of adults in the United States because of its system of randomly selecting participants, which suggests that every household in the country has an equal chance of being contacted to be polled at any given time. The results have a maximum margin of error of plus or minus 4 percentage points. This means if Gallup conducts the same poll 100 times at the same exact time, according to its website, the result to any question would come with four percentage points of the "true" figure in 95 of those surveys.

Still, your chances of being contacted by Gallup remain extremely small, as there are more than 105 million households in the country.

Online Polls
Just about every news outlet and political organization conducts their own online polls on their websites. This means the results will naturally skew toward those who already visit those websites or patronize those news outlets. Often, one side or the other will flood

a poll by asking like-minded people to go vote pro or con on a news site. Such polls are in no way an accurate portrayal of support for a given candidate or issue. Polling inside an echo chamber is always going to lean in the direction of the echo chamber.

One favorable point about Gallup polling is that the company makes its methods transparent, whereas most online opinion polls and surveys are just "click and go," so it's not clear in the latter case who exactly is being surveyed or what conclusions can be drawn. Gallup also identifies a population that a given poll is supposed to represent. For example, if Gallup conducts a poll about sports preferences, its polls would be directed to the age groups most likely to be sports fans.

Online polls make random sampling impossible, as they do not pursue subjects but allow subjects to come to them and vote by clicking. Media giants like CNN, MSNBC, and Fox will conduct online polls that most likely will skew in favor of their existing political bias, as will any liberal or conservative media outlets of any size. Why? Because the polls are on their own websites, so their own audiences will be the main respondents. Results will therefore not be indicative of the general public consensus.

Online polls make random sampling impossible, as they do not pursue subjects but allow subjects to come to them and vote by clicking.

Poll Presentation

According to the Pew Research Center, which conducts studies into polling practices, when it comes to election polling, "Determining voter preference among the candidates running for office would appear to be a relatively simple task: just ask them who they are going to vote for on Election Day. In fact, differences in how this question is asked and where it is placed in the questionnaire can affect the results." Pew research shows that most voters have made up their minds who they plan to vote for by the time they are polled, but for those who haven't made up their minds, specific features about a question and how it is asked can make a difference in the results.

For example, does the question include the vice presidential candidate for each party? Is the party affiliation made clear? Are third-party candidates included in the poll? Is the order in which the candidates are listed itself a bias? Do answers change depending on the location of the polling? There are many ways to present a poll question, from the super-simple "this or that" choice (hotdogs or hamburgers?) to more complex methods with more options to choose from.

Weighting

There is also the question of "weighting." For example, say a pollster recognizes that only 7 percent of their sample comes from people of color even though people of color make up 14 percent of the public. The pollster may then count the response from the people of color twice, to reach the 14 percent mark. Or they might weight another population down to meet its public percentage. This is not too much of a problem when we know the demographic factors involved, such as race, gender, or age, for example. It is a way to try to represent those demographics without adjusting the results too much.

Upweighting and downweighting isn't always an accurate or fair way to conduct a poll, however. Say you are polling a group of people who are mostly Democrats. Should you upweight the Republican representation to correct the sampling to be more accurate with demographics? Or would that be a form of tampering with the results, building in a bias for partisan purposes? Another concern is reporting the results of a poll that differs greatly from what other polls are saying: should the poll be weighted to bring the data closer to the mean reported in other polls?

Polling Reliability

One especially important question applies specifically to exit polling that occurs when people leave the ballot box location. Do people always tell the truth in polls about who they voted for? Might some people feel a fear of retribution if they don't answer in a specific fashion? Will someone answering an exit poll answer in a manner they think shows them in a favorable light, such as not showing a race or gender bias? Will a Democrat in a highly Republican neighborhood want to admit they voted the Democrat

Do people always tell the truth in polls about who they voted for? Might some people feel a fear of retribution if they don't answer in a specific fashion?

ticket up and down the ballot? According to the Pew Research Center, in the 1980s and 1990s, there was a pattern of polling errors involving African American candidates that raised questions about whether some voters were reluctant to say they voted, or would vote, against a Black candidate.

This also brings up the point that some demographic groups are less likely to engage in polls, which means they are not represented accurately in predictions about who will vote and how. People who refuse to participate in polls skew the results toward those who like to take polls, thus leading to inaccurate outcomes.

An interesting new propaganda tactic is to create or commission a poll that appears to come from a noted news source but is done by a hired research company and used to make it appear that a certain candidate is losing or winning. This was done in 2020 when a Fox News Poll was released showing incumbent Republican presidential candidate Donald Trump losing by a wide margin to any of the three primary Democratic contenders at the time—Joe Biden, Elizabeth Warren, and Bernie Sanders. The poll was not conducted by Fox at all but was commissioned to two firms, Beacon Research and Shaw & Co. Research, and consisted of a sampling of 1,000 random registered voters. Calling it a Fox poll gave the appearance that the conservative news channel viewership did not support Trump.

The same survey asked respondents if they thought Trump would be reelected. By a 46–40 percent margin, respondents said yes. Inconsistencies like this demonstrate that surveys and polls are enough to inspire a major headache.

News organizations and other polling groups have been known to deliberately skew numbers in order to create panic or spur action towards their candidate of choice.

This tactic is used on both sides of the political spectrum to make it look like the opponent has been abandoned by his or her own party. These so-called suppression polls (undertaken or publicized for the purpose of discouraging a subset of voters) are often found on biased news media sites or on the sites of political candidates or parties. A more accurate poll would not take place just among viewers of one news channel or members of one party, but some media outlets thrive on conducting polls that make their side look like the winning side as a method of influencing voters still on the fence, reasoning that everybody wants to be on the winning side of history.

Many polls are pretty blatant about skewing toward a particular ideology. If you survey 1,000 people at a conservative event, they will tell you they are voting heavily for the conservative candidate. If you survey 1,000 people at a liberal event, well, you figure it out. Yet people swallow up the results of polls as if they are gospel truths and wonder why the election results often don't match up. Poll people on the street in a neighborhood, and the results will reflect only that neighborhood. Call people on their cell phones, and the results will reflect only those who answered the call and agreed to take the poll.

An opinion poll doesn't always measure true public opinion. Instead, it may be designed to represent the opinions of a selected segment of the population, and thus the results will be skewed coming out of the gate. If it is conducted by a news site or broadcast channel, no doubt it will already lean in the direction of the channel's ideology. Tracking polls look at ongoing opinions and results over a number of polls conducted over a specific time period and may offer more insight into changing public opinions. This is valuable, but it brings up another problem. Public opinion does change, and voters who may have been "vote red till I'm dead" or "vote blue no matter who" six months ago may have since changed their tune. Is there such a beast as a truly accurate poll? For an election, the end result may be the only sort of "poll" that counts.

Nonetheless, polls can indicate who will be voting for whom, how many people prefer Coke to Pepsi, whether people believe climate change is occurring, and who prefers dogs to cats (but what if you love both equally?). They are samplings of the vast body of opinions of those polled, even if they may not always reflect the millions who have never been asked to take part in a poll or been inclined to seek one out. Pollsters from legitimate firms seeking the most unbiased random sampling will insist that their methods work and that they have mastered the science behind everything from which methods to use for their polls to how to deal with low response rates.

Whenever you see or partake in a poll, look for transparency in the sample methods and any other pertinent information that indicates how objective the pollster is and how randomly sampled the audience being polled is. You also have to ask what the motive is behind the poll. Is it to make something seem more popular so others will be influenced to support it? To sway the voters by showing them how wrong they would be voting against the leader of the poll? To show how many people support one particular candidate to prompt people to donate to the other one? To find out if you prefer your hamburger with or without pickles? And who is paying for the pickle poll: a pickle company or the anti-pickle industry?

Peer Propaganda and Social Media Activism

*"To swallow and follow, whether old doctrine
or new propaganda, is a weakness still dominating
the human mind."*
—*Charlotte Perkins Gilman*

Some of the most effective propaganda tactics come not from our government and political leaders but from our peers. Social media has opened up a whole new can of worms called "peer propaganda." The tools can include inspiration and information, but they can also include shame, guilt, showing off, and competitions for attention and appreciation. Celebrities, politicians, and regular people post and troll and comment and attack via social media in mostly futile attempts to coerce or persuade others to accept their point of view, or at least tell them how wonderful they are for expressing it.

The adage that "no good deed goes unpunished" has never rung truer, particularly when the good deeds are being done more for the ego fix of the doer than to help someone less fortunate or contribute to the betterment of society. And woe are those who don't get on board the conformity train of virtue signaling—that is, showing off one's own goodness—for they shall be humiliated and dishonored, if not unfollowed, unfriended, or blocked. We are much more inclined to feel the damage from propagandist tactics used on us by family, friends, and colleagues than those used by the government. People closer to us have more power to influence us, for better or for worse.

Add to this the hundreds or even thousands of strangers we friend or follow on social media, and it's become impossible to get through the day without offending someone or drawing the wrath of some opposition group.

VIRTUE SIGNALING

"Look at how virtuous I am!" That's the not-so-subtle message behind what is known as virtue signaling. You may think virtue signaling was created along with social media, but you'd be wrong. Charles Darwin wrote in his famous work *The Descent of Man, and Selection in Relation to Sex* in 1871 that the evolution of sex and sexual selection rested upon the preference for certain traits that attracted mates, and outwardly signaling moral values was one of those traits. It was a way to convey information to a prospective mate that one was worthy of being selected for sex.

Nowadays such signaling may be focused less on getting laid than on stroking our own egos, puffing up our proverbial peacock feathers to make ourselves look good to others, and feeling good about ourselves. When we engage in virtue signaling, we are asking to be accepted. We are showing our ability to conform and our stance on a particular issue. We don't even have to act on our virtues. All we need to do is express the right sentiment or perhaps look like we are acting, making sure to get a selfie or video to prove it on our social media.

It's not just telling the world what we believe in and support, or oppose, that is important. It's how we do it that gets it labeled a

It's been called "humblebragging" for its sneaky way of making us look like we are truly humble even as we tell everyone who will listen how awesome we are.

social phenomenon, and one closely linked to the "look at me" culture of today. It's been called "humblebragging" for its sneaky way of making us look like we are truly humble even as we tell everyone who will listen how awesome we are. Other labels are "hashtag activism" and "slacktivism," apt descriptions for this rather lazy way to feel like we're contributing. It's a way to offer token support to serious issues and garner a sense of superiority while doing so. It looks and sounds an awful lot like, "Hey, so sad that this awful event happened, but look at me, look at me, look at me!"

Celebrities, athletes, religious leaders, and politicians are known for their virtue signaling, which often backfires on them when more base aspects of their character are revealed. It gets even worse when it involves "cringebolism."

CRINGEBOLISM

The use of symbolic images and gestures to show how virtuous and righteous we are is often cringeworthy. Hence, "cringey symbolism." Think of politicians holding up the Bible even as they are accused of less than holy behaviors. Think of MAGA hats and waving flags of every color and type, or thousands of marchers wearing pink hats to support feminism, or self-centered celebrities making videos singing songs about peace after starring in violent movies, or claiming to "take responsibility" for racism and ask forgiveness from those they may or may not ever have dishonored.

In the summer of 2020, cringebolism was everywhere. President Trump was ridiculed for holding up a Bible during a photo op in front of a church near the White House, having just violently scattered peaceful protesters to clear the way for his picture. The photo op drew an uproar from those who quickly accused Trump of being anything but holy, let alone a practicing Christian. But the pandering went both ways, as it tends to do. During the Black Lives Matter protests of May and June in 2020, which were sparked by the slow death of George Floyd under the knee of a police officer, Speaker of the House Nancy Pelosi and other prominent Democrats set the cringebolism meter into overdrive when they posed for a picture kneeling in honor of Floyd while wearing kente cloths. The fabric is a traditional cloth of the Ashanti people in Ghana worn for special occasions, and the cloths had been given to the congresspeople by the Congressional Black Caucus and had been worn for other events before this one. Many people took offense to the photo, however, finding it both an empty pose and exploitative of an important African symbol.

Speaker of the House Nancy Pelosi was criticized for wearing kente cloth at a George Floyd memorial. People said she was pandering to the black community.

One favorite way for people to show their support for a cause (and inadvertently engage in cringebolism) is to turn their social media profile a certain color or show a designated image on a chosen day of the year, such as an American flag or a ribbon of a certain color. For many who do this, it reflects an honest sense of support and desire to effect change, but for others it's a way to jump on the bandwagon and look like they care. For the remaining 364 days, very few people continue to use the symbolic profiles, returning instead to their default settings.

The danger of this form of public display is that if you forget to change your profile to support the cause or choose not to conform, or if you genuinely have issues with the subject being supported, you might be shamed by those who have decided that your profile picture is indicative of your character and overall virtue. Virtue shaming can arise anywhere, so be careful what you post, what you use for a profile picture, and what you express as your personal opinion. You may be shamed for not agreeing, conforming, going along to get along, getting in line, toeing the party line, or jumping on the bandwagon.

Shame culture and cancel culture have created a shift in the freedom of expression on social media. Now many people won't say publicly what they really feel, mean, or think for fear of retribution and marginalization, relegating such opinions to private groups with others of like mind. Which leads us back to the aforementioned echo chamber.

One common example of virtue signaling and cringebolism is the response to horrific events with the offering of "thoughts and prayers." This standard expression of dismay offers none of the outrage or action that are necessary for change. It's considered by many to be lazy activism—sanctimonious crumbs offered in a situation where even the whole cake is not enough. Political engagement in the social media age frequently becomes more about the person posting than what they are posting about.

On the flip side of this is outrage culture, which instead of "thoughts and prayers" to pacify uses anger and rage to excuse destruction, violence, and harm to others. Vandalism prompted by outrage against police brutality, for example, might become not only excusable but acceptable. Early on during the largely peaceful protests in the spring and summer of 2020 in many American cities after George Floyd was murdered by police, for example, some protesters engaged in violence and destruction.

TREND ACTIVISM

Why is it some people only show up to protest or get on board a social justice cause when it's the popular thing to do? Social media has expanded the phenomenon of trend activism, where people suddenly grow a conscience and pay attention to situations or causes only when enough other people start showing their support.

Celebrities genuinely care about many causes, and they give money and time to support things important to them. Occasionally, though, activism becomes more about making the celebrity look good than directing attention to the cause. One has to wonder how many celebrities would engage in charitable activities if the cameras were off. This same accusation might be leveled at the average person now who makes sure to get good selfies and videos of themselves engaged in "activisming" at whatever march, protest, or cause is popular at the moment.

Occasionally ... activism becomes more about making the celebrity look good than directing attention to the cause.

The atmosphere of virtuous self-display has created a new moral code for people on social media, one that has moved away from guilt culture to shame culture. In a guilt culture, you judge yourself or your actions by how your conscience feels, good or bad. In a shame culture, you judge yourself or your actions by how the community feels about or labels you. Shame is worse because it marginalizes you as an outcast. If you don't do what everyone else is doing to support "the cause of the month," you are a bad, bad person who just doesn't care.

Just as hashtags trend on social media, so, too, do topics to care about and get involved in, but they have to either be relevant to a recent event or news headline or supported by the right combination of celebrities and power figures to make the grade.

For a while, child sex trafficking or human organ trafficking are trending, and then for a while it's police violence or #MeToo. Trend activism suggests we pick and choose our causes based upon what we are told is important or by what makes the headline news.

Mitch Hall wrote a powerful opinion piece for the *Federalist*, called "Stop Virtue Signaling on Social Media and Help Someone," dated June 23, 2016. The piece decried the armchair activism, virtue signaling, and shaming culture the author was seeing after the mass shooting at an Orlando nightclub eleven days earlier and the subsequent push for gun control. Hall wrote, "The development of this shame culture has not only created a misguided moral system wherein actions are judged based on one's inclusion or exclusion from a certain group, but it has also rendered political activism into much more of a selfish enterprise—as an opportunity for individuals to promote themselves alongside a political issue."

Hall went on to give students credit for the many boycotts, protests, and walkouts they engaged in, but he also suggested that a person's physical presence was no longer required to be included in any given movement. "Tweeting out a popular article or publishing a Facebook essay about how much you care, all from the comfort of your bedroom, conveys a person's commitment without him actually having to do anything meaningful," he pointed out. Could this brand of slacktivism do more harm than good to a movement?

By contrast, some observers call upon critics of virtue signaling to stop "shaming the shamers" and to acknowledge the positive aspects of putting up a black or pink square on their Facebook profiles. The calling out of those accused of being virtue signalers might do more harm than good, according to Rachel E. Greenspan in her June 13, 2020, *Insider* article, "Politicians and Influencers Have Been Accused of 'Virtue Signaling' during Police Brutality Protests, but the Callouts Could Do More Harm Than Good." Greenspan took the stance that most people who engage in virtue signaling do have real moral concerns.

Perhaps it's the delivery that causes the criticism. Greenspan wrote that "Republicans, liberals, and many others charac-

The calling out of those accused of being virtue signalers might do more harm than good....

terized Congressional Democrats donning kente cloth, a Ghanian fabric, and kneeling for a moment of silence in Floyd's honor as virtue signaling." She went on to say that in that particular instance the label fit, since the Democratic Party was never able to bring about real change when it came to systemic racism.

But the author pointed out how attacking people in general for virtue signaling ignores the fact that being motivated to virtue signal does not mean the feelings are inauthentic.

In a January 2020 research study by Jillian Jordan and David Rand, published in the *Journal of Personality and Social Psychology*, the researchers identified three motivations behind virtue signaling:

- Personal experience with the subject matter (such as having yourself been shot in a mass shooting or beaten up by a police officer). This type of person always posts about the issue and doesn't care about the "reputational outcomes" of doing so.
- People who are influenced by the desire to look good in the eyes of others, but are still authentically concerned and genuinely motivated to help. This fits the Kente cloth photo op, which served both to make politicians look good, but was also no doubt fueled by their authentic desire to make a positive statement.
- People who act out of bad faith and only share their virtues to look good. This is the ego-serving post, the cringey video, the celebrity selfies at a somber protest.

In her *Insider* article, Greenspan encourages activists to go beyond the posting and do something more tangible. She quoted Dominique Roberts, an activist quoted widely on social media, as saying: "Posting a black square is totally fine—to stand in solidarity and amplify our voices—but you have to graduate. People should be able to grow from mistakes they made."

Perhaps we should accept social media virtue signaling and all that goes with it as the "new normal" and be happy people care enough to even go that far. Social media allows everyone to have their voice, and does it really matter what level of participation someone gives when we don't know their motives or limitations? Perhaps they can't attend protests because they are sick. Maybe they're broke and cannot donate to a cause. Maybe all someone can muster the courage, strength, or energy to do sometimes is keep the flow of a message going from one person's page to their page and to the next by liking and sharing.

Armchair activists can have their place in helping to better humanity. Sometimes just being a decent person is a revolutionary act.

PERFORMATIVE ALLYSHIP

When a nonmarginalized group professes solidarity with and support for a marginalized group in a selfish, self-serving, or harmful way to the marginalized group, it is known as performative allyship. The group professing alliance gets the reward of praise, attention, and acknowledgment for its virtuous actions, like a trophy or a pat on the back for being such a social justice warrior. The group may even take it upon itself to use violence or other unwanted forms of protest that the marginalized group does not endorse or want to accept.

Some people believe allyship allows those involved to do things that are harmful with the excuse that they are "just trying to help" and are making personal sacrifices in their own eyes to help the oppressed and underprivileged. During the George Floyd protests in May and June of 2020, self-proclaimed antifascists, sometimes called "antifa," committed acts of disruption and violence in the name of helping the Black Lives Matter cause. However, many in the BLM community did not want violence to mar the messages of their protests. Even media commentators and many politicians and celebrities excused the looting and burning because they felt it made them look like they were on the right side of justice.

Anti-Fascists (known as Antifa for short) have been accused of causing acts of violence at demonstrations and otherwise disrupting peaceful marches.

Sadly, too many people, including celebrities who felt guilty about racism and the unjust treatment of African Americans, decided to draw attention to themselves through virtue signaling and performative allyship. This happens with any protest movement, as was seen with the previous year's marches related to feminism and immigration. Humans have egos, and for many, it's more important they feel good about themselves than actually devote time, energy, or money—without public acknowledgment—to the cause at hand. Another consideration is a short attention span that has people jumping on one bandwagon briefly before jumping off for another.

BLOCK, UNFRIEND, UNFOLLOW

Every neighborhood has the old man who is always yelling at those pesky kids: "Get off my lawn!" Social media has those, too. They are people who cannot engage in a discussion of other viewpoints and block, unfriend, or unfollow anyone who challenges their points of view. It's peer pressure to the nth degree, because instead of bullies on a playground, they're all over Facebook and Twitter and Instagram.

Imagine the pressure to self-censor your ideas and opinions, even on your own social media page, because if you voice them, you will be cut off from friends, family, or colleagues who don't agree with you. Just one hour on Facebook reveals people posting "If you like _____, get off my page!" or "If you voted for _____, do not ever speak to me again." With nary a thought to the fact they may be banishing people they love, they proclaim that their lawn is not meant to be trod upon by anyone with a different opinion or perception, especially when it comes to politics. "Get off my lawn" has become "get off my page" and has contributed greatly to censorship, anxiety, depression, intimidation, and the dissolution of relationships.

Too many people attack others instead of engaging in grown-up debate and discourse, trying to learn from each other and find some common moral ground.

Everyone is entitled to host who they want on their social media pages, but purposely cutting off anyone who disagrees is a form of denial and closed-mindedness that leads to confirmation bias and serves the propagandists by reinforcing ideologies and vilifying those with opposing ideologies. It plays right into the hands of politicians and leaders eager to exploit ongoing divisiveness and intolerance. And cutting off others for their beliefs can indicate hypocrisy for the person claiming to be the tolerant and open-minded one. Some of this comes from a lack of civility and polite discourse. Too many people attack others instead of engaging in grown-up debate and discourse, trying to learn from each other and find some common moral ground. The ability to project our most base behaviors is easier on social media than in real life because we can avoid facing the repercussions. Often the people on the attack are strangers or using fake names.

When an attack or insult comes from family or friends, it's hard to swallow down a response, and you have to decide what is worth more, the relationships or a quick venting of opinion. Social media has become a weapon that, like a playground bully, can bruise, harm, and even destroy others by making them feel marginalized, isolated, and shamed just for voicing their opinion and being who they are. If this is what social media has become, no wonder those who own the platforms find it such fertile ground for social engineering and mass manipulation.

Information Warfare: Fighting Back against Propaganda, Disinformation, and Manipulation

"The propaganadist's purpose is to make one set of people forget that certain other sets of people are human."
—Aldous Huxley

"I have certain rules I live by. My first rule, I don't believe anything the government tells me."
—George Carlin

Propaganda is insidious. It is pervasive. Often, it's blatant. Other times, it's subtle. Once you see it in action, you cannot unsee it. But how do you fight it, stop it, or avoid it when it is everywhere you turn?

Identifying propaganda and helping others to see it remove much of its power. When you are aware you are being manipulated, you don't allow it to happen anymore. Propagandists rely on our short attention spans, hoping we won't remember the past and the patterns of their manipulations. Unless we have a specific reason for doing so—say, for researching a book—we have little reason to store old news stories in our memory chambers when there is so much more demanding our attention. We have a limited amount of processing capacity to deal with an overwhelming amount of current information. The horrific false flags and major disasters of yesterday fade from our memory, and our emotional reactions to them diminish over time—no doubt a survival necessity—until the next one comes along and we must react and respond all over again.

We can only take so much.

The media we are exposed to is a huge part of the problem. It's confusing, muddled, spun, and distorted. Facts get buried in opinion, assumption, allegation, and accusation. Media outlets report stories before they get all the facts because they want to be the first to break the news. Then as new facts come to light, the stories seem to change.

The media we are exposed to is a huge part of the problem. It's confusing, muddled, spun, and distorted.

A perfect example of muddled news comes in two stories that emerged during the spring and summer of 2020 amidst the COVID-19 pandemic and the protests against racism and police violence. These show how the media makes finding the bare facts as difficult as finding a needle in a haystack. Whether they do it on purpose to fulfill their financial backers' agendas or as a result of shoddy reporting, it matters not. You are left with the haystack.

Newsweek reported the week of June 21st, in its story "No Evidence Black Lives Matter Protests Caused COVID-19 Spike," that despite the hundreds of thousands of protestors who hit the streets in 315 of America's largest cities to support Black Lives Matter, there was no evidence of a spike in COVID-19 cases following the two-and-a-half-week time period after protests. This would be well within the incubation period of 7 to 14 days that the CDC and the WHO had cited earlier in the year. The *Newsweek* article drew its information from a study titled "Black Lives Matter Protests, Social Distancing, and COVID-19," published by the National Bureau of Economic Research. The study referenced a "median incubation period" of 5.1 days, "with 97.5 percent of individuals experiencing symptoms within 11.5 days."

Yet in another story the same day, "Oklahoma Reports Highest Ever Daily COVID-19 Cases," *Newsweek* mentioned both a spike in COVID-19 cases in Oklahoma and a Trump rally in Tulsa two days before. Did this now mean the virus incubation period was just one or two days? Though the story did not claim a direct link to the rally—in fact, it stated, "Although Saturday's rally was not the cause of the most recent spike, experts fear it will make matters worse in coming weeks"—conservatives railed against the article's insinuation that the two were connected. *Newsweek* also published other stories throughout June with conflicting reports about spikes in cities where protests occurred. Here are some of the conflicting headlines:

A protestor complains about media unreliability during a march against COVID-19 restrictions.

"Houston Protestors Begin to Fall Ill with Coronavirus after Marching for George Floyd," from June 16.

"Two Weeks after Protests over George Floyd's Death Began, New Coronavirus Cases in Minnesota Continue to Drop," from June 10.

"Hawaii Health Official Says Protests Caused Coronavirus Spike," from June 19.

There were a few others, too. The point here is, what is the truth? Did the protests lead to spikes in virus cases or did they not? Why would *Newsweek* post a study saying they did not after weeks of posting stories to the contrary? Could the infection pattern have progressed differently in different regions?

Also in June 2020, the WHO reported that asymptotic spreading of COVID-19 was rare, citing in a press conference international contact tracing data that suggested WHO officials were not finding a "secondary transmission onward" of the novel coronavirus. People began questioning the need for stay-at-home orders and the closing of certain businesses over what the WHO cited as less of a danger than previously believed.

Cut to two weeks later when the WHO backtracked that stance, stating now that instead of asymptomatic spread being "very rare," the rate was "simply unknown" at this time. Scientists and researchers flocked to respond with varied opinions as to the true rate of spread, but the truth remained that the public was confused.

Did the confusion arise because this was a novel virus and scientists were learning on the fly? Or were there hidden agendas beneath the decisions to release information by the CDC, the WHO, the media, and the government? Sadly, the conflicting information did nothing to encourage trust in all of those organizations.

DEADLY DISINFORMATION

Decades ago, commercials for cigarettes appeared frequently on television. How cool those commercials made smoking seem! Too bad the product the tobacco industry was promoting was deadly and would result in millions of deaths from cancer in subsequent decades. The food industry uses propaganda and disinformation, too, to get us to buy their products, but in matters of health and survival, it behooves us to learn how to identify and deflect it. Our lives may depend on it.

During the 1960s, the sugar industry paid scientists to perform research studies playing down the links between sugar and heart disease and instead placing the blame on saturated fats, according to internal industry documents published in the 2016 *JAMA Internal Medicine* journal. These documents showed a five-decades-long barrage of research into nutrition and heart disease that identified saturated fats as the main culprit behind heart disease, while exonerating sugar. The studies were paid for by the sugar industry.

Every little Helps!
"*Don't be angry Daddy,*
it's for ST. DUNSTAN'S"

SMOKE
ST. DUNSTAN'S
VIRGINIA CIGARETTES
The quality is as excellent as the cause.

20 FOR 1/-   10 FOR 6D.

This 1922 ad shows a child smoking a cigarette, much to his parents' amusement. The caption says it's okay because money from this brand went to a charity for war veterans. Cigarette ads of the 1920s often showed children smoking.

According to Anahad O'Connor in the *New York Times* article "How the Sugar Industry Shifted Blame to Fat," published September 12, 2016, this was a concerted propaganda campaign that involved the Sugar Research Foundation paying three

Harvard scientists to publish a review on sugar, fat, and heart disease that featured hand-picked studies minimizing the links between sugar and heart disease, and promoting the links between fat and heart disease. Meanwhile, Coca-Cola was paying millions of dollars in funding to researchers to downplay the links between sugar and obesity.

To make a long story short, these faulty and fraudulent studies became the foundation of a decades-long propaganda push to eliminate fats from our diet and to push low-fat foods and products. For decades, consumers were told that cutting out saturated fats and eating white breads and processed low-fat foods would make them healthy. The result? A rise in obesity until the jig was up and the fraud was exposed.

In "Big Fat Lies—A Half Century of Sugary Propaganda Has Made Us Sick," published by *Healthline* on August 15, 2019, Brian Krans writes that the sugar industry uses money to manipulate the diet of American citizens. This is similar to the way corporate entities use money to manipulate mainstream news media. Krans writes that the sugar industry, Big Sugar, restructures conversations around health and choice by, among other tactics, establishing front organizations to guide the dialog in their favor. They pay consultants to speak at conventions and testify at public hearings, and they steer research in their favored direction. They redirect and deflect.

"During the 1960s," writes Krans, "the sugar industry steered public policy away from recommending reduced sugar consumption for children because it caused cavities. Like the tobacco industry, it was able to protect itself from damaging research. It achieved this by adopting 'a strategy to deflect attention to public health interventions that would reduce the harms of sugar consumption rather than restricting intake,' according to an investigation using internal documents." The sugar industry repeated this process when it came to obesity.

We are talking about multibillion-dollar industries that are aggressive about their propaganda tactics. They know the science is there showing they are creating products that make people sick and even cause death. But it's all about the bottom line, and these corporations and industries bank on the fact that the vast majority of consumers will never bother to do their own research into what's in their water, foods, medications, products, air, and so on.

The internet and social media groups make it easier than ever to spread a big lie from a big corporation or business. Until we all start doing a little research on our own and not taking everything at face value, propaganda will continue to promote hazards to our health and well-being just so someone else can make a buck.

NEWSFASTING

The best way to avoid or deflect propaganda is to take a news fast. Don't watch the news, national or local, for two weeks. You will get any important news from your friends and across social media, but you do not need to be exposed to the constant bombardment of manipulative stories meant to coerce you into behaving and thinking a certain way.

There is an old saying that what you give your attention to, you give your power to.

Try it, and see how it clears out your brain, making it better able to process what is going on in your life on a day-to-day basis. There is an old saying that what you give your attention to, you give your power to. Now and then sticking your head in the sand works to renew and refresh your spirit to face the further media onslaughts to come.

Do some self-care or get involved in some altruistic projects during the time you'd ordinarily binge on CNN or Fox News. Take a social network fast while you are at it, to avoid the negativity, judgment, and spread of viral misinfo and disinfo. If you feel compelled to check the headlines, watch a local news report rather than the more politicized cable news outlets. Local news gives you the headline stories and the news you need to know from your area. Then turn it off and proceed with your newsfast.

DO NOT FEED THE FEARS

According to the article "How to Size Up Propaganda" from the American Historical Association, "No matter how we define it, the principal point on propaganda is this: Don't be afraid of it."

Some propaganda is good. It tells us to brush our teeth at least twice a day and to recycle plastic bottles to stop them from ending up in landfills. Not every news story, commercial, advertisement, or piece of information is meant to lead us down some dark and shadowy road. And not everything is propaganda in the first place. When we are feeling afraid and untrusting, we become paranoid even of good or neutral information. The American Historical Association goes on to state: "Those who spread an unreasoned fear of propaganda base their preachments on the unscientific notion that propaganda by itself governs public opinion."

There are many factors that influence public opinion, and there exist "specific information and sound knowledge of facts, presented without any propagandic motive whatsoever," that constitute an extremely important factor in the formation of public opinion.

The AHA suggests some simple propaganda fact-checking when presented with a news story or piece of information. As yourself:

- Is it really propaganda? Is there some individual or group consciously trying to influence public opinion and action? If so, who are they, and what is their purpose?
- Is it true? When you look at independent reports, do they show that the facts are accurate? Did the comparison show that the ideas or information are soundly based?

Those two questions are priceless for getting a better grip on identifying propaganda, but you might also ask yourself:

- What is the source of the propaganda?
- Who benefits most from it?
- Who is being touted as the authority figure?
- Who are the financial backers? (Follow the money!)
- Why this, and why now?

Applying this kind of critical thinking alleviates fear and feelings of being disempowered because knowledge gives you a foundation from which to respond or act. Instead of just following the norm or toeing the party line, believing every word of the news as gospel, you can "learn to discern"—to engage your gut instinct and intuition, along with your intellect, to determine the source and purpose of a news story or event. This overcomes conditioning and the possibility of being manipulated because you will better understand the factors below the surface and more readily spot inconsistencies in the official narrative.

When people unquestioningly do as they are told, they are probably operating in fear. Fear of their government, fear of not conforming, fear of retaliation. But identifying fear when it arises

When people unquestioningly do as they are told they are probably operating in fear. Fear of their government, fear of not conforming, fear of retaliation.

and facing it directly allow you to figure out where it is coming from, what it is trying to tell you, or what it is trying to protect you from. Once you acknowledge those fears, you can better control them and make wiser decisions, including how you interpret news and propaganda, which requires a clear, sharp mind. Our conditioning keeps many of us from ever side-stepping fear to engage in critical thinking to solve problems. Instead, we give in to "fight or flight" programming that serves no one.

In a particularly harrowing situation such as a terrorist attack or the threat of war, facing fears is critical to keeping yourself from giving in to impulses and emotions that could harm you or your loved ones. It also keeps you from falling prey to the temptation to join the fear-mongering crowds on social media and spread viral information that is not true or is itself fear-based, serving only to increase the size of the existing pool of negativity and panic. During times of chaos and strife, the world needs clear-headed thinkers as leaders, not impulsive, overemotional panicked people who don't know where to turn for information and assistance.

STOPPING COERCIVE CONTROL

The techniques of coercive control used in cults and on victims of domestic violence have much to teach us about similar abuses we suffer at the hands of propagandists. Recognizing coercive control is the first step to preventing it. You will know when someone is attempting to use and abuse you, force you to embrace an ideology you do not believe in, or discard values and ideals you hold to be true.

Healthline's October 10, 2019, article "How to Recognize Coercive Control" by Cindy Lamothe lists 12 signs that you are being coercively controlled:

1. Isolation from friends, family, and support systems (isolation and marginalization)
2. Lack of privacy; your activity is constantly monitored (surveillance)

A thermal camera detects shoppers with fevers in this still shot. Many people are becoming uneasy with the increased surveillance popping up in businesses and public places, especially with the onset of the COVID-19 pandemic.

3. You are denied freedom and autonomy (e.g., phone taken away, no shopping, no school, no work)

4. You experience gaslighting—psychological manipulation in which a person or a group covertly sows seeds of doubt, making a person or group question their own reality, memory, perception, or judgment, often evoking in them cognitive dissonance or low self-esteem (manipulation)

5. Name-calling, criticism, judgment, put-downs—to make someone or a group feel inadequate, stupid, and worthless (disempowerment)

6. Limiting your access to money (disempowering, crippling)

7. Reinforcing traditional gender or race roles (stereotyping)

8. Turning others against you (isolation and marginalization)

9. Controlling your body and health (e.g., mandated medical procedures)

10. Making unfounded accusations, perhaps out of jealousy (shaming and guilting)

11. Regulating your sexuality (lack of body autonomy)

12. Threatening your children, loved ones, pets (intimidation)

All of these are tactics used not just by individuals but also by governments, military, religious and cult leaders, and extremist groups to take away someone's power or autonomy. These tactics work for the domestic abuser, and they work equally well for anyone who wishes to abuse you for their agendas and purposes. You also must look out for attempts to control the flow of information to you, which is censorship, and to make you dependent on your abuser. Creating a state of emotional and physical dependency is a surefire way to control another human being or even an entire population. An example might be a national emergency that destroys the economy, but the government comes through with stimulus checks and free food, creating a complete sense of dependency upon them. People who cannot work or earn money turn to the government for their very basic survival needs. We see this all the time in cults where members must give up their life savings and material possessions to depend entirely on their new "family." Of course, there is a difference between purposefully created deprivation, as induced by a cult, and a natural or economic disaster, in which governments exist in part to help their citizens survive. We would all be wise to remain mindful of the difference.

Creating a state of emotional and physical dependency is a surefire way to control another human being or even an entire population.

During the 2020 COVID-19 pandemic, the government gave out stimulus checks to assist families who were out of work and out of food. The amount was paltry compared to the need, but for many people, it became a lifeboat to stay afloat in. A sum of money added to weekly unemployment checks served to keep many laid-off workers fed and sheltered. As a result of the sum added to unemployment checks, some low-income workers temporarily made more money while they were out of work than they did at their jobs, raising concerns that they would not want to return to work once their employers were able to hire them again. Whether this was an example of created dependency, minimum wages being too low to begin with, both, or something else is a continuing debate.

Another powerful technique to effect coercive control is to change the source of authority. This happens when the normal authority figures are replaced by more totalitarian ones that the population must submit to. Gone are local, state, and regional authority figures, replaced by a single dictator or regime. Once that authority figure usurps all others, it becomes difficult to remove them from their pedestal without great effort, even violent revolution. History offers numerous examples.

Gaslighting alone is enough to destroy another human being, or group of human beings, because it plays into our sense of perception of reality and our place in it. When we are gaslit, whether by a lover, a family member, the media, or the politicians in power, we experience tremendous cognitive dissonance and confusion. We are exposed to people who are adept at wearing us down, using what we love as weapons against us, lies and lies about lies, an occasional positive action to keep us off balance, and the ability to get us to completely question and reevaluate our own reality.

Gaslighting is a great brainwashing method because of how it strips down a person's sense of internal self and external reality. But once you know the techniques, you can see it happening and stop it in its tracks. This is the last thing the propagandists in our lives want: for us to wake up and smell the coffee. Once we smell this brand of coffee, though, we no longer want to drink it.

DEPROGRAM YOURSELF

Those lucky enough to escape from cults, or those rescued from them, are put through a rigorous and intense deprogramming to remove the embedded beliefs of the cult and allow the brain, namely the subconscious, to program in new and more empowering beliefs. Propaganda is a form of brainwashing meant to reprogram our sense of identity, personality, behaviors, actions, thoughts, and most foundational sense of reality. While we don't need the intensive deprogramming methods required to get out of a cult, the principles are similar.

To deprogram from propaganda requires the use of critical thinking and analyzing our own beliefs. It involves digging deep within our subconscious to hold up our most entrenched beliefs, many of which we might not even be aware, to the light of day. We must ask ourselves:

- What is the belief?
- When did I start believing this belief?
- Is this a belief I agreed to, or was it imposed upon me by family, peers, society, or someone else?
- Does this belief make sense to me now?

- How is this belief helping me? Hurting me?

Journaling the answers helps to make it more of a tangible exercise. Once you start to track your beliefs and examine the ideologies you follow, you can begin to sense whether or not they reflect your own choices or those of others. So much of what we believe comes from our parents when we are children, then our peers, educators, government, media, and now social media. Never examining the thought behind our thoughts leaves us open to manipulation, coercion, and the cult mentality that enslaves us to someone else's life agenda.

Newsfasting helps. Learning to detach from the emotional overload allows us time to decompress and open our eyes to the good in life—to the honesty and authenticity around us that gets drowned out by the lies and distortions of the mainstream media talking heads. We start to hear our own voice again and to form our opinions based on that inner voice rather than on what is popular on Facebook or what some pundit tells us we should believe.

Staying away from negative people and avoiding those still embedded in their political, religious, or social righteousness also allows you to rid your mind of their agendas so you can fill your own well with what serves you. Be careful, though. There are tons of articles online advising ways to deprogram yourself out of being a Republican, voting Democrat, believing in UFOs, liking cheese, and so on. These are just another form of brainwashing written by those who benefit from you doing what they want you to do, guiding you back to what you are trying to break free of in the first place.

Take a break from the onslaught of TV and online news and read a book or enjoy the outdoors. This allows you time to decompress and reassess your life.

Ideally, you want to be yourself again—or a better version of the person you were before you let the propagandists have a field day with your brain—and rid yourself of the programming that has been dumped into your subconscious since childhood by both well-meaning and not-so-well-meaning people. If you feel inclined, you can look into self-hypnosis or working with a hypnosis program designed to reprogram your mind for positive benefits and rid it of old, stale, and destructive beliefs and paradigms. You've heard the saying "garbage in, garbage out," and it works for your life just the same. What you program in (or allow programmed in) shows up in your external reality as your health, success, happiness, relationships, and career.

Know thyself. The truth will set you free, but it will piss you off first. Once you acknowledge how pissed off you are that you've been lied to, manipulated, and sabotaged, then you can begin the journey back to a state of empowerment that comes from operating from your own chosen programming instead of someone else's.

CRITICAL TIMES REQUIRE CRITICAL THINKING

Learning to detect the baloney from the filet mignon requires critical thinking skills. Fortunately, you can learn such skills any time. In his book *The Demon-Haunted World: Science as a Candle in the Dark*, the late author, scientist, and visionary Carl Sagan included a chapter titled "The Fine Art of Baloney Detection," in which he examined types of deception and how to think critically about them via his "baloney detection kit." This "kit" was a set of cognitive tools Sagan believed could fortify the mind from falsehoods, like the fake news of today.

He listed nine tools:

1. Wherever possible, facts must be independently confirmed.
2. The evidence should be debated by knowledgeable proponents of all points of view.
3. Seek out scientific experts, not authorities.
4. Think of all the different ways something can be explained, then think of tests to disprove each one. What survives is the hypothesis that cannot be disproved.
5. Do not get too attached to a hypothesis just because it's yours.
6. If what you're explaining can be measured, measure it; quantify it numerically.
7. Every link in a chain of an argument must work, not just most of them.
8. Remember Occam's Razor: when faced with two hypotheses that both work to explain the data, pick the simpler one.
9. Ask whether the hypothesis can be tested or falsified.

Sagan also encouraged people to avoid the most common fallacies of logic and rhetoric, such as ad hominem argu-

The late astronomer and science writer Carl Sagan shared a strategy with his readers on how to detect "baloney."

ments that attack the arguer and ignore the argument itself; appeals to ignorance by claiming things that have not been proven false must therefore be true; observational selection, which consists of counting the hits and forgetting the misses; and "slippery slope" arguments, among others.

The key is to better understand and evaluate our own arguments before we try to present them to others or to evaluate the arguments of others.

Critical thinking requires important skills to allow us to objectively analyze and evaluate a situation so we can make an informed judgment. It requires the ability to engage in independent and reflective thinking and to use our ability to reason rather than depend on emotion. Effective critical thinking skills allow us to understand the links between two or more ideas; determine the relevance of ideas; build and appraise our own arguments; approach problems consistently and systematically rather than out of passiveness or emotion; find errors and inconsistencies in our own arguments and those of others; and reflect on our beliefs and values.

Without the ability to evaluate different points of view, we are unable to determine their validity.

Without the ability to evaluate different points of view, we are unable to determine their validity. We also need to keep an objective stance and look for the weak points in an argument or point of view to determine the strength of the idea. Taking notice of the following helps us evaluate propaganda and rhetoric when we are presented with it, especially in the media:

- Who said it?
- What exactly did they say?
- Where did they say it?
- When did they say it?
- Why did they say it?
- How did they say it?

These are the tenets of good journalism and reporting—the *who*, *what*, *where*, *when*, *why*, and *how* that should be in every news story. When we evaluate the news media, we should be asking these questions and looking deeper for possible agendas and motives, such as "Who benefits financially or politically from this?" "Who is financing this?" and "Who wins and who loses from this decision?"

Just as it benefits us to become critical thinkers and decision makers in our personal lives, we must become critical consumers and viewers of mass media to avoid being taken advantage of, lied to, deceived, and manipulated. We have to learn how to look at a news story and find "just the facts, ma'am." We need to seek alternative sources to corroborate those facts within and outside of the mainstream media. We need to make smart assessments of the implications of a news event and ask if there is a benefit to a particular person, group, or political agenda.

One of the most important ways to become a critical consumer is to understand the relationships between the media and advertisers, governments, politicians, special interests, lobby groups, and competitors. All of these play a role in what news is presented and how it is done. In their fabulous booklet *The Thinker's Guide for Conscientious Citizens on How to Detect Media Bias and Propaganda in National and World News*, Dr. Richard Paul and Dr. Linda Elder use critical thinking as the foundation for their tools and concepts, and they offer several reasons why manipulating critical consumers of news is difficult:

- Critical media consumers study alternative perspectives and know how to interpret events from multiple viewpoints.
- Critical consumers analyze news constructs the same way they analyze other representations of reality.
- They notice questionable assumptions implicit in stories.
- They notice what is implied but not openly stated.
- They notice which points of view get a favorable light and which don't.
- They notice the agenda and interests the story serves.
- They learn to identify viewpoints embedded in a story.

They also ask some key questions, such as:

- Who is the audience?
- What point of view is being promoted?
- Which stories are making the front page, and why?
- Which stories are being buried behind the front-page stories?
- Is there any important information buried in the article that is not being talked about on the news?

The savvy critical news consumer knows that a big, bold headline story can hide an even more important one, especially one that is damaging to powerful people. They know to read more than just one quick news item to get the whole picture. They also know that the whole picture may change as more information is made available, so they take what they read with a grain of salt.

These are just a few of the ways critical thinking can be applied to the identification of propaganda when it presents itself. The authors state, "To find sources of information supporting the dominant views within a culture is not difficult. The problem for most of us is finding well-thought-through voices that question the mainstream news." We need to strengthen these muscles to locate mainstream and dissenting views that are articulate and insightful if we want to understand the full range of views on any issue. And of course, first we have to identify those views, which requires us to 1) locate a full range of views, and 2) locate well-informed sources for each major position.

"The media world we inhabit is without exception a world of spin," stated the May 7, 2004, *Wall Street Journal*. The only way we can overcome the spin of the world is to identify it, analyze it, break it apart, shed light on it, and counter it with facts and truth once we find it.

FIGHTING CENSORSHIP

On June 22, 2020, Breitbart, a conservative media outlet, reported that the online superstore and media service Amazon removed from its playlist a documentary titled *Killing Free Speech*. The documentary was about censorship, and it was censored by Amazon.

The biggest slippery slope we can slide down is the one that muzzles us of free speech but also denies us access to information simply because it serves someone's agenda to do so. Censorship is a wound that grows and can eventually threaten to take away all of the rights and liberties that make America a free country of free individuals. When someone else decides what we have access to—what we can say, wear, do, think, and be—we are no longer free.

Fighting censorship can mean everything from getting off social media platforms that censor or writing to them in protest, to boycotting companies and media outlets that censor important information. It can mean doing your own research and distributing it. It can mean looking beyond the official narrative to the one the primary sources aren't telling you about, or the story they want to distract you from.

The fight to end censorship is not just for writers, journalists, reporters, and whistleblowers. It affects every one of us. We might not mind if it's happening to someone else, but we certainly don't want to be the one being censored. Should even Hitler have been allowed to give speeches? Yes, if we truly believe in free speech, because free speech requires that we defend even the speech we find offensive. Censorship assumes we are too stupid or lacking in discernment to identify the information we want and need.

When is censorship a violation of free speech and when is it protecting people from hate speech, propaganda, and lies?

From the website Reformed Health, which has experienced censorship by social media outlets over many of its articles and videos about natural health and vaccines, came a scathing statement:

> Censorship hinders free thought and progress. Facebook censorship stops new ideas from entering the marketplace. And quite frankly, those who promote Facebook censorship—or any organization that TELLS you what you ought to believe is TRUE or FALSE (who is not God)—that person is weak minded and not interested in knowing the truth.
>
> When organizations feel they need to censor people from the truth, it is for one of two reasons.
>
> 1. They think the population is too stupid to find out the truth on their own.
>
> 2. They are trying to sway public opinion to their way of thinking.
>
> Do you want Facebook telling you what to believe? Are YOU too stupid to check the facts for yourself? That's what Facebook thinks. Or else ... they are trying to sway you to their way of thinking—so you don't need to think on your own.

Speaking of Facebook and censorship, the social media platform went head to head with the right-leaning activist group Project

Veritas in June of 2020 when a Project Veritas sting caught on hidden-camera footage almost a dozen Facebook post moderators working for a company called Cognizant openly claiming they banned, blocked, and flagged Republican and pro-Trump posts even though they did not violate community standards or the platform's rules. The third-party moderator company announced that it would scale back content-moderation services for Facebook after the scandal, and after former content moderator Zach McElroy turned whistleblower and confessed that about three-quarters of all posts flagged for "civic harassment" were right/conservative leaning.

This is just one example, and to be fair, no doubt the same kind of selective cherry-picking of posts occurs on both left-leaning and right-leaning sites. Propaganda is rampant on both sides of the political posting spectrum. Censorship is not just about burning books or rock albums in a bonfire. It occurs in ways the public is not even aware of, and it breaches the trust of users of media sites and social media platforms who believe they are being leveled with.

Here are some tips to help you fight censorship:

- Get informed on the issues so you can speak to what is being censored or left out.
- Complain to the sources that are censoring. In your complaint, list the facts you know the sources are leaving out of their story. Be polite. No one likes to be talked down to.
- Boycott sources of censorship; put your money where your mouth is.
- If someone shares information you know is false, stand up for the truth and ask them to consider looking at the evidence and facts.
- Post on social media about things you have seen censored and offer facts. Try not to be preachy or condescending, as that turns people off regardless of how accurate your message may be.
- Find and support alternative news and media sources that do not censor.
- Support organizations that fight censorship and promote freedom of speech, such as the American Civil Liberties Union, Judicial Watch, the Electronic Frontier Foundation, National Coalition against Censorship, and Project Censored Top 25 Censored Stories and Project Censored Radio, which identify and list the top censored news stories each year.
- Post correct and censored facts in the comments sections of similar articles or ones that present a counterversion of what you know has been censored.

- Buy banned books.
- Speak up when you see someone else being censored, even if you disagree with what they are saying. If we all lose the right to freely express ourselves, we all lose.

FINDING SOURCES THAT WORK FOR YOU

Some news agencies, notably Associated Press (AP) and Reuters, are widely recognized as exhibiting no bias in their reporting. Many other mainstream media outlets, however, lean right or left—sometimes by publishing the AP or Reuters stories within a certain framing or embellished with a certain spin—and most of us can figure out which. There are dozens, if not hundreds, of smaller media outlets that have their own agendas, and these don't necessarily constitute a sinister plot to brainwash the masses. Outlets owned by people or groups with political preferences do express those preferences in the stories they publish or broadcast. Why? Because either their funding sources want them to or their audience demands it. If Fox News suddenly went to the extreme left, it would lose its base audience. If CNN suddenly lurched rightward, it would lose its audience. This is understandable.

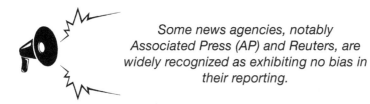

Some news agencies, notably Associated Press (AP) and Reuters, are widely recognized as exhibiting no bias in their reporting.

But if you seek your news with as little spin as possible, or at least want to know ahead of time who leans center, right, or left, there are some resources you can use. Watchdog and media bias organizations exist that do the work for you of producing guides and lists of news outlets and their political stances, but beware that many have their own spin depending on who runs the organization, where their funding comes from, and the results, which may differ with your own experiences watching those news outlets. This is fine if you are told up front that the media guide is directed to viewers who prefer to lean right, or lean left, but this author found some "reputable nonpartisan media bias rating sites" that showed their own bias. Who watches the watchers?

Two of the bigger and more transparent media bias watchdog sites are the Pew Research Center and AllSides.

Pew publishes a guide of news media outlets on the political spectrum. On its website, Pew promotes transparency and even includes a link to its tax documents to show its contributors. Its focus is more on the ideological placement of the audience than the intent of each news outlet, but the information is valid. Pew lists on a chart which news sources are used and determined trustworthy based on individual political values, conservative or liberal, to measure the political leanings of the audiences and what sources they prefer. Its website also features other analyses of the media and bias among viewers.

AllSides is chock full of charts, lists, and analysis of media outlets of all sizes. Using multiple sources for its information, All-Sides rates news media according to its own system to classify news sources as left, center, or right. Some of the components of this system include crowdsourcing, surveys, use of third-party resources, internal research, and research conducted by outside sources. AllSides regularly conducts blind surveys across the political spectrum, editorial reviews, user feedback ratings, and multipartisan analysis. Its focus is on online news outlets, unless specifically noted.

According to its website, "AllSides Media Bias Ratings help you identify different perspectives so you can know more, understand more, and think for yourself." It rates the bias levels of almost 600 media outlets and writers with the intent to free people "from their filter bubbles so we can better understand the world—and each other."

Let's take a look at AllSides's latest findings.

Media Sources Leaning Left

Note that some of these sources began in the center before moving or being perceived as moving toward the left.

- CNN
- MSNBC
- Yahoo
- NPR Editorial
- PBS *NewsHour*
- *New York Times*
- *Washington Post*
- Huffington Post
- *Mother Jones*

- Politico
- Slate
- *New Yorker*
- *Atlantic*
- *Time*
- *Newsweek*
- Alternet
- The Intercept
- Buzzfeed
- Vox
- *Guardian*
- *Washington Post*
- CBS
- ABC
- NBC
- Daily Beast

Media Sources Leaning Center
- *Wall Street Journal* (online only)
- BBC News
- Associated Press
- Bloomberg
- The Hill
- Reuters
- *USA Today*
- *Christian Science Monitor*
- NPR (online)
- *Forbes*

Media Sources Leaning Right
- Fox News
- Breitbart
- OANN
- Daily Wire
- *National Review*
- NewsMaxx
- Daily Mail
- Daily Caller
- *New York Post*

- Federalist
- Judicial Watch
- CBN
- Reason
- Drudge Report
- *American Spectator*
- RT
- *Wall Street Journal* (newspaper only)
- *Washington Times*

With new media outlets like the right-leaning One America News Network (OANN) and others popping up each year, AllSides asks users to submit new sources. Many of the sources listed above may only lean slightly in one direction, while others may be more extreme. AllSides breaks down all of this and allows users to filter for news outlets of a specific lean or bias.

There are other watchdog sites out there as well, offering their mission statements on their websites.

Media Matters of America, founded by David Brock in 2004, is a left-leaning nonprofit organization with the stated mission of "comprehensively monitoring, analyzing, and correcting conservative misinformation in the U.S. media."

FAIR—Fairness and Accuracy in Reporting, founded in 1986 by Jeff Cohen and Martin A. Lee, is a self-described "national media watchdog group" with progressive and liberal leanings that monitors news media for inaccuracy, bias, and censorship, and also works to advocate for more diversity of perspectives in media. FAIR calls attention to the corporate ownership of the media and is against media monopolies and conglomerates.

Judicial Watch is a conservative foundation that "fights for accountability and integrity in law, politics, and government" and also focuses on censorship, media bias and propaganda, and legal issues.

Ad Fontes Media puts out a detailed media chart that is regularly updated, featuring larger news sources organized by political lean and accuracy. A perusal of its results shows a lean toward the left.

The University of Michigan Library Research Guides are hugely informative, but they lean left as indicated by the slant toward the authors, articles, and research they suggest.

The *Wall Street Journal*, a right-leaning outlet, conducted an experiment that ended in 2019 called "Blue Feed, Red Feed" that placed actual Facebook posts of news stories side by side to show them from a liberal and conservative point of view. Comparing and contrasting can be quite an eye-opener. On its website for the project, which shows the archived results in full, the *Wall Street Journal* stated:

The *Wall Street Journal* did a study in 2015 comparing news stories posted on Facebook with how the same stories were written about in liberal and conservative news outlets.

> Facebook's role in providing Americans with political news has never been stronger—or more controversial. Scholars worry that the social network can create "echo chambers," where users see posts only from like-minded friends and media sources. Facebook encourages users to "keep an open mind" by seeking out posts that don't appear in their feeds.
>
> To demonstrate how reality may differ for different Facebook users, The *Wall Street Journal* created two feeds, one "blue" and the other "red." If a source appears in the red feed, a majority of the articles shared from the source were classified as "very conservatively aligned" in a large 2015 Facebook study. For the blue feed, a majority of each source's articles aligned "very liberal." These aren't intended to resemble actual individual news feeds. Instead, they are rare side-by-side looks at real conversations from different perspectives.

Though this study was done in 2015, it remains a valuable tool to understand the way those of a different ideological affiliation interact with the same news content.

Doing a search for media watchdogs pulls up a number of organizations, big and small. Some are mentioned here. They, like the news media they report on, must earn your trust and respect, so do your own research on each.

That a media watchdog group leans right or left doesn't necessarily mean the information is bad or inaccurate, as many of these sites seek to offer another perspective to one they feel is more prominent in society and the current dialog, or to balance out an inequality they perceive in reporting. You can usually tell by the focus of a group's headlines, studies, or results if there is an in-house predisposition toward one end of the political spectrum or another, but again, that doesn't mean you should automatically discard its findings. Even groups and websites with a decided political tilt may offer good information or factual data worth considering.

Want to know the number-one media bias tracker on the market? You. Yes, you. Use your own discernment and watch or read the news on a particular outlet yourself. Do some comparison shopping between a decidedly right spinning outlet and a decidedly left one. Look for common factual elements, and challenge yourself to locate the embellishment, spin, bias, and propaganda on both sides of the political spectrum. Just separating out the who, what, where, when, and how elements of a news story works wonders at getting the information that counts while avoiding the opinions and commentary that get piled on top of it.

FIGHTING THE DISINFO MACHINE

Disinformation isn't always easy to spot, but the same principles apply as with spotting propaganda. Once you see it, you can then avoid it and do your part not to spread it. Nowadays all media outlets have email addresses where viewers can write to report inconsistencies and mistakes in news reporting. Holding these outlets accountable must start with the viewers, who need to demand they are not being lied to, manipulated, or fed false news stories meant to mislead and distract them. See something, say something, and let them know you won't be giving them your support if they engage in spreading disinformation.

Often there is a section for comments at the end of opinion pieces and news stories posted online, so make use of it with facts that make your case for correcting falsehoods. But be polite. Being hostile and condescending gets you nowhere. Sometimes the reporters or writers don't know they are spreading bad information, and if you can prove it to them, they will post a retraction or correction. At the very least, people will read your comments and be made aware of the problem.

It's easy to get a news outlet to correct misinformation and mistakes in reporting. But be ready for a struggle when you identify disinformation because it might be intentional. Come prepared with some proof as your ammunition.

Spotting disinformation on your social media feed is easy once you know what to look for. Often it comes in the form of shared stories or memes, which are passed along by people who don't take the time to look closely at what they're sharing. Bad information goes viral just as easily as good information. Keep this in mind, and pause before you retweet, repost, share, or like. There are some simple questions to ask to evaluate the information:

- Is it an original, sourced news story, or is it an opinion piece?
- Who shared this with me or created it?
- What account is sharing this? When was the account created? Do they share things from all over the world at all times during the day and night? Could this be a bot? Do I know them well? Do I know their political point of view?
- Why was this shared with me in particular?

If someone shares an important news story and you aren't sure about the facts, you can search for corroboration online at other news outlets before spreading it to someone else. Also be mindful of who posted it or shared it with you and their motives and political leanings. If it came from a stranger or a shady-looking profile, delete it. It could be spam or clickbait. A good rule of thumb is to beware before you share, or you'll be known as "that person" who spreads fake news.

SOCIAL MEDIA AND SEARCH ENGINE ALTERNATIVES

As Facebook, Twitter, and Google are engaging in more and more censorship, shadow banning, and invasion of privacy, some alternatives have arisen. Social media sites like Parler, Minds, and MeWe are hoping to entice users with the promise of no censorship or privacy invasion, and although they don't have the reach of the bigger social media sites, they promote their services as far more user-friendly.

Parler is a fast-growing social networking service originally launched in 2018 and marketed as a Twitter alternative especially

Social media sites like Parler, Minds, and MeWe are hoping to entice users with the promise of no censorship or privacy invasion....

Kremlin Disinformation Techniques

The Center for European Policy Analysis, a nonprofit, non-partisan public policy institute, published some of the common techniques used by the Russian Federation to spread disinformation:

- Ping pong—The coordinated use of complementary websites to springboard a story into mainstream circulation.

- Wolf cries wolf—The vilification of an individual or institution for something you also do.

- Misleading title—Facts or statements in the article are correct, or mostly correct, but the title is misleading.

- No proof—Facts or statements that are not backed up with proof or sources.

- Card stacking—Facts or statements are partially true.

- False facts—Facts or statements that are false. For example, an interview mentioned in an article that never took place, or an event or incident featured in a news story that did not occur.

- False visuals—A variant of false facts, this technique employs the use of fake or manipulated provocative visual material. Its purpose is to lend credibility to a false fact or narrative.

- Denying facts—A variant of "false facts," this occurs when real facts are denied or wrongly undermined. The facts of an event might be reported, but an attempt is made to discredit their veracity.

- Exaggeration and overgeneralization—This method dramatizes, raises false alarms, or uses a particular premise to shape a conclusion.

- *Totum pro parte*—The "whole for a part." An example: portraying the views of a single journalist or expert as the official view or position of a government.

- Changing the quotation, source, or context—Facts and statements are reported from other sources, but they are now different from the original or do not account for the latest editorial changes.

- Loaded words or metaphors—Using expressions and metaphors to support a false narrative or hide a true one; for example, using a term like "mysterious death" instead of "poisoning" or "murder" to describe the facts of a story.

- Ridiculing, discrediting, diminution—Marginalizing facts, statements, or people through mockery, name calling (i.e., *argumentum ad hominem*), or undermining their authority. This includes using traditional and new media humor in order to discredit on nonsubstantive merits.

- Whataboutism—Using false comparisons to support a prefabricated narrative or justify deeds and policies.

- Narrative laundering—Concealing and cleaning the provenance of a source or claim, such as when a so-called expert of dubious integrity presents false facts or narratives as the truth. Often, this happens when propaganda outlets mimic the format of mainstream media. A common technique is to feature a guest "expert" or "scholar" on a TV program whose false fact or narrative can then be repackaged for wider distribution. For example, "Austrian media writes that ..." or "A well-known German political expert says that...."

The Moscow Kremlin, the seat of the Russian government, is home to expert propagandists who have made the export of false information into an art form.

- Exploiting balance—This happens when otherwise mainstream media outlets try to "balance" their reporting by featuring professional propagandists or faux journalists and experts. The effect is to inject an otherwise legitimate news story or debate with false facts and narratives. This technique is common in televised formats, which feature point–counterpoint debates. Propagandists subsequently hijack a good-faith exchange of opposing views.

- Presenting opinion as facts (and vice versa)—An opinion is presented as a fact in order to advance or discredit a narrative.

- Conspiracy theories—Employing rumors, myths, or claims of conspiracy to distract or dismay an audience.

- Joining the bandwagon—Creating the impression that the "majority" prefers or understands an issue in a certain way.

- False dilemma—Forcing audiences into a false binary choice, typically "us" versus "them."

- Drowning facts with emotion—A form of the "appeal to emotion" fallacy, this is when a story is presented in such an emotional way that facts lose their importance.

- Creating the context—Most commonly found on broadcast news programs, it creates the context for a prefabricated narrative by preceding and following a news story in such a way that it changes the meaning of the news itself.

for those who have been banned from Twitter, Reddit, YouTube, and Facebook. It's a worldwide site that requires registration and focuses on protecting the free speech and the rights of users. It has a larger concentration of conservative voices, as well as those who are opposed to Big Pharma and have been censored on other formats for their antivaccine content. Parler has a more lenient attitude toward free speech, which can be extremely off-putting or offensive to some, but it does not allow violence or pornography. CEO John Matze named it "parler" from the French word for "to speak." It has drawn many prominent conservative voices and a large alternative health following. Parler never shares user data, a huge plus for those tired of having their information sold by Facebook to the highest bidder.

Minds is an unusual free and open source distribution social network. Founded in 2011 by Bill Ottman and John Ottman as an alternative to Facebook, it has become a popular social network for those eager to engage in intellectual and philosophical conversation, as well as take advantage of free speech and protected privacy. The site requires registration but allows it to be anonymous, and Minds prides itself on its radical transparency and promotion of free speech. What makes Minds different is that it uses blockchain, a record-keeping technology, to reward members with ERC-20 tokens, a form of online currency. Users can use their tokens to promote their content or to crowdfund other users through monthly subscriptions to their exclusive content and services, making it the first "crypto social network." It has been criticized for some extremist neo-Nazi content, which it then banned from the platform.

MeWe was founded by Mark Weinstein in 2012 as another alternative to the usual social media suspects. It made its official debut during the 2016 South by Southwest festival and was honored as the 2016 Start-Up of the Year for Innovative World Technology. MeWe requires registration and touts its commitment to user privacy and control. Users can post text and images as on other social networks, and they have their own "home feed" and access to online chat, groups, and privacy settings for posts. MeWe's stand-alone messaging is called Privacy Mail and is available for Androids and iPhones. The phone app also includes a custom camera. MeWe is a free service and plans to stay that way. It was the top trending social media app in 2018, with continued growth ever since thanks to strong privacy rights and less censorship.

For those opposed to the censorship and banning of video content on YouTube and Vimeo, give BitChute a try. Founded in 2017 by Ray Vahey, the video hosting service was created as an alternative to the content rules on other video hosting platforms. BitChute can be a bit intimidating, as it contains a lot of conspiracy theories, conservative viewpoints, radicalism, and alternative viewpoints on religion, politics, health,

Now owned by the Sgrouples company in Culver City, California, the MeWe social network markets itself as an alternative to Facebook because it has a greater focus on data privacy, but it has been criticized for not moderating content very well.

Big Pharma, and everything else. According to the BitChute website, "BitChute aims to put creators first and provide them with a service that they can use to flourish and express their ideas freely."

BitChute guidelines are spelled out directly and serve as the community principles expected to be followed. They state that BitChute is about free expression, people power, individual responsibility, decentralized distribution, opportunity to succeed, and empowering creators. The site does not support oppression or incitement of violence, platform bias, mob rule, censorship, illegal content, or exploiting creators. BitChute aims to foster a place "where users can express themselves, their thoughts and/or opinions for open discussion, without unjust criticism or discrimination."

For those seeking a search engine that not only doesn't censor the results but protects search history and privacy, nothing beats DuckDuckGo, the go-to search engine for those who are tired of the political leanings and sneaky analytics and algorithms of Google. DuckDuckGo is the most popular alternative search engine promising privacy and security. It was launched in September of 2008 and created by Gabriel Weinberg, who claims his search engine "does not collect or share personal information. That is our privacy policy in a nutshell."

DuckDuckGo recently improved its search quality by removing search results for companies acting as content mills, which Weinberg claimed are lower-quality sources of information designed to specifically rank higher in Google search indexes. DuckDuckGo filters out pages with tons of advertising, too. It gets its search results from over 400 sources and also includes crowd-sourced sites like Wikipedia. In 2010 DuckDuckGo introduced anonymous searching for search engine traffic using the Tor network, and in 2011 it introduced a voice search compatible with Google Chrome voice search extension.

There are over a dozen other alternative search engines, many operating by country or region. Do your due diligence in researching their privacy policies, search term storage, and information sources. Opt for a private search engine that does no tracking, won't save your search histories, and allows you to extract information with as few clicks as possible to keep your footprint down. Also check how each search engine makes its money and where it is headquartered. "The more you know...."

PRIVACY TIPS

Because propaganda is so intertwined with privacy rights (the more they know about you, the more they can use you to their advantage), here are some basic tips for staying a bit more under the radar.

Use a VPN. A VPN is a "Virtual Private Network" that allows users to send and receive data across shared or public networks without leaving a data fingerprint. It routes what you are doing on-line through some other computer somewhere else in the world, so that your location and identity are impossible to track. VPN is software you can download and install like any other and is easy to use, even if you're not a techie type. VPNs make it look as though your computer is not your computer by creating a fake identity that is routed through other sources so you cannot be pinpointed.

Older email systems such as AOL, Yahoo, and Gmail are often used as surveillance platforms, so try something with end-to-end encryption, such as ProtonMail.com.

Avoid using Google Search or Chrome as your browser, be-cause they track keystrokes and every visited webpage. Find an alternative like Brave, a free, open source web browser that blocks ads and tracking.

Bing and Yahoo search engines draw their search results through Google Search. Use DuckDuckGo instead.

If possible, avoid using Google Home and Amazon Alexa devices in your home as they are always recording and sending information back to Google or Amazon.

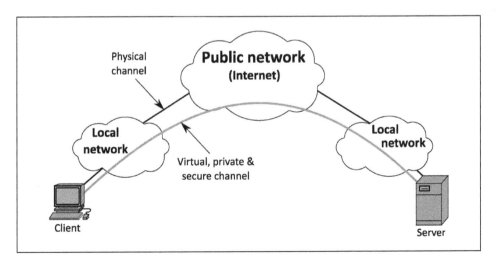

A Virtual Private Network (VPN) helps users protect their identities by routing data through other computers in another part of the world. This makes the original user difficult to track.

The Amazon Alexa service, which is connected to by devices such as this Amazon echo dot, record and track information that you provide for marketers to use.

Your cell phone is always listening, especially if you have an Android or if you have Siri on an iPhone. Check your privacy settings and turn off Siri and voice activation apps, and always check to make sure your camera and microphone are turned off in various apps like Zoom and Skype.

Regularly clear out caches, cookies, search histories, and browser histories.

Change passwords every three to six months. Avoid using easy-to-decipher passwords such as "1234." If you need to write down your various usernames and passwords, keep the list in a safe, and do not carry it on you when you leave the house.

Cover the camera on your desktop or laptop computer when not using it for Skype or Zoom sessions, and be sure to turn off the microphone and camera in your desktop settings.

It can be frightening to realize that even when your cell phone is off, it still records conversations you have. Consider leaving it in another room when not in use, or get creative and turn on some speed metal and let the phone spies suffer!

If you choose to continue using Facebook, Twitter, Reddit, Instagram, YouTube, or Google Search, or to continue to watch mainstream news media, that is absolutely fine, because all of these sites and outlets have many positives, including access to friends and family, joining groups, keeping up on local events, engaging in discussions with like-minded folks, and having access to volumes of information. A simple awareness of how these and other sites and outlets deliver you the goods is often enough to start seeking out information on other sources, or you may prefer to weed it out for yourself where you are already. Nobody demands you get off Facebook or stop watching YouTube or refuse to buy something on Amazon. It's your choice, and freedom of choice is what we are all fighting for in the first place. Just remember: *caveat emptor*!

SWITCH SIDES FOR A DAY

This exercise requires courage, open-mindedness, and tolerance: Try for one day to only look at news outlets that lean in the opposite direction of your political identity. Try for one day to pretend you are a conservative if you're a liberal, or vice versa, and seek out conversations, memes, posts, and threads on social media from that viewpoint. Read them in an attempt to understand why others have such a different perspective and perception from your own. You will often find it is not because they are hateful or evil but because they have a different set of life experiences that conditioned them or led them to embrace a set of beliefs. Just like you did. You may come to realize that they see things differently, and because of that, they have different preferences in what they vote for or against. Everyone we think is our enemy thinks the same thing about us, when there may be no enemy. Just different people.

Chances are you will feel enraged and indignant at first when you see and hear people speaking out against what you believe in and for things you find unacceptable, but keep going. Remember that not everyone thinks the same, believes the same, or understands the same, and it can be an empowering and enlightening adventure to examine why. You might even end up finding some things you agree with and maybe make friends outside the echo chamber you've become used to. People can change. They can expand their definition of who they are, and sometimes that happens when they are exposed to new and different points of view.

People can change. They can expand their definition of who they are, and sometimes that happens when they are exposed to new and different points of view.

So give this a try, if you have the courage to do so. Take one week and see if it changes your perspective. Every morning, check the headlines on left-leaning media, such as CNN, MSNBC, or Yahoo. Then, go to a number of right-leaning media outlets, such as Fox News, OANN, or Breitbart. Maybe choose three of each. Plan to visit these same sites each day as part of your experiment.

Write down the headlines on each outlet, and then write down the same news story headlines on the opposing media outlets. Read all the stories on both sides and make a list to compare and contrast them. Then write down just the facts of the story— the who, what, where, when, and how. This will allow your brain to start seeing how a media outlet, depending on its political slant, can bias a story in one direction for its audience.

Looking at both sides of the media to see how they cover one particular story so differently is eye-opening, and once you see the propaganda at work, you will never unsee it.

Imagine how little control our media, politicians, and world leaders would have over us if we all found out we have common ground and common goals, even as we respected our measurable differences. Yes, we are going to be different. Different people are inclined to believe in different things. Would we prefer to be clones with no individuality? Not at all. People must be allowed to be who they are and to evolve into something better if they choose. The majority of humans want to live and let live, and they prefer to do so in peace.

Propaganda works best when it can set one group or ideology against another and create chaos and disorder. Without that division, the manipulation loses its power.

TRUST THYSELF

Ultimately it comes down to trusting yourself, your discernment, your gut, and your intuition. Propaganda plays upon our fears and lack of information, but there is a part of us all that senses when we are being lied to, manipulated, or coerced. We sense the con job and the used car sales pitch. We feel it in our gut when the stories don't line up or the facts presented contradict themselves.

Trying to teach others what you've learned once your eyes are open is a mixed bag of tricks and treats. Some people might be receptive. Most will not. Often, having a conversation with someone who still drinks the proverbial mainstream media Kool-Aid will feel frustrating because no matter how many facts you offer, they will refuse to accept them. The best you can do is be empathetic. No doubt there was a time in your past when you refused to see the truth. Trust that your own journey to acquire more knowledge may be enough for now.

Perhaps the propagandists of the world rely on our lack of self-trust. They feed off it and use it to their advantage where they can. The term "sheeple" is given to those who follow others and do what they are told, like sheep being herded by a big, bad dog— or like sheep being led to slaughter, never questioning where they are going or why.

Learning about propaganda and disinformation opens our eyes, our minds, and our hearts to all the ways we have given up our most prized possession—our personal power. Often, we give up our collective power just as willingly. Informing ourselves means we are no longer willing to believe everything we are told. We must research it for ourselves.

Propaganda relies on our isolation and separation from others. Yes, we may be on social media, but that doesn't equate to person-to-person contact. The powers that be want us divided, fighting it out on social media over point A so they can slip in point B while we are distracted. Conversations easily become relegated to angry, hostile posts agreeing with this or disagreeing with that. Do people see each other in person anymore? Radio host Celeste Headlee says in her TED talk *10 Ways to Have a Better Conversation* that a great conversation consists of honesty, brevity, clarity, and a healthy amount of listening. She encourages people to "Go out, talk to people, listen to people. And, most importantly, be prepared to be amazed." Can you imagine how much less power propagandists would have over us if we talked to, listened to, and learned from each other? Instead, our media tells us who to hate, avoid, and fear.

Can you imagine how much less power propagandists would have over us if we talked to, listened to, and learned from each other?

It's time we all opened our eyes. It's time to set aside emotions and look for the facts even if they don't align with what we believe to be true. Facts are facts. Until we stop relying on how we feel about something, we will attack those who feel differently, and we will forever be prisoners of propaganda. Our feelings come from our experiences, and our experiences are ours and ours alone.

Shifting to facts requires a drastic shift in perception, and for many people, sadly, that day may never come. They will go to their graves believing their side was right and just and the other side deserved to suffer. They will defend until their dying breath their own right to speak and think freely, while denying that right to anyone who disagrees. Then suddenly something happens and a shift occurs. Eyes open wide. Hearts and minds expand.

Identifying and seeing something means you can never unsee it. Like the cloud that looks like a sailboat, or the pattern on Grandma's den wallpaper that looks like Tom Cruise, or the shape of a turkey on your piece of burnt toast, once you see it you cannot *not* see it. You didn't see it before, and then it was pointed out to you, maybe by someone else who saw it first. You took notice. *You saw it.* Now you can point out the sailboat right away and show it to others who cannot see it. Why? Because your entire perception changed. Something that was not a part of your reality now is.

You woke up—or "got woke," as the expression is now.

That, and that alone, is your most powerful weapon against the propaganda machine. You cannot dismantle a machine you don't even know is there. You need to see it first—how it works and operates, how it influences and affects you and the world around you. Soon you start to see how it hurts you and others, how it divides instead of unites. How it plays one side against the other and pushes agendas that rarely benefit anyone other than the powerful elite.

Then you need to decide whether or not that machine needs to be taken apart or exposed. You have the means of doing so. It's called knowledge.

Use it.

FURTHER READING

"53 Admitted False Flag Attacks." Global Research. September 3, 2019. https://www.globalresearch.ca/53-admitted-false-flag-attacks/5432931.

Acun, Mustafa. "Propaganda Instruments in the Civil War: Poems, Songs, Pictures, and Cartoons." Medium.com. July 17, 2018. https://medium.com/@AcunMustafa/propaganda-instruments-in-the-civil-war-poems-songs-pictures-and-cartoons-20fe0d6d3f57.

Benkler, Yochai, Robert Faris, and Hal Roberts. *Network Propaganda: Manipulation, Disinformation, and Radicalization in American Politics.* New York: Oxford University Press, 2018.

Bernays, Edward. *Crystallizing Public Opinion.* New Hall, CA: New Hall Press, 2019.

Bernays, Edward, and Mark Crispin Miller. *Propaganda.* New York: IG Publishing, 2004.

"A Brief History of Propaganda." iLab. February 21, 2014. https://ilab.org/articles/brief-history-propaganda.

Brodie, Richard. *Virus of the Mind: The New Science of the Meme.* Carlsbad, CA: Hay House, 1996.

"A Citizen's Guide to Understanding Corporate Media Propaganda Techniques." Films for Action. November 3, 2012. https://www.filmsforaction.org/news/a-citizens-guide-to-understanding-corporate-media-propaganda-techniques/.

Collins, Glenn. "The Psychology of the Cult Experience." *New York Times,* March 15, 1982.

Collins, Katie. "Edward Snowden Says Facebook, Amazon, and Google Engage in Abuse." CNET. November 4, 2019. https://www.cnet.com/news/edward-snowden-says-facebook-amazon-and-google-engage-in-abuse/.

Deikman, Arthur J. *The Wrong Way Home: Uncovering the Patterns of Cult Behavior in American Society.* New York: Beacon Press, 1990.

Dolan, Eric W. "Study: Conspiracy Theorists Are Not Necessarily Paranoid." PsyPost. May 10, 2018. https://www.psypost.com/2-18/05/study-conspiracy-theorists-not-necessarily-paranoid-51216.

Elder, Linda, and Richard Paul. *The Thinker's Guide for Conscientious Citizens on How to Detect Media Bias and Propaganda in National and World News—Based on Critical Thinking Concepts.* Tomales, CA: The Foundation for Critical Thinking, 2008.

Epstein, Robert. "How Google Could Rig the 2016 Election." Politico. August 19, 2019. https://www.politico.com/magazine/story/2015/08/how-google-could-rig-the-2016-election-121548.

Faulkner, Neil. "The Official Truth: Propaganda in the Roman Empire." BBC Online. February 17, 2011. https://www.bbc.co.uk/history/ancient/romans/rtomanpropaganda.article.01.shtml.

"Favorite Piece of Propaganda?" *Journal of the American Revolution.* July 2014. https://allthingsliberty.com/2014/07/favorite-piece-of-propaganda/.

Gillis, Alex. "The Rise of Junk Science." The Walrus. March 27, 2019. https://thewalrus.ca/the-rise-of-junk-science/.

Greenspan, Rachel E. "Politicians and Influencers Have Been Accused of 'Virtue Signaling' During Police Brutality Protests, But the Callouts Could Do More Harm Than Good." Insider. June 13, 2020. https://www.insider.com/virtue-signaling-social-media-george-floyd-protests-racins-2020-6.

Grossman, Taylor Lee. *Brainwashing: The Science of Thought Control.* Amazon Kindle Services. 2019.

Hassan, Steven. *Combating Cult Mind Control: The Guide to Protection, Rescue, and Recovery from Destructive Cults.* 30th ed. Amazon Kindle Services, 2018.

Hastings, Michael. "Congressmen Seek to Lift Propaganda Ban." BuzzFeed News. May 18, 2012. https://www.buzzfeednews.com/article/mhastings/congressmen-seek-to-lift-propaganda-ban.

Herman, Edward S., and Noam Chomsky. *Manufacturing Consent: The Political Economy of the Mass Media.* New York: Pantheon Books, 2002.

Herrington, Boze. "The Seven Signs You're in a Cult." *Atlantic*, June 18, 2014. https://www.theatlantic.com/national/archive/2014/06/the-seven-signs-youre-=in-a-cult/362400/.

Hirst, K. Kris. "Behistun Inscription: Darius's Massage to the Persian Empire." ThoughtCo. November 1, 2019. https://www.thoughtco.com/behistun-inscriptions-dariuss-message-170214.

"How Can We Fight Corporate Propaganda?" Rabble.ca. September 2017. https://rabble.ca/blogs/bloggers/views-expressed/2017/09/how-can-we-fight-corporate-propaganda.

Hudson, John. "U.S. Repeals Propaganda Ban, Spreads Government-Made News to Americans." ForeignPolicy.com. July 14, 2013. https://foreignpolicy.com/2013/07/14/u-s-repeals-propaganda-ban-spreads-government-made-news-to-americans/.

Ingram, David. "More Governments Than Ever Are Using Social Media to Push Propaganda, Report Says." ABC News. November 4, 2019. https://www.abcnews.com/tech/tech-news/more-governments-ever-are-using-social-media-push-propaganda-report-p1076301.

Jones, Marie D., and Larry Flaxman. *Mind Wars: A History of Mind Control, Surveillance, and Social Engineering by the Government, Media, and Secret Societies.* Pompton Plains, NY: New Page Books, 2015.

———. *Viral Mythology: How the Truth of the Ancients Was Encoded and Passed Down Through Legend, Art, and Architecture.* Pompton Plains, NJ: New Page Books, 2014.

Jowett, Gareth S., and Victoria O'Donnell. *Propaganda and Persuasion.* Thousand Oaks, CA: Sage Books, 2012.

Krans, Brian. *Big Fat Lies—A Half Century of Sugary Propaganda Has Made Us Sick.* San Francisco: Healthline, 2019.

Kujawski, Mike. "Misinformation vs. Disinformation vs. Mal-Information." Medium.com. September 5, 2019. https://medium.com/@mikekujawski/misinformation-vs-disinformation-vs-mal-information-a2h741410736.

Lamothe, Cindy. "How to Recognize Coercive Control." Healthline. October 10, 2019. https://www.healthline.com/health/coercive-control.

Leetaru, Kalev. "The Daily Mail Snopes Story and Fact Checking the Fact-Checkers." *Forbes,* December 22, 2016.

Lichfield, Gideon. "21st-Century Propaganda: A Guide to Interpreting and Confronting the Dark Arts of Persuasion." Quartz. May 13, 2017. https://qz.com/978548/introducing-our-obsession-with-propaganda/.

Ludden, David. "Why Do People Believe in Conspiracy Theories?" *Psychology Today,* January 6, 2018.

Mark, Joshua J. "Behistun Inscription." Ancient History Encyclopedia. November 28, 2019. https://www.ancient.eu/Behistun_Inscription/.

Marrs, Jim. *Population Control: How Corporate Owners Are Killing Us.* New York: William Morrow, 2015.

McCowan, David. "How WWI Food Propaganda Forever Changed the Way Americans Eat." The Takeout. March 15,

2017. https://thetakeout.com/how-wwi-food-propaganda-changed-the-way-america-17987_59481.

Meerloo, Joost A. M. *The Rape of the Mind: The Psychology of Thought Control, Menticide, and Brainwashing.* Amazon Kindle Services/Hauraki Publishing, 2015.

Mercola, Joseph. "Google—A Dictator Unlike Anything the World Has Ever Known." Mercola.com. May 5, 2020. https://articles_mercola.com/sites/articles/archive/2020/05/10/google-and-your-privacy.aspx.

———. "Google and Big Tech Bought Congress." Mercola.com. January 7, 2020. https://articles.mercola.com/sites/articles/archive/2020/01/07/google-big-tech-bought-congress.aspx.

———. "Harvard Professor Exposes Google and Facebook." Mercola.com. March 28, 2020. https://articles.mercola.com/sites/articles/archive/2020/03/28/surveillance-capitalism.aspx.

Mitchell, Mary Niall. "Rosebloom or Pure White, Or So It Seemed." *American Quarterly,* September 2002.

"NDAA 2013: Congress Approves Domestic Deceptive Propaganda." RT USA News. May 22, 2012. https://www.rt.com/usa/news/propaganda-us-smith-amendment-903/.

O'Connor, Anahad. "How the Sugar Industry Shifted Blame to Fat." *New York Times,* September 12, 2016.

O'Connor, Caitlin, and James Weatherall. *The Misinformation Age: How False Beliefs Spread.* New Haven, CT: Yale University Press, 2018.

Oltermann, Philip. "Revealed: How Associated Press Cooperated with the Nazis." *The Guardian*, March 30, 2016. https://www.theguardian.com/world/2016/mar/30/associated=press-cooperation-nazis-reveaeled-germany-harriet-scharnberg.

Oransky, Ivan. "Science Sting Exposes Corrupt Journal Publishers." *Scientific American,* March 23, 2017.

Pillar, Paul R. "The Iraq War and the Power of Propaganda." *The National Interest,* September 14, 2011. https://nationalinterest.org/node/1216.

"Power to the Picture: The Evolution of Propaganda." UK Independent. October 23, 2011. https://www.independent.co.uk/arts-entertainment/power-to-the-pictures-the-evolution-of-propaganda-2075321.html.

Ross, Rick Alan. *Cults Inside Out. How People Get In and Can Get Out.* Amazon CreateSpace Independent Platform, 2014.

Sasse, Ben. "This New Technology Could Send American Politics into a Tailspin." *Washington Post,* October 19, 2018. https://www.washingtonpost.com/opinions/the-real-scary-news-about-deepfakes/2018/10/19/.

Scandling, Michael. "If It Bleeds, It Leads. No Matter Whose Blood It Is." Stand. February 27, 2018. https://www.stand-league.org/blog/if-it-bleeds-it-leads-no-matter-whose-blood-it-is.htm.

Sirota, David. "How the '80s Programmed Us for War." Salon.com. March 15, 2011. https://www.salon.com/2011/03/15/sirota_excerpt_back_to_our_future/.

Stanley, Jason. *How Propaganda Works.* Princeton, NJ: Princeton University Press, 2016.

"Stop Virtue Shaming on Social Media and Help Someone." TheFederalist.com. June 23, 2016. https://thefederalist.com/2016/06/23/stop-virtue-shaming-on-social-media/.

Taylor, Philip M. *Munitions of the Mind: A History of Propaganda from the Ancient World to the Present Era.* Manchester, UK: Manchester University Press, 2003.

Toews, Rob. "Deepfakes Are Going to Wreak Havoc on Society. We Are Not Prepared." *Forbes,* May 25, 2020. https://www.forbes.com/sites/robtoews/2020/05/25/deep-fakes-are-going-to-wreak-havoc-on-society-we-are-not-prepared/.

Took, Robyn. *Symbiotic Radicalisation Strategies: Propaganda tools and Neuro-linguistic Programming.* Edith Cowan University Research Online, 2015.

"Understanding Cognitive Dissonance (and Why It Occurs in Most People." Cleverism. March 14, 2019. https://www.cleverism.com/understanding-cognitive-dissonance-and-why-it-occurs-to-most-people/.

Vinton, Kate. "These 15 Billionaires Own America's News Media Companies." *Forbes,* June 1, 2016.

Williams, Phil M. *The Propaganda Project.* Amazon Kindle Services/ Phil W. Books, 2016.

Wood, Molly, Kristin Schwab, and Stephanie Hughes. "How Social Media Brought Political Propaganda Into the 21st Century." Marketplace.com. October 23, 2017. https://www.marketplace.com/2017/10/23/how-social-media-brought-political-propaganda-21st-century/.

INDEX

NOTE: (ILL.) INDICATES PHOTOS AND ILLUSTRATIONS.